CHAMPIONSHIP

HOLD'EM

Limit Hold'em Cash Game Strategies
Tournament Tactics • Practice Hands

T. J. Cloutier & Tom McEvoy

Championship Hold'em
Limit Hold'em Cash Game Strategies,
Tournament Tactics, Practice Hands

by Tom McEvoy and T. J. Cloutier

Copyright 2000 by Tom McEvoy,
T. J. Cloutier and Dana Smith

First Printing: January 2000
Revised Edition: January 2002

Library of Congress Catalog Card Number: 99-76814

ISBN 1-884466-00-1

Editor: Dana Smith

Cover Design: Christene King

Photos courtesy of Larry Grossman
and Card Player Magazine

Cardsmith Publishing
4535 W. Sahara #105
Las Vegas, NV 89102

www.pokerbooks.com

CONTENTS

Chapter 4

Things to Think About ...

Chapter 5

Things to Think about ...

ACKNOWLEDGMENTS

We gratefully acknowledge the contributions of other poker players and theorists to this book. Erik Seidel was gracious enough to write the foreword and critique the tournament strategy chapter. His suggestions have been valuable to us and we appreciate his thoughtful insights.

In order to fine-tune some of the concepts and strategies in this 2002 revised edition of Championship Hold'em, we sought the advice of several well-known hold'em players. Daniel Negreanu, tournament champion and Card Player comunist, spent a lot of time detailing his insightful suggestions and we are particularly thankful for his help. Steve Badger, another respected tournament champion and Card Player columnist, gave us several valuable suggestions which we sincerely appreciate. We also thank David Sklansky for sharing his insights with T.J. during the 2001 World Series of Poker.

For the 2000 version, professional player Walter Fong offered his expertise in the cash game chapters. We appreciate the suggestions of tournament player Don Vines and, of course, we thank tournament champion and author Ken Buntjer for his endorsement of Championship Hold'em.

As always we are indebted to our publisher and editor, Dana Smith, whose creativity and diligence have led to the inception and publication of our Championship Series of books.

No book is a success without readers. We thank you for purchasing Championship Hold'em. We sincerely believe that it not only will increase your expertise but will augment your bankroll as well. It is our intention that the advice herein will help you get to the winners' circle far more often than you ever dreamed possible. We'll be there waiting to offer you our heartfelt congratulations and shake your hand! ♠

FOREWORD

by Erik Seidel

Erik Seidel is the all-time limit hold'em money winner at the World Series of Poker. In 1992 he won the $2,500 limit hold'em tournament and in 1994 he won the $5,000 limit hold'em championship event. In 1997 he played at the final table in all three WSOP limit hold'em tournaments. Seidel placed fourth in the $10,000 no-limit hold'em championship event in 1999 and currently is ranked ninth on the list of top money winners at the WSOP.

When Tom McEvoy and T. J. Cloutier publish a book, it presents an extraordinary opportunity for those of us who are interested in improving our poker skills. Here is a chance to look into the minds of two players who have been in the trenches for many years, successfully competing against the top players in the world.

Tom and T. J. recognize that limit hold'em is an amorphous game, a game in which there are very few set answers on how to play. Every session and every player is different — we need to constantly respond to these changing conditions in order to play hold'em well. Hold'em can accommodate many different styles of play, each of which can be successful. California players tend to play faster than Las Vegas players and generally are more aggressive. Europeans tend to limp more often and play more flops.

We may have our own particular ideas on starting requirements and strategies, but in the heat of battle these might change. A top player such as Huck Seed can be the tightest player at the table one session and, depending on game conditions, will be the most aggressive the very next day. It is this type of thoughtfulness and flexibility that often distinguishes the top players from the rest of the field.

T. J. and Tom understand this concept and have written *Championship Hold'em* not only to show you how to *play* like an expert but how to *think* like one as well. Even though this is a hold'em book, you can apply the lessons that you learn here to all the other poker games you play.

In my opinion the section on tournament play by itself is worth many times the price of the book. Here you have Tom McEvoy, a former World Champion and fifteenth on Binion's list of top money winners, and T. J. Cloutier, a man who many people believe is the best tournament player in the world, sharing their thoughts with you.

In addition to Tom's accomplishments at the tables he also has contributed to the success of many people currently playing major tournaments through his private lessons and books. It is indeed rare that a player at Tom's level of expertise is willing and able to share with us what he has learned from hard experience. Tom is worth the price of admission on his own but in this book we also have the "T. J. kicker," or as we say in hold'em parlance, top pair-top kicker.

I have been playing tournaments for 11 years and during that time, nobody has won tournaments with the consistency that T. J. has shown. He seems to have a free pass to the final table at half of the tournaments he plays. Although he makes it look easy, T. J. is one of the toughest competitors in every poker game. He has been at the final table of the World Championship three times, a feat many times more difficult than winning it. T. J. also has won more big-money tournaments than anyone in poker.

So enjoy! You are in very good hands with T. J. and Tom, and I expect that as a result of reading *Championship Hold'em* you will be in many more. ♠

INTRODUCTION

T. J. Cloutier

We believe that anyone with some talent for poker can become a winning player at limit hold'em. All it takes is basic knowledge, good skills, examined experience, the ability to read your opponents, and an adequate bankroll.

The Purpose of This Book

Championship Hold'em is for all players, novices and professionals alike. We believe that we have put enough in this book that it will help anybody, at any level of competition. If you want to play hold'em seriously, we suggest that you move up a notch as soon as you increase your knowledge and experience enough to play at a higher limit.

As you progress, we want you to find a lot of information in this book that will help you as you're moving up the ladder. This includes you tournament players who begin your career in low-limit events on your way to advancing all the way up to the World Series of Poker. We give you tips to use as you're scaling the tournament ladder, tips that will help you become more competitive so that you'll have a better chance to win when you sit down with the big boys. If you're already there, we believe that this material can help to bring you back to the basics when you get off the winning track, as sometimes happens to even the best of us.

Spring training in baseball is devoted to practicing the fundamentals over and over again. Twenty-game winning pitchers and .300 batters practice the basics, going through the same routine time and time again to fine tune their skills.

This is why it looks so easy when they're on the field of play, but it *isn't* easy — it just looks that way because they've done it so many times. Because professional players sharpen their basic skills every spring, they're able to continue to perform at a high level for years and years. We hope that this book will become a practice manual, a spring-training guide, for poker players who already play at the advanced level but need reminders here and there.

In golf it's called training your muscles to do a certain thing. The pros go out and hit balls time and time again so that by repeating their strokes over and over, they will have the same swing every time. In poker the reason that you go back and reread the books and reevaluate your play is so that your mind becomes strict — you're training your mind so that you won't keep making the same mistakes.

Remember that when you're losing at poker, *two* factors are involved, not one. You aren't just getting your hands beat, you're playing bad — and playing bad goes hand in hand with losing. The best players in the world play bad in some situations. We all make mistakes that we *know* we're making *when* we make them. But if you have trained your mind to listen to your first instincts and they say "Don't raise. Don't make this call," you won't do it. You won't make those mistakes if your mind is right, but if it isn't right you'll fall into all the traps that go along with losing.

Just as baseball and golf pros work hard on the basics to create a uniform performance on the field and on the links, we want you to be able to use this book to train your mind so that your game will always be in top shape at the tables. Ever since our other books were first published, I've had many, many players come up to me and express their thanks, saying something like "I was doing this, I was doing that and I knew better — I *knew* that I was doing things wrong. So I went back and reread your book, and reread it and reread it again, and I picked up something different every time. Now I'm not making those mistakes." These were not beginning players, either — they were *players*. If more advanced players can get a lot out of reading books, imagine the benefits of study and practice to less experienced players.

Why Do People Play Limit Hold'em?

People play particular poker games for different reasons: One game might be easier for them than another, or one game might suit their personality better than any other one. A lot more people are playing limit hold'em these days than any other poker game. Some of the reasons for its popularity are:

• Players like action. Hold'em games often have a lot of multiway pots and action players like that aspect of the game.

• The smaller-denomination chips that you play with make it look as though the pots are enormous. Playing with $5 chips in the $15-$30 games, you see all those chips piled up in the center — which triggers some sort of chemistry in the average player. We used to play $5-$10 games with $5 chips and the pots didn't look nearly as big as they are when the house puts $2 chips on the table in a $6-$12 game. It's a psychological ploy that the casino uses to attract people to the game.

• Unlike no-limit hold'em, limit hold'em is a game in which you usually cannot get broke on one hand.

• A lot of people can play a lot of hands in limit hold'em.

• Limit hold'em is deceptively simple. No card memory is required as in seven-card stud. If you know the basics of poker, you can always tell from the board cards which hand is the best one possible. That hand might not be out, but at least you know what it is.

Using The Strategies In this Book At Various Limits

There always seems to be some doubt in players' minds as to whether the strategies outlined in any poker book apply to all limits of play from $2-$4 to $200-$400. We believe that the strategies we suggest in "Championship Hold'em" can be successfully applied to any hold'em game that you play, no matter what the limits.

No player in the world wins every time he plays, not even the best of the bunch, but the better players will win at any limit over the long haul. If you use the strategies that we suggest, you should be able to beat any game in the long run.

In addition to your poker skill and hold'em strategy, your percentage of wins also will be influenced by how strong the competition is and how you're running on that particular day. Just because someone says that you should average one and a half bets per hour doesn't mean that you will win exactly that amount every time you play. You might get a rush of cards and clean the table off in one hour — or you might lose your buy-in and have to go back to your pocket.

I can't think of a single time when I considered playing in a game where I thought that I could win one and a half bets an hour. Tom and I don't think in terms of what a particular hour's worth of play will win or lose. We know that the standard deviation during an hour's play in a $10-$20 game can be $400 or $500, which is more than what your hourly win normally would be if you're a winning player, or what your usual hourly loss would be if you're a losing player.

If you're a good player, what matters most is which game you're sitting in and how the chips are flowing. If you're sitting in a good game your expectation might be ten bets an hour if you hold any cards. Or if you're in a tough game with a lot of strong opponents, you might have a negative expectation even though you're a winning player overall.

Getting Your Slice of the Pie

Ol' man Dean told me years ago back in Houston that playing poker professionally is the toughest way in the world to make a living because so many people are trying to cut themselves a little slice of the pie, and there's only so much pie to get after the house gets its piece and you tip the dealers. You don't have access to the whole pie — you only have access to one little slice of it.

Never forget that it's all one big poker game. Sometimes, even professional players get caught up in the action and forget that. Some players literally cannot go to bed until they have gotten even, so they play marathon sessions until they either collapse from lack of sleep or the game breaks. These are people whom I consider to be problem gamblers.

Understand, however, that I don't consider people who play poker to be gambling. There is enough skill in the game so that if you develop your abilities, you can win at it. Skill may not win in any one session, but it will win overall. It is the other types of players who are gambling — players who don't know the principles of the game and do not have a solid foundation in it, or players who know them but choose to ignore them. It is these people who are gambling, who go on tilt and play the marathon sessions. And that's ridiculous.

Remember this: There is only one Doyle Brunson and there's only one Chip Reese. You don't have to beat Doyle or Chip in a game to be successful at poker. You can be a winning player without ever achieving what they have achieved. The players who make the most money at poker, and at limit hold'em in particular, are the ones who simply are the best players in their particular games. You don't need the talent of a world-class player. If you have a big skill edge over your opponents, you have a better shot at making money at poker. In fact, if you're the best player in your game you may have a bigger earn than some of the star players who play against other stars. In the bigger games, these poker stars often are playing against each other and their individual earns may not be that great because the talent among them is so close.

Another thing to remember is that if you're the best player in your local game at home, maybe that's the game you *should* be playing. When you go out of town to play a tournament, a lot of other players in that event also are hometown champions and you may not be able to beat them. It's certainly worth taking a shot, but always know your own skill level. If you're beating the game at home, *play* the game at home.

We've all heard the old cliche that Las Vegas is the graveyard of hometown poker champions. And you can say the same thing for some of the bigger, aggressive games in California too. Being a hometown champ doesn't necessarily mean that you won't succeed somewhere else against stronger competition, it's just that if you cannot adjust to it or don't have the skills to beat it you aren't going to continue to get the results that you have become accustomed to.

It takes a while in a new place to learn the people, to set up a book on them. When you come to Las Vegas, you get to know some of the locals who always play in the same game, but you also have a steady stream of non-locals in those games, some of whom are your bread and butter and others who play better than you thought they could. The locals want to dodge each other and play the tourists, they're just hoping to break even against each other. This doesn't mean that they won't play against other locals in the game, it just means that they give each other a lot of respect in the game.

Always remember that the pie isn't that big. And if that pie is being eaten up pretty fast by the guys who play in the game all the time while you're in there trying to get your little piece of it, a lot of times that piece isn't available to you. You may end up with just the crust. ♠

1

KEY CONCEPTS FOR WINNING AT LIMIT HOLD'EM

T. J. Cloutier

When I first began thinking about this topic, Tom laid the foundation for it by saying, "Players are telling me that it seems to be harder and harder for them to win at limit hold'em these days, and at almost all other forms of poker too. Many more people are playing hold'em now, which has replaced seven-card stud as the most popular casino poker game, and most of them aren't playing 'according to the book,' especially at the lower limits. Sklansky laid out standard hold'em hands by position several years ago, but a lot of people aren't playing by those standards anymore.

"We're getting into a new brand of hold'em in which people are playing hands out of position, more players are in pots, and the betting is more aggressive than it used to be. Under these changing conditions, what does it take these days to win a few bucks at hold'em?"

While it's true that some things have changed in poker, there are other things that will never change. No matter how the game is played, you still have to have enough skill and your share of luck to beat it. The principles of winning that we will discuss in this chapter are listed on the next page. They are what I consider to be some of the requisites for becoming a winner at limit hold'em. I suggest that you copy the list and review it before every session you play.

Key Concepts for Winning at Limit Hold'em

- Be in a Good Frame of Mind
- Watch Your Opponents
- Develop a Table Presence
- Don't Get in Too Deep
- Switch Gears When You Need To
- Search for a Suitable Game
- Play Within Your Bankroll
- Don't Let Losing Affect You
- Play in a Game that Compensates Your Skill Level
- Play Small Connectors in Selected Situations Only
- Remember that Kickers are Important
- Avoid Long Calls on the End
- Always Try to Save Bets
- Stick to Your Standards
- Bring Your A-Game to the Table

Be in a Good Frame of Mind

When you get up in the morning and you decide to play poker, there should never be any doubt in your mind that you can win. If you have any doubts — this isn't your day, you have other things on your mind, you've been running bad — and you can't devote your full attention to the game, you shouldn't play.

Frame of mind means, "If I get the cards, I'm going to win." It's a feeling of confidence. You feel good, you know your abilities. And you know that you're going to play the whole table — you're not going to try to single out one player. A lot of times, when you single out one player (usually the loosest player in the game) you run into trouble because the other guys are trying to do the same thing.

Years ago, Bobby Baldwin mentioned that when you go to play cards, you should dress comfortably because you're probably going to settle into a game and play for a while. You might even play longer than you expected to play, so you should be comfortable with your clothing *and* yourself.

Watch Your Opponents

You must learn all you can about your opponents. Know the kinds of hands they will play, when they will play them, and whether they will bluff. When you come to a table, you've made the decision to play in that game, no matter what the limits you play. If you're playing in Los Angeles or Las Vegas where there are lots of games to choose from, you have chosen this particular game.

Usually, you will know one or two of the players but if you don't, you should spend your first 15 to 45 minutes concentrating on what you see going on at the table. Of course, you'll be playing your best hands during that time, too, but mostly you are trying to find out what kinds of cards your opponents are playing, what kinds of hands people are raising with, how they play their hands. If they raise with an ace-big and the flop comes with three baby cards, do they automatically bet if you check to them? This is easy to determine: A lot of times, a player will raise with A-J and the flop will come with something like 8-5-2. A couple of players who called his raise preflop will check to him and he will bet; and they call the bet. Then on fourth street comes another rag, they check to him, and he also checks (or sometimes, he might bet again). But he almost always will bet on the flop with two big overcards.

The reason you're watching the action so closely is to answer the question, "Will they do this?" If you find out that they will, then you can check to them, let them bet, and then come back over the top of them (check-raise) on the flop; or if you have a big hand, just flat call. Then check again on fourth street, let them come again, and then take their money.

You will see players like this at every table. If a good player has raised before the flop, he usually will put in one bet on the flop unless, for example, he has a big pair and the flop comes with overcards. Say that the good player has two jacks and the flop comes with an ace, king or queen. Unless it's checked to him, he won't bet. If he does bet, and you have top pair — if you've been selective on what you call raises with — then you should be able to play with him.

Another reason you're watching your opponents is to answer, "Does this guy raise with only premium hands, or does he raise with hands like 10-9 or 6-5 suited?" A lot of guys raise with connectors, suited or unsuited. If your opponent is that type of player and the flop comes with medium cards, you know that he might be there.

These are just two reasons why you're watching what everyone at the table does: Who is passive? Who is aggressive? A lot of people play in a tight mode, never raising the pot. If an overcard comes, they would never think of betting. If they have two jacks, for example, and an ace or king comes on the flop, they would never consider betting the hand. You have to know who these guys are.

As you watch their play, you also will find out which players will take off aggressively on the flop even though they don't have a made hand yet, bet it again on fourth street, and bet it again on fifth street to try to win the pot, thinking that maybe you're on a draw and don't have anything to call them with. You need to know who will do this.

You are watching the cards that they show down at the end, as well as their betting patterns. Some players will never play a hand from early position without bringing it in for a raise, no matter what kind of hand they're playing. You need to know who they are, as well as which players will just flat-call from early position with a hand like A-Q or A-J instead of raising with it. They usually will stand a raise with the hand, but they don't want to raise it themselves until they see where they are. Then there are the ones who seldom play any hands from up front, but will play more hands from late positions.

Develop a Table Presence

Your table image is important to your overall success in limit hold'em. Deception, confusing your opponents about the type of player that you really are, is the essence of developing a table presence. It is also important to be able to switch gears from more conservative play to looser play depending on the ebb and flow of the game, the nature of the players who are in it, and which players have left the game.

What you want to do is give the "illusion of action," as Tom puts it. "You want players to think that you're an action player who raises a lot, when what you're actually doing is raising selectively when you have a hand," he adds. "Your table image is all about deceiving your opponents as to what kind of player you really are. One way to do that is to always bet your hand as though you have what you are advertising."

In an exceptionally loose game, you may deliberately take a tight image if they're going to give you action anyway. It all depends on how observant your opponents are, which is another factor in your image: Does it matter to them that you are playing either a lot more hands or a lot fewer hands? If you're in against a lot of conservative players, you sometimes will appear to be a kamikaze pilot because you're doing most of the raising. They are allowing you to take command of the game and not contesting you, so you're winning a lot of pots that are up for grabs, ownerless pots that are just waiting for an owner to take possession of them. If that's the situation, you can be the grabber of these ownerless pots.

If you're up against maniac players who are super aggressive, you won't be able to outgamble them so you give them the illusion of action to try to make them think that you're gambling with them when you're actually only gambling with your better hands. Of course, this doesn't mean that you'll win with your good hands all the time, because these are the types of players who will come after you anyway and put beats on you. They will go farther with marginal hands that you wouldn't play in the first place.

I like having a table image that allows me to win some showdown hands because I have such a presence at the table that people are afraid that if they make a move at me, I'm going to chop them off. You want to instill a little fear in your opponents because when they are afraid of you, you sometimes can get free cards. Or when nothing comes on the end, you might be able to steal the pot with just a high card because they're afraid that if they make a move you'll go over the top of them.

If I could get into a game and not be known, I would want things just as Tom and I have described here, but neither one of us can go into a major cardroom with anonymity. So, I have to use the other type of presence, the intimidating presence that instills fear in them. I don't do it by my voice or body movements, I just do it by my reputation and maybe some of the plays that come down.

Of course, we're talking about some of the higher limit games here. Table image is less important at the $4-$8 level than it is at the $40-$80 limits. Many of the very low-limit players play exceptionally loose and don't pay attention to you anyway. Generally they are fearless, they don't care who you are or what kind of plays you're making. They only know what their cards are and they're ready to gamble with them.

If you're a "name" player in a tournament, that image can be beneficial to you. So many times we've heard, "Oh, *you're* at my table?! What a tough table!" And I'm looking around thinking, "Boy, this looks like a piece of strawberry shortcake compared to some of the tables I've played."

The other night I started at a tournament table that supposedly was the toughest one in the whole room. I looked around and there was Sergio on one side of me and Mario Esquerra on the other side and some other tough players. "This is gonna be a good table," I'm thinking to myself. And then even before we started playing, this Russian stands up and says, "This is the toughest table I've ever been at in my life!" And I'm saying, "Good, this is gonna be an action table. These guys are here to play." In the first hand that I saw played at this supposedly tough table, a guy raised with A-9 offsuit and another dude called him with A-4 offsuit! "They're right — this is a tough table!" I'm smiling to myself.

Don't get me wrong here: Sergio and Mario are fine players, it's just that they're action players. They're not waiting for the nuts to put their money into the pot, especially in no-limit hold'em. For example, I saw a play in which Mario brought it in for a $200 raise and a guy on the end reraised him $600, all that he had left, so that Mario could not win any more money than that after the flop. He called the reraiser with a pair of fives. The guy had A-K and Mario flopped a five and broke him. To start with, I wouldn't have raised with the two fives before the flop and I sure wouldn't have called a reraise with them but for some players it works, even at the final table.

Don't Get in Too Deep

Limit hold'em isn't like no-limit or even pot-limit hold'em. In no-limit and pot-limit, you can lose your original buy-in, go into your pocket and bring out another buy-in, win one hand and get even or come out a winner. But suppose you buy in to a $20-$40 limit game for $500 and you lose it. Then you buy in for $500 more and you lose that, too. Now you're $1,000 stuck. How hard is it to get that $1,000 back? How many hands do you have to win at $20-$40 to recoup your money? Usually, $1,000 is within range but if you're in $1,500 or $2,000 you're in trouble. Where your earning rate is anywhere from one to three big bets an hour, how many hours do you have to play just to get even? Is it better to continue playing when you're not running so good, or is it better to quit and come back another day?

Switching games usually won't do it. If you're playing good hold'em, it isn't the players you're up against, you're just not "on" that day, your hands just aren't working out. So if you're playing in a metropolis where you can play poker any day of the week, pick a different day.

Limit hold'em is not a game to get buried in — it's a game to get winner in. If you're comfortable just stay and play and win some more. But just to be sitting in a seat doesn't make sense, does it? If you're reading this book you want to be a winning player, you're not there just to sit down in a game for the recreation. You hope that most of your opponents are recreational players — the idea is to let *them* get in deep, *you* don't want to be the one who gets drowned. With one or two buy-ins you usually can see how things are going to run for the day — if you're playing good. If you're just giving your money away, it doesn't matter. If you're in there making long calls (overcalls with marginal hands) with hands such as K♠ 7♠, playing any two suited cards, you're not going to win anyway. (One of the biggest mistakes that people make in limit hold'em is playing any two suited cards.)

My advice is that when you sit down in a particular size game, ask yourself, "What is this game worth? How much can I win in this game? If I hold a lot of hands, what can I win? If the cards break even, what can I win?" And when you first sit down, you should always say, "If things don't work out, I'm going to cut my loss. I'm going to quit at a certain point." And then you should stick to it. Getting buried just for the sake of playing simply isn't worth it.

Suppose you've won between $300 and $800 five days in a row at the $20-$40 game and you've put together $2,500 to $3,000. Are you willing to give away five days' work in one day? This just doesn't make sense, yet it happens time and time again. I never think along the line of, "I'm in $1,500. If I get $500 of it back, that's a score." But if I'm in for $1,500 and I happen to get even, I feel that I've won $1,500. One time back in Texas, Everett Goulsby got in for $20,000 in a $30-$60 hold'em game. He stayed for four solid days and got even, but the chances of that happening are astronomical. Everett was a great player, but he had a real ego problem. "These guys aren't gonna beat me," he was thinking. I guess he might even have gone for another $20,000, but that would've been ridiculous.

"I should be able to beat this game," a loser thinks, but that type of thinking gets players into a lot of trouble. A lot of times, you'll get into a game where one guy's just throwing off his chips, but he's destroying two or three players along with himself. He's raising every pot with any two cards and you're calling him with decent hands. You're getting unlucky and somebody else is getting his money ... but they're getting your money, too. It's like my wife used to tell me, "Every time it's a good game is when you lose!" That isn't true, of course, it's just that the maniacs can drag you through the mud. I've seen some very good players in limit hold'em go off like a cannon — they get buried in the game and buy rack after rack after rack. Doesn't make sense, does it?

Switch Gears When You Need To

To me, switching gears means things such as, "When do you call with second pair? With third pair?" You've been observing your opponents throughout the game and you've seen what they do in various situations. Suppose that a guy has raised the pot before the flop and it comes with little cards. You've put him on two big cards. You check to him and he bets. You've made a pair on the board, either first, second or third pair. You call his bet. You've switched gears and now you're calling him with a hand that is a lot less than what you usually would call with. You need to know which opponents you can make the call against and which ones you can't. Is it a good practice? No, not usually. It's only a good practice when you're certain of where you are in the hand, and you know that based on your observations of your opponents.

Or maybe the board comes 10-8-2 and you have two sevens in your hand. When do you know this hand is good against someone who is betting? You've put him on two big cards. He makes the bet and you call with confidence. You switched gears on the flop, because ordinarily you wouldn't be calling when there are overcards on the board. The men know when to do this and the boys don't. Then an ace, king or queen comes on the turn. Now what do you do with the hand? Are you good enough to throw it away if he bets again? How disciplined are you?

Now suppose you have two fours in the hole in a multi-way pot. The flop comes A-K-2. Is it worth your while to call one bet, or a bet and a raise, to try to snag a four to make a small set and maybe win a big pot? I say no. You have no straight or flush draws — just two cards in the deck twice, so you have four outs. You're already more than a 10-to-1 dog with two cards to come. The number of times that you will win with this hand versus the number of times that you'll take the chance just doesn't compute. Yet players do this all the time in limit hold'em. This type of play is what "makes" limit games. If someone else takes that chance and makes a big drawout on you, you just have to hold yourself in and say, "Good play." Then think to yourself, "Go ahead, try it again!" You're in there for the long-run gains, not the short-term wins.

Dana Smith, publisher and editor of the Championship Series.

Search for a Suitable Game

Limit hold'em is the most popular ring game in casinos, both in Los Angeles and Las Vegas as well as on the East Coast and the Gulf Coast. More casino games today are limit hold'em than any other type of poker. You usually will find four or five tables of the same size of hold'em game in the larger cardrooms. This is why you should learn to pick and choose which game you want to play in.

If you play in one of these large cardrooms, you probably will have to put your name on the board and take the first game that's available when your name is called. You usually have to get in the first game so that you can get on the list to move to another one. Always keep the game in mind that you want to play in. And which game is that? It's the game that you have the best chance to beat. You should always try to get into a game where the chips are moving. Sometimes you have to be patient to get into a better game. Of course, if you just want to play, what difference does it make which game you play? But if you want to be a *winning* player, always search for the best game available to you, the one that you have the best chance to beat.

Play Within Your Bankroll

Say that you've been playing $5-$10 and have built up a decent enough bankroll — and you've learned enough — to move up to $10-$20 or $15-$30. You have to use the same way of playing that won for you at $5-$10, but you have to feel comfortable at the higher limits. Now you're playing for more money; your wins will be bigger, your losses will be bigger. But you still use the same concepts that made you a winner at $5-$10.

I don't care if you're playing $500-$1,000 or $5-$10, it's still limit hold'em. Some players might get into "power poker" at the higher limits, but limit hold'em is the exact same game at every level. You'll hear people say that there are better players at the higher limits. Not necessarily. Some of the toughest games I've ever played were $5-$10 hold'em games. They're tough to beat. Why? Players are comfortable playing at that level and they sit back, knowing that it's going to cost them $7 a round (with $2-$5 blinds), and wait and wait and wait for hands. The only difference in the higher-limit games is that it's going to cost you a few more dollars each round, so most people are going to play a few more hands. Eventually, you will get the same results if you get the same cards and play the same way that you played at the lower limits.

I firmly believe that you have to be willing to play within three different limits if you're going to make a living playing limit hold'em. If you're comfortable in the medium-limit game, you should search for that limit plus one a step higher and another a step lower. If you're a $20-$40 player, you should be ready to play $15-$30 or $30-$60, one limit on either end of your preferred limit. You should be comfortable playing in all three limits and then find the best game available. A very good $15-$30 game is better than a bad $20-$40 game.

You've heard that the little games, $2-$4 or $4-$8, are pretty loose. I think that the bigger games are sometimes even looser than they are at the lower limits. The difference is that you get more drop-ins, more recreational players, in the smaller games. When you move up, there aren't as many drop-ins so the pool of players is smaller and there are supposed to be more "players" at the higher limits. The smaller games are designed strictly for the house, with the (proportionately) bigger rake breaking at least one player an hour. Furthermore, your win is practically nothing. You might buy in for $100 to win $20 — you might as well just put that $100 in the bank.

Let me tell you a little story along these lines: I remember a bad beat I once took with two aces in a loose high-limit game. I was playing $50-$100 limit hold'em at the Garden City Club in San Jose. I raised it with pocket aces and got called in three spots.

The board came A-10-7. Somebody bet, an Asian player called, and I raised. They both called the raise. On fourth street came a five. Check, check, I bet. The first guy threw his hand away and the Asian called. On the end came a four, making the board A-10-7-5-4 . The Asian bet and I raised. He reraised and I called him. Then he showed me 3-2 in the hole!

True story — he had called a bet and a raise on the flop to catch something to draw to, picked up a middle buster on fourth street and called the double bet, and on the end came his straight card. I've seen a lot of bad things, but that's the worst play I've ever seen.

Don't Let Losing Affect You

Several poker mathematician types have mentioned that you should average a certain number of bets per hour when you play poker. I think that notion is erroneous. Say that you don't win a hand in the first hour and then you win five or six hands in the second hour without losing one — that's higher than one and one-half bets an hour, isn't it? Even if you haven't won a hand in two hours, you still play the hands you're supposed to play and don't worry as much about *when* you play them.

A lot of times you're going to sit down in a poker game and not hold any hands. In that case, you shouldn't lose any more than the antes since you haven't had any playable hands. Losing or not getting any cards should never affect your play: You don't call just to be calling.

Suppose you're playing $20-$40 and you're in the $20 blind. The pot gets raised and it's up to you. You don't just call with some trash like 9-2 just because you're halfway in the pot already. You don't make a $40 loss out of a $20 loss. You're always hoping that you'll pick up a hand in the blind that you can win with, but if you don't pick it up, release the hand. Why chase when you know that you're taking the worst of it? The whole idea of poker is to get the best of it and have it work for you, have it stay the best.

But you see so many people making that automatic call out of the big blind, figuring that they already have one-half the bet in the pot. I love those kinds of players because I want to get some of their money. Sometimes they luck out when trash comes on the flop, but not often enough to overcome their bad play. It reminds me of horse racing: The best horse doesn't always win the race. And in limit hold'em, the best starting hand probably doesn't win even 50 percent of the time if it gets more than two callers. In multiway pots where people are in there with strange hands, all sorts of things can happen when those three cards come out on the flop.

Remember that not everybody plays by the book. They read the books and then play their own style. Many beginning players and new tournament players have given me good comments on our books. A lot of players are reading them over and over, incorporating things that they have read into their own styles of play. You can get out of any book what you want to get out of it. Out of the knowledge that you are given, you just have to search out those parts that work best for you.

Play in a Game that Compensates Your Skill Level

If you're a serious player, you have to figure that your time is worth X-number of dollars an hour and you should play in a game that will compensate you accordingly. Playing poker is your job. If the minimum wage is $5.50 an hour and you follow the guidelines of only making one or one and a-half big bets an hour at $5-$10, that's about $8 to $12 an hour. You might as well be working at a regular job! Then at least you know you'll get paid. For a recreational player, it's fine to play in the small games, but as a player who wants to win money, you're better off saving up enough money to play at limits where you can really win something.

If you are a working pro or a serious player accustomed to playing $20-$40 or higher, I don't believe in playing a low-limit game to pass the time until your preferred game starts. If a $20-$40 game isn't open and there's no list for it, why not hop in your car and go to another casino? It isn't that unusual for someone to lose $500 in a $5-$10 game. Can you afford to lose $500 in a game in which you probably cannot recoup that size a loss?

I've also seen $5-$10 players get stuck in their regular game and jump into a higher game, but since they're just as bad at the higher limits as they were at the lower limits, they get stuck even more trying to get back what they lost in the first game.

Play Small Connectors in Selected Situations Only

Suppose you're holding small connectors in one of the last two positions and four or five players are already in the pot. If it hasn't been raised and it doesn't appear that you will get raised, why not play them? Or if it's a multiway pot that has been raised and it is unlikely that one of the two or three players behind you (the button and/or the two blinds) will reraise, why not take a flop? This is a very good time to play suited (or unsuited) connectors such as 5-4, for example.

If you flop to your hand, you probably will be the only one playing those cards. You may trap somebody holding big pairs or two high cards. What makes these hands worth playing is that you might win 15 or 20 bets with them, whereas if you don't flop to the hand, you can throw it away at a cost of only one or two bets.

But I don't suggest calling with the small connectors from just any position — only from late position. Coming in from early position with them, or raising with them, just sets you up to get killed. Suppose you raise, someone behind you reraises, and you call. Then you don't flop to the hand, or maybe you flop third pair. With three bets already in the pot, you're tied to the hand and think, "I'll take off one more card and try to catch either my other card or a third one of these." And I don't suggest playing the small connectors very often in tournaments *unless* you have a ton of chips because you can burn up a whole lot of chips if you don't make the hand.

Remember that Kickers are Important

We used to play $2 limit hold'em back in the old days in Shreveport just for something to do. I had been playing draw poker and lowball for years, but when I first started playing hold'em just give me any ace and I'd play it. I was like a lot of these guys today, a lucky Leopold who didn't care a thing about having a kicker. But I learned fast. By about the third time I played hold'em, I had good kicker values.

In all forms of hold'em, the kicker is very important. Sometimes, though, whether you play a hand with a weak kicker depends on who your opponent is. Say that you have A♠ 7♠ and the flop comes A-K-2. Your opponent bets into you. Do you call him or not? Usually, you would call him in limit poker — but if you know that he only plays aces with decent kickers, you would throw the hand away. Again, knowing your opponents is the key. And always remember that any bet saved is a bet won.

Another type of hand that you see players calling raises with in multiway pots is big-little suited cards such as K♠ 6♠. I think that's horrible. First of all, if you're going to call with a big spread, you should always have the nut-flush draw. I'm not saying that I won't call with a hand like A-7 suited from a late position in an unraised pot, although I would rather have the ace suited to a wheel card (and obviously, you're going to play ace-face suited). But say that it's been raised and called in two spots and you hold A-J offsuit. You have to throw that hand away. However, if the A-J is suited the combined value of being suited and being in late position gives you enough of a price to usually call.

It is the big-little suited hands such as Q♦ 7♦ or J♣ 4♣ that are treacherous. Invariably, it seems that when you flop to the hand, you flop top pair. Then somebody bets into you and you call — with no kicker — and end up just wasting your money.

Avoid Long Calls on the End

In limit hold'em games when you get to the end of a big pot and a scare card comes at the river — a flush or straight card, or an overcard to your pair — and someone bets into you, a lot of players will say to themselves, "I think I'm beat, but I'm going to make the call anyway just in case I have the best hand." They make what I call a "long call."

Say that you do this ten times during a session, you call that big bet on the end when you know that you shouldn't. Those bets that you lost probably are what you would have won for the day. Making the long call on the end when you figure that you are beat is the biggest sin in all of limit hold'em. How about the call that you make when you have no pair on the end? Or when you call at the river with an A-K that has never been helped?

Maybe you called because you thought the bettor was bluffing. It's OK to call somebody for a bluff once in a while, but you can almost count on one hand the amount of times that someone bluffs in a multiway pot in limit poker. It just isn't worth your while to make the call, so just quickly determine who has won the hand and get on with the game.

In tournament play, making the long call is really bad. Say that you've been in the tournament for a long time and have $1,000 in chips. You're playing $100-$200 limits and call the $100 bet before the flop. Then you call $100 on the flop and $200 on the turn. Now you have $400 in the hand and someone bets into you at the river. You think that he has destroyed you, but you call anyway. Now you have only $400 left from your original $1,000. This simple math should show you that you simply cannot make those kinds of calls. Or maybe you were leading all the way and at the end, your opponent takes over the lead. It's like Ivory Snow, it's almost 99.99 percent pure that he has you beat ... but you call him anyway.

Always Try to Save Bets

The long call is the worst play you can make in limit hold'em, yet it is the mistake most often made in all forms of limit poker. You have to save those bets. People justify these calls because of the size of the pot, but ask them to justify it at the end of the day when they don't have any money left! You might say, "I was running unlucky." You weren't running bad, you made bad calls. You were unlucky that they caught their cards, but it sure wasn't a lack of luck that made you give your money away after they caught their cards.

Remember that a basic axiom of all poker is, "A bettor be, a caller never be." Unless you're calling for a reason. Suppose it's raised before the flop. On the flop it's checked around to the raiser. He has a big ace, but no pair. Instead of also checking, he leads at the pot. Then it gets back to one of the guys who checked and he pops it. So what does the original bettor do? He has no *reason* to call, but he *automatically* calls anyway. Now he has wasted two bets, his bet and the one he called. If he had checked it to start with, he could have gotten a free card and saved two bets.

Now suppose his card doesn't come off on fourth street and someone bets into him. He folds, but he has already wasted two bets that he didn't have to lose. Sometimes a player will bet with nothing because he figures that nobody else has anything either and they'll throw their hands away. Against one player I can understand it, but against two or more players who have checked to you, forget it. You have to save bets.

Stick to Your Standards

Many of the limit hold'em games these days are played multiway. Suppose you know that in the game you're playing, most of the pots are going to be played multiway. Should you change your starting-hand requirements. Should you play more hands? No to both questions. You should let your opponents play more hands while you maintain your own standards.

First of all, you're going to put a little fear into your opponents because you haven't played very many hands so that when you're in a pot, they're going to think that you're in there strong. This is where a little tighter image comes in handy. It is a fallacy that just because there are five people in the hand, you need a better hand to play. If you're playing your standard hands, you already have a good hand to start with. In a five-way pot it might be worth your while to take a flop to small pairs because if you flop the third one, you can win a big pot. You don't often flop that set and it costs you money, but that's the nature of the limit game.

T. J. Cloutier wins the Limit Hold'em championship in 1997 at the World Poker Finals tournament at Foxwoods Resort and Casino.

Always Bring Your A-Game To the Table with You

When you sit down, have your A-game in mind and stick to it. Leave your B-game and C-game at home. Any time you play, you should be willing to play your A-game. The hardest thing to do in poker is to play your A-game all the time, to play the way that you know you should.

When it comes to the decision, should I play this hand or should I do this or that, ask yourself, "Is that in my A-game?" That should run through your mind at all times. But what happens sometimes is that when you get into one of those loose games or wild games, you falter. Don't — losing and playing bad go hand in hand.

I say to bring your A-game with you every time you play, but I'll bet you can't do it! There's not a player alive who brings his A-game with him every single time. Doyle Brunson made a statement at the opening of the Tournament of Champions: "I have made myself a promise. I have promised that I will try to win this tournament instead of just showing up and throwing off my chips. I have decided that if I'm going to put in the hours to play this tournament, I'm going to try to win it." Which means that he was going to play his A-game all the way through. He did. And he came in fourth.

Doyle is one of the greatest gamblers who has ever lived and even he admits that he doesn't play his A-game all the time. But if you can put yourself in the frame of mind to not let anything bother you, to play the game the way you know how to play it best, you're going to win. Maybe not today, maybe not tomorrow, but over a year's time you will win. ♠

2

TYPES OF HOLD'EM GAMES:
HOW TO ADJUST YOUR PLAY

Tom McEvoy & T. J. Cloutier

Not all hold'em games are created equal. How you play the game in certain situations can be radically different from how you play under other conditions. In this chapter, we discuss how to adjust your strategy for various types of games. Look for answers to these questions:

- How can you best adjust your strategy to beat today's rammin'-jammin' games?

- What about changing your play in shorthanded games? In tight games?

- How do hand values change in jackpot games?

- Should you defend the "kill" in kill-pot games?

- Is there a difference in how you play in rake games and time games?

- How does the blind structure affect your play?

- How can you beat the maniacs? The weaklings? The rocks? The foxes?

Rammin'-Jammin' Games

Rammin'-jammin' (loose-aggressive) hold'em games are prevalent in California and the East Coast, not just at the lower limits but at the $10-$20, $20-$40, even $40-$80 limits. These loose-aggressive games are often referred to as no-fold'em hold'em, or California-style hold'em. Here are some things that you can do to adjust to these types of games.

TJ: If you're in a rammin'-jammin' game, you want *them* to do the rammin' and jammin', not you. You're not going to outgamble these people or outbluff them. If you're in a pot, you're always in there with a hand. They're still going to ram and jam and build a nice pot for you. You don't want to fall into their trap just because they're rammin' and jammin'.

Tom: In games where they're capping it with hands like 9-8 suited and two fours, I might want to play a few more hands selectively, hands that I may not normally play in capped pots, such as A-J suited or A-Q.

TJ: Limit hold'em is a big-card game, so you're going to play those hands anyway, aren't you?

Tom: If I'm playing a Nevada-style game with expert competition and it's raised and reraised by solid players before the flop, I'm not going to play A-Q or A-J. But against loose players in the rammin'-jammin' games, I'm going to play them. However I'm not going to take all that heat with hands such as two fours or J-10.

TJ: Which again gets down to knowing your opponents. But in these loose games, you're going to play the big cards like A-Q, A-J, K-Q suited. You're going to see the flop with those hands, but if you don't flop to them don't be a fool like the rest of them, get rid of them. Don't chase.

Tom: You don't just keep calling when all you have is overcards and they're firing into you, like so many loose players do. Loose players will raise with A-K, get three callers, and keep playing it even though they hit nothing on the flop. They'll never give up an A-K, even when it's obvious that someone has hit a pair. If the flop comes with something like 9-8-4, they will bet with their A-K instead of checking to try to get a free card, get check-raised, and continue playing it. This is a terrible play.

TJ: Or say that you are in the pot with low connectors like 7-6. The flop comes 4-4-3, giving you a middle buster. It's a rammin'-jammin' game where everybody's playing everything and they're all trying to take a card off. You need a five to make your straight. But if anybody has made a set of fours on the flop, there's a good chance that they also have a five (or even a three) to go with it because they're playing those little connectors too. So if the five comes and you make your straight, where are you? Your opponent may have filled up with the card that made your straight.

As far as I'm concerned, anytime that a pair hits the board and a player continues drawing to a middle-buster or an open-end straight in a multiway pot, he's a stone fool. You have to get rid of a straight draw when a pair hits the board because you might already be up against a set — and even if you make your hand, if someone also hits his hand and fills up, you're a gone goose. There's nothing worse than making your hand and losing all your money because you were drawing dead to start with.

Tom: In these rammin'-jammin' games you can play a few more hands selectively, but still play a bit tighter than the opposition. And play very solid on the flop and thereafter.

TJ: Also, you should not check the best hand in these loose games. Even if you flop the stone nuts, don't check it because your opponents are going to ram and jam some more and you'll get more money into the pot by betting than you will by checking. Don't give them a free card — even if you lead at the pot, they probably won't believe that you have the nuts and will keep on betting and raising until the end.

Tom: The nice thing in these types of games is that if you get the nuts and lead with it, not only do they *not* give you credit for it, they also *raise* you and then you can three-bet them and get in more bets than you would have if you had slowplayed the hand.

TJ: In a regular limit hold'em game, you might get a big-big hand and check it on the flop because you want to get a call on your double bet. But that goes out the door when you're in a rammin'-jammin' game. You lead at it with the little bet because you know that they're still coming. In these types of games, if they have draws they're going to go all the way to fifth street even though they might be drawing dead. So get all you can get out of your good hands.

Tom: They will take the worst flush draws, the worst straight draws, and keep coming with them. These players will play the 8-7 suited, flop a four-flush, and push it — so what if you have the A-Q in their suit? They don't seem to take that possibility into consideration. They will never give you credit for a higher flush until they've lost four or five bets to you.

Naturally, there is a frustration factor in these loose games when they chase down your legitimate hands or your big pairs and you don't get there. So, you have much bigger fluctuations in your bankroll.

TJ: But you expect those fluctuations. In a rammin'-jammin' game, you're lucky if you win 50 percent of the time when you started with the best hand. You can't let it bother you, you can't let it change your play, because over a period of time you're going to end up with the money. You'll win more money in the long run, but in the short run you'll have much bigger swings. When your good hands hold up, they'll be earning extra action that they wouldn't ordinarily earn so you'll win a lot more bets with them. Eventually, the luck factor will balance itself out.

Tom: At the lower limits, you will find many people playing any-ace and even any-king. You love those kinds of players. The only time that I can see playing those kinds of hands is when I'm in the small blind in an unraised pot and I can call for one-half a bet just because I'm getting a good price on it. Even then, if I flop to it I have to play with caution after the flop. Actually, I don't think you lose much by just passing from the blinds. Virtually never play these kinds of hands.

TJ: A lot of players talk about playing low connectors *suited* as though they must be suited in order to play them. Although being suited gives you a mathematical edge, playing low suited connectors can get you into trouble in rammin'-jammin' games when the flop comes in your suit. Why? Because the pots usually are multiway and if the flop comes in your suit and there is any substantial action, there's a good chance that someone else has the same suit with higher cards, in which case you'll be drawing dead to the flush. Of course, you can get away from the hand if the flop comes suited (if you're smart) because you realize that you're drawing to a baby flush. But if the flop comes with three different suits and you flop the nut straight or a draw to it, that's a different story. In that case, you have a playable hand.

Tom: Now let's look at playing medium connectors in a loose game. Suppose you have 9-8 and you decide to play it from an early position because you figure that the pot will be played multiway. The flop comes A-6-5. I have actually seen players lead with an inside-straight draw in this type of situation.

In my opinion, if you lead with this hand you're making two mistakes: (a) Playing medium connectors from up front, and (b) Leading into the field. Leading when an ace is on the board is way out of line, especially when you know that in these loose games players are quite likely to be playing any-ace. There is a strong possibility that someone will raise you, thus costing you even more money to continue with the hand.

A lot of people also play small pairs from any position, so you may already be up against a set. Given the loose game conditions, you want to play the small and medium connectors as cheaply as possible and certainly not from a front position.

Kill-Pot Games

Kill-pot games are popular in cardrooms across the country, especially at the lower limits. Sometimes these games are set up in a $6-$12 hold'em game, for example, where the betting goes to $9-$18 (a half-kill betting structure), or in some places the betting doubles (a full kill) to $12-$24. But most of the time, hold'em games are set up with a half-kill. If it's a $10-$20 game, whoever wins a pot that is more than a specific amount (usually $150-$200) has to kill the pot and the game limits move up to $15-$30. Or he may have to win two pots in a row to become the "killer."

In a typical $10-$20 game, the kill button is placed in front of the winning player, who has to post $15 no matter what position he is in. The small blind remains at $5 and the big blind stays at $10. The sequence of play is the same: The first person in front of the big blind has to either call the $15 or raise to $30. In most cardrooms, the killer must act in turn (he does not get last action.)

Just the fact that the bets are 50 percent more than usual entices some players to come into the pot. Rather than intimidating them, the bigger limits encourage them to play more. They won't sit down in a higher-limit game, but they'll play in a kill-pot game and they'll play looser than they usually would.

TJ: Any time the kill is behind you (he can act after you do), you need an even stronger hand than normal to enter the pot. Why? Because there's a very good chance that someone will come in for a raise, possibly even the killer. It also is less likely that you will be able to make a play at the pot and get people to fold because with that extra blind in the pot, somebody usually is going to play.

Remember this, too: When you start out in a regular game (with no kill) and it gets changed to a kill-pot game, the guys who want to change it usually are the ones who have more money sitting in front of them than the normal players might have in the game. It's bad for players on a limited bankroll because these other guys have enough of a bankroll to play the higher limits and they don't.

Tom: If the kill is based on winning two pots in a row, I have a lot less incentive to play the next hand with less than premium cards, especially since I know that I will have to kill it. Naturally if I have a premium hand when I am the killer, I'm going to bet it for value, since I figure to win more with it at the higher level.

Blind Structures

Tom: In $15-$30 cash games the small blind is $10 and the big blind is $15, which means that you are far more likely to get involved defending the small blind since it is two-thirds the size of the big blind. With the small blind two-thirds the size of the big blind, the $15-$30 cash game is unusual in that you will find more multiway pots.

Also, in the $30-$60 game the blinds are often $20-$30 since most casinos issue $10 chips for that game. Therefore, you have to expect the blinds to defend more often when you are attacking — you can't routinely expect both blinds to lay down their hands because they will be a bit more liberal in defending. This means that you will need to have a little bit better starting hands to attack with, unless the blinds are supertight players, in which case you can take a few more liberties against them. The point is that any time the small blind is two-thirds the size of the big blind, you probably will get involved more often in defending your blinds, and other players will be defending their blinds more often too.

TJ. From a practical standpoint, when the small blind is two-thirds the size of the big blind, players will defend it more often whether they should or not. Consequently, there usually are more players in the pots. You have to factor this into your strategy.

Tom: Definitely. In what I call a "normal" hold'em game in which the small blind is only one-half the size of the big blind, you have far less incentive to defend your small blind. In the $10-$20 game, for example, the blinds are $5-$10 and in the $20-$40 game the blinds are $10-$20. In this structure, not only are you out of position if someone raises but you also must have a much better hand to defend with.

TJ: Your criteria for the hands that you play should be the same for any size game that you play. If you're going to play $10-$20, it takes a certain amount of money to enter the game. If you're going to play $100-$200, it still takes a certain amount of money to get into that game. In relationship to your bankroll, your criteria for starting hands should be exactly the same no matter what limit you're playing. Whether you buy in for $500 in a $10-$20 game or $5,000 in a $100-$200 game, your criteria for starting hands must be the same.

The only time that a good player should worry about defending his blinds with weaker than his normal starting hands is when he cannot be reraised — this is criteria A-number-one. You have to be in a position where the raise was early enough and the callers are behind you so that there is nobody between you and the original raiser who can reraise. This is the only time that you can lower your standards when you are in the small or big blind.

If you are the small blind and know that the big blind is pretty tight and isn't a blind defender, you aren't worried that much about just this one player. That is the only time that you can call a raise from the small blind with a slightly weaker starting hand, such as a small pair. But like I said, the criteria for entering the pot should be the same in that spot as anywhere else unless you cannot be reraised.

Then you look at how many players are in the pot. If there are four or five players already in and you have 5-4 suited or even offsuit, why *wouldn't* you call? You know that if you flop to the hand, you're going to make a lot of money in this pot. If you don't flop to it, you can get rid of it. But if it's reraised before it gets to you, who wants to put in three bets with this hand? Or four bets if it can get reraised again before it gets back to you? You're just giving that money away. And you see it happening all the time: People defend their big blinds in limit poker. I think that one of your money earners at the end of the day is the bets that you save from not defending your big blind. Another bet that you can save at the end of the day is not making the long call.

Remember, too, that you are always out of position when you are in the blinds. Always. Of course, you can sometimes use that to your advantage. You are in the perfect position to check-raise, or if you get a big flop to your hand, you can lead at it hoping that someone behind you will raise so that you can reraise, so it isn't always terrible to be out of position. Of course the only player that you have position over in the big blind is the small blind. Position has always been emphasized as a major factor in hold'em. Although it isn't as major a consideration in limit games as it is in no-limit, position is still a very strong consideration in limit hold'em

Tom: You sometimes can win pots from a front position simply by putting pressure on the pot, if you have the right table image and the game conditions are favorable. While it is true that position is sometimes overrated, if you entirely ignore position in limit poker, you do so at your own peril.

T. J. Here is an example. Suppose you're in the big blind with a J-9 in an unraised pot with four limpers. The flop comes J-3-2. You have to act first. What do you do with your hand? Do you lead with it? No, you check it. Some people would say to bet it, but I don't go along with that because you have no kicker. Now if there are only two people in the pot besides you, then you can lead with the hand, but with more than that you should check it.

A Tip from the Top
You do not have to bet money
to find out where you stand in a hand.

You hear players say, "I bet to find out where I'm at." That's terrible. Why take a chance on losing two bets? If you bet the hand, you're willing to call one raise on the flop. With a flop of J-3-2, you're willing to call one raise in a limit game — but if you're beat, you could have saved two bets by not leading at the pot. It's OK for you to check this hand on the flop. That way, if it's bet and raised before it gets back to you, you can dump it without its having cost you a penny. You do *not* have to bet money to find out where you stand in a hand.

The blind that you posted isn't your money any longer anyway. Just consider it a loss. When people talk about defending the blind they think they're talking about defending their money, but they aren't — that money doesn't belong to them, it belongs to the pot. The pot is ownerless until somebody claims it at the end by either showing down the best hand or having no one call the final bet.

Most of the people who are getting broke playing poker are players who will never lay down the big blind. They just automatically call — and they're forever rebuying. Believe me, since that blind comes every nine or ten hands it's going to eat you up."

Tom: A typical winning pro wins maybe a bet and one-half or possibly two bets an hour. If he routinely defends his big blind with a bad hand, he has just lost an hour's worth of pay. Caro says that more pros lose more money from their play from up front in hold'em games, from the blinds through first or second position, than they do from any other play. I agree with him 100 percent. You see, a lot of pros think that because they are better players than the opposition they can play more hands. And they probably are right about that. But when they play more hands that are marginal out of position, they're kidding themselves.

Rake Games

The lower-limit games, $6-$12 and smaller, are almost invariably rake games in all casinos. In Nevada $10-$20 and $15-$30 and sometimes, $20-$40 games also are raked. Whether a game is a rake game or a time-collection game affects the strategy for playing that game. (Mike Caro has discussed this concept in greater detail than we will go into in this book.) In particular, if you are paying a time collection you don't have a lot of incentive to take many walks away from the table because you're paying for your walking time as well as your playing time. In rake games you can take more frequent breaks, especially just after you've taken a big loss on a hand, for example.

Also, as opposed to time-collection games, the rake in the smaller-limit games is much stronger. In other words, you're paying more proportionately to play in a rake game than you're paying to play in a time game.

TJ: Suppose you're playing in a $1-$3 game such as those played in a lot of cardrooms in California. You can buy into this game for $20. At least three players an hour are losing their original buy-ins to the rake — the rake is breaking three players an hour, and sometimes it's even higher.

Tom: Yes, and this is why it is so difficult for low-limit players to make money at poker. And this is why I tell my students who are hoping to play professional-level poker that they must play at the $10-$20 limit or higher to make a living. Even though the competition is weaker in the lower-limit games, players are paying so much more to play than they would in the higher-limit, tougher time-collection games. Of course, you can scratch out some money playing $6-$12 because the players at those limits are so weak, but you can't make a decent living from the small games. If you're a recreational player, it's fine to play the low-limit games — enjoy yourself. Just remember that the house is raking $60 to $90 an hour off the table and even more if it's a jackpot game. This is why so many players are walking around stuck, not playing until they can raise enough money for their next buy-in — the rake has taken its toll on their bankrolls.

Therefore if you have the skills and the money to play $10-$20 or higher, I strongly advise you to buy in to a time game. Even if the $10-$20 game is raked, the house usually takes only about $2.50 from each pot rather than the $3.00 that it extracts from the smaller games.

TJ: However, this doesn't mean that you should begin your poker career by playing at the higher limits. If you are a beginning player and you aren't going to risk a lot of money in a poker game, I suggest that you begin by playing real small to learn the game and learn to watch your opponents. If you want to become a *player* — and I am assuming that anyone who buys a poker book wants to become a player — once you learn the basics, you have to move up to games in which you can make some money. There comes a time when you must move up.

Remember that all the small-limit games, $1-$3 through $5-$10 are designed for the house. If the house had its way, it would keep every game $6-$12 and under. The house doesn't want to break anybody on any one play, they want them to come back day after day after day. And all the money winds up in the drop box. But there's nothing wrong with playing the small-limit games until you have learned enough to move up. Just consider the rake to be a part of the cost of your lessons.

If you move up before you have learned your lessons, even though the cost is smaller in the time games, the expense of playing against better players in the bigger games is too high. Why not learn for an average "tuition" of $60 to $100 a day rather than learning at a cost of $500 to $1,000 a day? If you're shopping in a supermarket, you're looking for the deals, aren't you? It's the same in poker: You're shopping for a cheaper way to learn your lessons.

Time Collection Games

Tom: California casinos usually collect a time fee on games that are $10-$20 and higher. Nevada casinos generally collect "time" for $30-$60 games and higher. In the East and on the Gulf Coast, policies are similar to the West Coast with casinos taking time collections on $20-$40 games and higher. Each cardroom has its own policies, but it is almost uniform for every casino to collect time for games that are $30-$60 and higher. In California the time fee is the highest and in Nevada it is the lowest.

Even though the collection is less expensive in Nevada, Las Vegas players still are considered stronger than those in other parts of the nation (rightly or wrongly), even though there are many strong professional players in all of these locations. Even in higher-limit games, you often see more loose action and more weak players in California and on the East Coast than you do in Las Vegas. So, even though you may be paying somewhat more in collection fees in other locales, you often are up against weaker players, which can help to offset the higher time fee.

In the "California" hold'em games, the rammin'-jammin' games that we discussed earlier, you see people playing a lot more pots with marginal hands. California players have acquired a reputation for being super-aggressive and loose. In particular, Asian players in California casinos have been stereotyped as being super-aggressive and super-loose, which sometimes is the case — but never overlook the fact that some of the very best cash game and tournament players are Asian.

TJ: I have heard some players ask if you should loosen up your hand selection in time games. Here are my comments on that: Rake versus time games should not have any effect whatsoever on the hands that you play. If you have good criteria for your hands, your expectant win for those hands is good. In other words, if you're selective with the cards that you play, even though you're going to take some beats, you're not going to lose that many pots. When you're playing poker, if you come into a hand you expect to win that hand. If you're calling just to play a pot, that's ridiculous.

If you're playing a time game, you may not want to be away from the table very often since you're paying for your space in it by the half-hour or hour. In a rake game you'll usually see players walking more often, which can cause problems, especially in Las Vegas where the cardrooms often are located adjacent to the sportsbook and players get up frequently to place their bets.

It is our opinion that the only difference between playing in rake games and time games is that in rake games, you're often playing against fewer players because they are not penalized by being away from the table.

Bad-Beat Jackpot Games

Tom: Tied in with rake games, which usually are the lower-limit games, are jackpot or bad-beat games. For years these games dominated the action in low-stakes games in California until the State outlawed jackpot games. An extra dollar usually was extracted from each pot for the jackpot, which made it even more difficult to overcome the rake. In its infinite wisdom (a facetious comment on its lack of virtually any knowledge whatsoever about poker), the State Supreme Court banned jackpot games as types of lotteries, which could not be run in competition with the legalized State lottery.

There used to be a huge contingent of players who traveled around from casino to casino in search of the biggest jackpot. If the jackpot at a casino reached $40,000 or up for a small-stakes game, it drastically affected not only the numbers of players in those games but the strategy as well.

T J: Another reason that California outlawed jackpot games is that the casino always has "first count," meaning that nobody really knows how much money actually has been collected from players for the jackpot fund. There was no way to account for how much money had been collected or how it was collected or how it got into the jackpot pool. And that still is true in many casinos. Nobody outside of the casino staff is sitting there counting how much extra money has come into the jackpot pool.

The casino also can charge what it calls an "administrative fee." So, it is possible that the extra dollar that was dropped down the bad-beat slot didn't go 100 percent into the jackpot fund itself, maybe only a small percentage of it actually made its way into the jackpot. Players don't know the house's criteria for increasing the jackpot, they just see running numbers posted on the board. There might be fifty tables in play, so it's hard to keep up with what you think the bad-beat jackpot should total.

Tom: Even though player contributions to bad-beat jackpots have been outlawed in California, they are still taken in Nevada casinos, where jackpots are very popular. The most common jackpots in hold'em are getting quads beat by a better hand, or getting aces-full beat. This is why pocket pairs go up in value.

The major point here is that when the bad-beat jackpot gets big, the play changes. When the jackpot gets very high, certain hands no longer have negative positional considerations and should be played. Virtually any pocket pair, even as low as deuces, should be played even in first position. You aren't aiming just to win the pot, your goal is to win the $40,000 or $50,000 bad-beat jackpot. Therefore, you're playing any pocket pair from any position.

TJ: If the jackpot can be won by any aces-full beat by a better hand, you are going to play ace-rag, including A-2 or A-8 offsuit from any position. You're going to play ace-anything *before* the flop, but not necessarily *after* the flop.

Still, the higher your ace kicker, the better because then you also have a chance to win the pot itself if no one else also makes aces-full. If you have A-2 in a jackpot game and the flop comes A-A-6 and you're up against an A-6, if a deuce doesn't come, you're shut out of the jackpot. You might know that you're beat, that you're drawing dead, but you're hoping to get there anyway to win your part of the jackpot — and you end up losing money.

Tom: Suited connectors also have value in hold'em jackpot games. Just remember that the suited connectors can make straight flushes, but it is very difficult to make straight flush against straight flush in hold'em. That is far more typical of the split games such as Omaha high-low. In hold'em it's a lot easier to make losing aces-full when you're playing ace-rag or to make quads against quads.

Usually, you should play the suited connectors more conservatively than you would play ace-anything or pocket pairs. It might be OK to play them for a single bet (or a bet and a single raise), but try to avoid putting in a lot of money with suited connectors in a capped pot, even in jackpot games. Aside from shooting for the jackpot, your goal is to try to hold your own despite the rake so that you can at least break even or perhaps book a small win. It is possible to beat these games, you understand, but with the extra rake and the fact that you are deviating from proper playing strategy, you are doubly handicapped in your efforts to beat the game itself.

In most jackpot games, both of your hole cards must play in order to qualify for the jackpot. Shane Smith gives this example: Early in her career, she had A-10 in a $2-$4 hold'em game. At the end the board was A-A-8-7-A. An opponent with pocket kings had just called throughout the hand and won the big end of the jackpot with aces-full beat. Shane's kicker had to beat the board for the jackpot to be hit. Both of her hole cards (A-10) played because the 10 was higher than the other two cards on the board. But suppose the flop had been A-A-J-7-A. In this case, the 10 does not play because it does not beat the board. This is the rule to qualify for most bad-beat jackpots.

When a jackpot is hit at your table, in addition to the winning and losing players receiving the bulk of the money, every player at the table usually gets a small percentage of the jackpot. But if you have not been dealt a hand when the jackpot is hit, you do not receive your share of it. This is why, when the jackpot gets high, players often will not leave the table for hours at a time, even for a bathroom break. Some players will put their bladders on hold for an amazingly long length of time to avoid the possibility of being absent when the jackpot is hit. Also, the casino usually requires that a minimum number of players be in the game to qualify for the jackpot. That number usually is five or more, although it varies from cardroom to cardroom.

Because of the unique circumstances surrounding bad-beat jackpot games, you can get hung on to a hand longer when you know that you're beat but want to try to draw out on your opponent to try to hit the jackpot prize. For example, say that two aces are on board and you have a pocket pair in your hand. An opponent has been betting the hand all the way and you know that you are beat, but you stay in hoping that the third ace will hit the board so that you can qualify for the big jackpot.

Unlike a regular side game with no jackpot where you simply get away from your hand as cheaply as possible, you are forced to put in many extra bets if you choose to chase a hand that you know is beat. Or suppose there are two aces on board and you have an ace with a weak kicker (A-4, for example), and you think that an opponent is in the hand with an ace and a bigger kicker. You're hoping that you both hit your kickers — so that you will lose to him with a smaller aces-full than he has. This is the only time in poker when you're hoping to lose the hand!

Strategies that would make no sense when a big jackpot is not in effect have to be factored in to adjust to the potential jackpot payout. You see, when you're playing jackpot poker, what you're really shooting for is a big score that is way above the size of the limits of the game you're playing. With that as your main consideration, normal poker principles quite often go out the window. Therefore, fluctuations are higher because you're playing hands that you might not otherwise play, and you're staying in hands longer than you normally would. When you're playing any pair from any position and any-ace, whether or not the pot is raised, you can expect your fortunes to rise and fall like the tides.

Sometimes, too, you don't get full value for your good hands because the betting may be weak when a jackpot hand is possible on the board. Quite often players will not push their hands when they believe that they have the best hand because they want to keep other players in the pot. They are hoping that their opponents will either catch up or even beat them if they think they have a hand that may qualify for the jackpot. A good example is when a player makes aces-up on the flop. Say that Harry has an A-J and there is an A-J on board. He hopes to catch another ace on the board, and that an opponent also will fill up when the ace hits.

Or suppose he has a pocket pair that hits a set on the flop. He's hoping that the fourth card of his rank comes and that some-one else will either beat it or lose to it with a qualifying jackpot hand. For example, suppose you have the 10♥ 10♣ in the hole and the flop comes 10♦ 9♠ 8♠. You're hoping that someone has the suited connectors in his hand and makes the straight flush if the 10♠ comes.

Sometimes, players blunder in bad-beat jackpot games. When they think that they're beat at the end, they blank out when it comes to showing down a qualifying jackpot hand. This is another reason why experienced jackpot players will slowplay their winning hands. Another hand they might slowplay is one where they have an ace in their hand and two aces come on the board. They have flopped three aces, although they don't yet have a full house or quads. But instead of pushing this hand, they will check or just call in the hope that an opponent will improve enough to qualify for the jackpot. Again, they aren't getting full value for their hands.

It is important to realize that people do these things in jackpot games so that you don't get dragged into losing pots by betting less than the nuts when one of these players is slowplaying the nut hand. If you don't have a hand that may possibly qualify for the jackpot, you sometimes can avoid making payoffs to players who you know habitually slowplay monster hands in jackpot games. This is a legitimate strategy consideration in these types of games. It also is another time when it pays to know your opponents, which ones will slowplay the nuts and which ones will continue to bet their hands.

T. J. also recommends that you should be sure that the other players at your table know the strategies unique to jackpot games. There have been cases when a tourist has laid down a jackpot hand because he thought that he was beat at the end. Sometimes a new player won't realize that he is sitting in a jackpot game and, not understanding the full ramifications of the situation, will cost himself and other players to lose a lot of money. On more than one occasion, I've even seen a fight break out when a player laid down the "losing" jackpot hand and it cost everybody their share of the booty. Or a player may have folded his hand on the turn when he knew that he was beat — exactly what he should do in a regular game — and then realized that he could have won his share of the jackpot if he had stayed to the river.

Since the jackpot often is divided among all the players at the table, T. J. advocates that you educate any new player coming into the game if there is a question in your mind as to whether the newcomer understands correct jackpot strategy.

Remember that throughout this discussion, we are talking about games in which the bad-beat jackpot is big-big-big so that it makes it worthwhile taking the downside for the chance to hit big on the upside.

Since jackpots were outlawed in California, the casino now puts up 100 percent of the bad-beat funds. These jackpots seldom reach the stratospheric heights that they used to. Whereas some of the bad-beat jackpots used to reach sums in excess of $40,000, today it is more usual for them to be around $2,000 to $3,000. Therefore, strategy considerations for the jackpot games in California are minimized. It is in the megajackpot games in other states where you must alter your strategy to factor in the jackpot.

Jackpot games might be very passive when two big hands are out against each other, or they might be wild since so many extra players usually are in the pots with any pair. Many times, two people with monster hands are playing very slow, just check-calling in an attempt to keep everyone in the pot in the hope that they will qualify for the jackpot. But sometimes, too, jackpot games become very wild since players figure that everyone is going to call anyway if they have even a remote possibility of qualifying for the jackpot, so they will push their hands for all they're worth. In this case, the game more resembles a normal hold'em game in which you do a lot of betting and raising when you think you have the best hand.

Therefore, if you're playing against loose, liberal jackpot players who will play anyway, your strategy should revert to the way that you would play in a more normal type of game. Again, you need to understand the mentality of the table and know when premium situations arise. T. J. points out that if he were at a table full of players who did not know proper jackpot strategy, he would immediately try to transfer into a different jackpot game where players presumably would better know how to play "jackpot poker."

If the jackpot is big enough ($40,000 or more) I can understand why even professional players might want to take a shot at it. Generally speaking, however, T. J. and I don't particularly like jackpot games and do not recommend them to serious players who are trying to play either professionally or semiprofessionally. With the extra rake, they are hard to beat.

However I do understand the lure of jackpot games. If you're simply a recreational player and want to take a shot at making a big win, go ahead and play them. Maybe you'll get "lucky" enough to get unlucky, lose a big hand, and make a big score.

Shorthanded Games

TJ: Position is even more important in shorthanded games than it is in full ring games. The fewer the players in the game, the stronger the button position becomes. Because you always have last action when you're on the button, it takes less strength to raise from the botton position, or to call a raise before the flop. Hands such as A-10 and A-9 become stronger than they are in full rings and you can raise with them when you have the button. And the mid-sized pocket pairs (sixes-tens) increase in value no matter what your position is.

Tom: Remember too that in shorthanded games the blinds go around very fast. If your style of play is too conservative for short games where you will be playing against people who play fast, you're going to wind up with problems because a fast style suits a short game far better than a conservative style. Your conservative style may work well in full ring games but not in shorthanded ones. In fact, because I am a conservative player myself, I am better off playing in full ring games.

TJ: It all depends on what kind of game you like to play. I would *rather* play shorthanded with aggressive players. There are definite personal criteria for playing in shorthanded games. For one, you have to figure that your talent is at least equal to or better than the other players in the game. If you know that the two or three other players in the game are better at short-handed play than you are, why would you sit down with them? Let's face it, the best player does not win every time he plays and you may beat him on any given occasion, but in the long run, he will beat you. You're going to make enough mistakes that he will end up getting the money. Forget the cards — in his actual play alone, the better player will beat you.

Shorthanded games are very aggressive games, and so, if you're the type of player who waits for a decent hand to play, you may not get that hand during the game. Your aggressive opponent might win 50 pots to your one. It isn't like no-limit games where if you win one decent pot, you will be even with the man. In limit hold'em, you're 49 pots behind!

Tom: In limit hold'em you usually have to show down some kind of hand and when you're constantly being attacked by a barrage of raises — which often happens in aggressive shorthanded games — that can be hard to do. In other words, you have to win about as many pots as you have lost to make up the difference whereas in no-limit, you can win one pot and get even or ahead.

T J: Keep in mind that you can always come back the next day when the cards might be running better for you or when you might find a game to play in that is better suited to your particular talents. Just remember that if you get stuck in limit hold'em, it's super hard to get out. Then you consider it a win if you just get even.

Tom. I have a rule-of-thumb that applies to any game I play: Do not lose more in one session at a particular limit than you can reasonably expect to win the next time you play.

Tight Games

In tight games you can't win as much money, but they're still beatable. You need to do a bit more attacking, but be willing to slam on the brakes quickly if you get played with. You will be playing a few more marginal hands when you're the first one in the pot, when you're the aggressor. For example, you might raise in middle position with a K-J offsuit because your opponents aren't defending their blinds and not too many people are coming into the pot. It always takes a much better hand to call a raise with than it does to raise with yourself.

If they start playing with you, you have to slow down. It isn't that you're playing a lot looser, it's just that you're playing more aggressively with your marginal hands when you are the first one to enter the pot. I'm not talking about when somebody else has already slipped into the pot. Sometimes a tight player will slip into the pot with a better hand than the one you were considering raising with.

TJ: At first you become more aggressive. But after someone has already opened in front of you, you have to be more selective. Because your opponents are tight players who only come in with premium hands, you have to be more selective of what you call them with when they have come into the pot.

Tom: Any tight player who raises from the first two spots under the gun usually has aces, kings, queens or big slick. His raise should shoot up a red flag for you: You have to have the goods to contest him. Tight players are the easiest opponents to read because they are far more predictable than the loose aggressive players. You know where they are at all times, so you can play accordingly. If you can beat their best hands — or stay away from their best hands — you can win against them. A lot of them simply duck an attack, which is where loose, aggressive, bad players get into trouble — they continue to give action to the tight players when the tight players are on the attack. This is a huge mistake, akin to walking up a steep mountain.

TJ: I've seen it happen thousands of times. A guy who's been sitting in the game for half an hour without playing a hand raises the pot — and he gets four or five callers! You wonder, are these people not even playing in this game? Do they not see that this man hasn't played a pot yet? The only way I'd call that raise is if I had a big-big hand.

Most tight players don't trap. They just bet out for value. Tight players don't play in most pots. They have to be betting and getting calls in order to get any money into the pot. They don't want to miss a bet. Let me tell you about a play that comes to mind: We were playing the final table of a limit hold'em tournament at the Queens Classic. The limits were $2,000-$4,000 and the play was tight. It was raised by an early seat and called by the next couple of seats. I was sitting in the big blind with A-K. I didn't even put in the one extra bet, I threw it away. The second guy in the pot was slowplaying with aces and won the pot. I had thrown away A-Q a zillion times just because I knew the player who raised; I knew that he wouldn't play anything less than A-K.

I've been wrong sometimes, yes, but when you're wrong *not* making the call from the blind, all you've lost is the blind; or if you're elsewhere at the table, you don't lose a thing by not calling. But if you're wrong *making* the call, it's going to cost you a lot of money.

A Tip from the Top
A Player who cannot lay down
a winning hand, cannot win.

Tom: That's exactly what happened to me in the Tournament of Champions. A guy who was shortstacked raised from a middle position. He was a good player but I thought that he was pushing the panic button. We were at $800-$1,600 and he only had about $3,000 in chips. I thought that he could be in with a somewhat weaker hand, so I called him on the button with K-Q. I flopped a queen but his pocket aces held up. My mistake was in thinking that he might be weak because he was so short on chips, when he actually had been sitting tight waiting for a premium hand to put in his case money. I didn't give him enough credit and I ended up doubling him up. He came back to bust me later in the tournament when I made a flush and he made a full house at the river.

TJ: Remember that there are a lot of players in tournaments who will not change their criteria no matter how few chips they have. I've seen them ante all the way down to their last chips, even going through the blinds, waiting for a hand. If they either make the bet or call a bet, forget it — they have a *hand.* This is why you should never make a marginal call against them.

Tom: This opponent was a very solid, professional player. A solid player will read situations and make the best positional play he possibly can, whereas a tight player will simply wait forever for a premium hand and then try to peddle it. A solid player waits for good hands, but will play less than a premium hand if he thinks it is the best hand and the best situation. This is how most professionals play whom I classify as being solid.

TJ: A solid player might make a move at a pot (bluff at it) with less than a premium hand knowing that it could serve two purposes. He knows that making the bet gives him two chances to win — he might catch a card to win or he might blow somebody else out of the pot, show them the hand, and then get calls later on. A solid player will do this (set up calls for later on) whereas a tight player almost never makes a move at the pot.

One of the best things that can happen in no-limit hold'em is to make this type of play at somebody and then show them your cards. It can throw an opponent off his game. For the rest of the game, he will never know where you're at, there will always be that little bit of doubt in his mind when you're betting at him. Of course, you'd be a fool to do it to him again. You're doing it so that he will come after you later on when you have a hand.

This works in limit hold'em, too. It can make you money in the long run and it's cheaper to do in limit games because all you're risking is the one-limit bet. If you raise and he comes back over the top of you, you throw the hand away anyhow because you don't have anything.

Solid Aggressive Games

Tom: You are more likely to find solid aggressive games at the higher limits where everybody in the game can play well and they also are very aggressive. In contrast, the players in the rammin'-jammin' games we talked about earlier simply *love* to play, but that doesn't necessarily mean that they *can* play. When you're playing the smaller limit games, a lot of the players are not very good, or they may be tourists or even beginners, but when you get to the higher limits, it is seldom that there are more than one or two players who don't belong in the game, people who haven't played long enough to play that type of game well. If you're not a highly aggressive player, how do you adjust to these fast games?

Let *them* be the aggressor. If you're in a full ring game, just play more solid than they do and lay back a little bit. You'll find plenty of opportunities to pick them off because they don't slow down often enough. I've been playing some $75-$150 split-pot games in California recently, and these are not my best games (Omaha high-low and seven-card stud, eight or better). My best game probably is limit hold'em, but I've been beating the split games not because I am more creative than my opponents but because I am being *less* creative. I am sitting back waiting for better hands while they're out there skating around with all kinds of stuff. They're out on a limb continually, putting all the heat on the pot early, but when I come into the pot, I'm always looking down at three or four premium cards. I'm not nearly as aggressive as they are, but my win ratio is much better than theirs. I have learned that in these games, you simply have to start with better hands.

TJ: You can be successful by playing aggressively in short-handed games, but in a full ring game where everybody else is being ultra-aggressive you should be the solid player. Pick your spots. In these full aggressive games, lead at the pot when you have a hand. Lead and let them raise you so that you can three-bet them. Or you might wait until fourth street to make your move when the bet is double. Of course, if you have the stone nuts and can't be drawn out on, and they're still playing very aggressively, you wouldn't make your raise on fourth street — you would wait until fifth street because you don't want to lose them.

Tom: So long as you don't show any aggression in return, some of these very aggressive players just keep firing.

TJ: Let me tell you how a typical hand goes in this type of game: Somebody's playing a K-7 suited and the flop comes king-high. An aggressive player leads at it, you call him, and on fourth street he leads at it again. You just call with the best hand. Then at the river he leads at it for the third time, but this time you raise him. And he calls! He might study for a minute or two first and then decide the pot's big enough that he should make the call.

Tom: Occasionally, of course, he will wake up and figure out that he's beat and fold. But just as often, he'll pay you off with a hand that was never good to start with. So he's made about four mistakes in the hand — getting involved in the first place, betting again on fourth and fifth streets, and calling a raise at the river.

TJ: With more players in the pot, just realize that unless you have a huge hand you can't play it this way. If all you have in this situation is a king with a better kicker, you had better make your move by fourth street because you don't want to give him the chance to hit his kicker on fifth street.

Tom: Exactly. In that case, you also want to try to whittle out anybody else from the field. You see, when you have a marginal hand that probably is the best hand at the moment, you have to protect it by trying to narrow the field. You don't want to give any free cards.

TJ: In limit hold'em tournaments, free cards are a no-no — more so than in any other game played — because there are too many people who are calling the original bet on some sort of draw. Say that you flop a big hand and you check it, giving them a free card. There are just too many combinations out against you that they can hit for nothing that you cannot afford to give them that free card. For example, somebody may pick up a straight or flush draw on the turn — when they wouldn't have called if you had bet on the flop — and then draw out on you at the river.

Tom: It is inevitable that your fluctuations will be much higher in very aggressive games than they are in normal games. I have seen players who have made the biggest wins in these aggressive games also set the record for the biggest losses. When a super-aggressive player loses early, goes on tilt and starts chasing, it's a thing of beauty. Then he's liable to go for his lumps, he just doesn't pull up.

TJ: The type of player that you love to play against is the one who starts off winning real big. Then all of a sudden, all of his win is gone and he's into his pocket for his own money. This type of player is liable to go for a big-big number because he's already tasted the feel of the win and he thinks that he can get it back. And he'll go farther and farther and play looser and looser as he goes down the drain.

If you get a loose goose in the game who doesn't have any idea what he's doing, that's fun too. Maybe you're playing with good players, but this guy just happens to also be in the game, in which case just remember that you're not the only one who's trying to get his money — there probably are seven or eight other players who also are trying to pick him off — so don't get yourself trapped in the middle trying to alleviate him of all of his chips.

One of my secrets to limit hold'em is this: If I get loser, I tighten up. I figure that maybe I'm making too many loose plays, so I tighten up my game. Even though I'm losing, anything that I win from that point on I consider to be a win. ♠

T. J. Cloutier beams a victorious smile upon winning the Limit Hold'em championship at the 1992 Hall of Fame.

3

Things to Think About ...

BEFORE THE FLOP

Tom McEvoy

Hold'em is a thinking person's game. You start thinking poker the minute you leave for the cardroom and don't stop until the last hand is dealt — and even then, you're still analyzing the way you played, how your opponents played, and what you can do to improve your play.

As soon as the cards are in the air, you're thinking about the three main topics we discuss in this chapter:

(1) Which hands you're going to play.
(2) The nature of your opponents.
(3) The game conditions.

T. J. and I discuss these three concepts and other key factors to consider in hold'em games. Look for answers to these questions:

• **Is it OK to play small and medium pairs from any position in rammin'-jammin' games?**

• **What about playing ace-rag?**

• **How does the nature of your opponents affect your decision to enter a pot?**

- How can the "Two Limper Rule" help in making quality decisions before the flop?

- How have starting hand values changed in today's California-style games?

- How tight should you play?

- How important is being suited?

- Why can you expect wider fluctuations in so many limit hold'em games these days?

- How can you become a situational thinker?

To Play or Not to Play, That is the Question

In the following pages we will be discussing how to play various starting hands. Remember that what we tell you should be tempered by the types of opponents who are in the pot with you. For example:

(1) Are they likely to raise in early position with small to medium pairs?

(2) Will they raise with small or large connectors that are either suited or unsuited?

(3) Might they reraise with these types of hands from any position?

(4) Will they call raises with bad hands?

Always remember that table observation and awareness are still your biggest asset and advantage in hold'em.

Playing Big Pairs

With a big pair you have no positional considerations other than how to best maximize the amount of money in the pot. When you know that you probably have the best hand, your goal is maximize the money that you can win and reduce the chances of getting your hand outrun. Generally, this means that I won't slowplay a big pair in limit hold'em. I would rather raise with it, even under the gun.

Big pairs are aces, kings and queens. Jacks are what I consider to be a medium-big pair. There is approximately a 50 percent chance that one or more overcards to the jacks will land on the flop. An overcard isn't necessarily fatal to any big pair, but it does mean that unless you flop a set you can't be nearly as confident about your hand being good when there's an overcard on board. Naturally, the bigger your pair the less likely an overcard will flop.

The biggest problem that most players have with big pairs is getting wed to them and not releasing them when it becomes clear that they are beat. For example, suppose that you decided not to raise before the flop with two aces because five or six people were already in the pot and you knew that you couldn't drive any of them out with a raise. The flop comes 8-7-6 or three of a suit (and you don't have the ace of that suit). This is the type of flop that potentially offers something to everybody: straight draws, pairs and overcards. Don't get married to your aces. Remember that a big pair is still only *one* pair.

If there is any substantial action on the flop, you're already beat and easily could be drawing dead or would have to catch runner-runner to salvage the pot (two consecutive cards that increase the value of your hand). Any time you're in a spot where you have to catch runner-runner, I don't like your chances too much. You're wasting valuable bets in a probably fruitless chase. Always remember that bets saved are just as important as bets earned.

Playing Two Aces

I will play two aces strong from any position. The only time that I might consider slowplaying them is strictly when I think that if I limp with them, someone behind me will raise so that I can reraise before the flop to make a bigger pot. Always keep in mind that the more people in the pot, the more likely your big pair will get drawn out on, so you have to do your best to protect big pocket pairs by trying to thin the field.

Unfortunately, you can't always do that. In fact, Mike Caro thinks that if a lot of people already are in the pot, you will only make the pot bigger rather than narrowing the field if you raise with a pair of aces from late position. The bigger pot will give your opponents a better price to draw against you, so it might be better to just call with aces. I agree with him — I would consider just calling with pocket aces when my raise won't drive anybody out of the pot but will make it big enough that almost anybody who catches a piece of the flop will be getting the right price to draw to it, whereas if the pot isn't raised, they won't be getting the right price and will be making a mistake if they continue chasing after the flop.

Late Position. The beauty of not raising with two aces from late position in multiway pots is that nobody will put you on aces and when they hold up, you can win a nice pot. And when the flop is unfavorable to the aces (three connecting cards or three flush cards when you don't have the ace in that suit), you can quietly muck those bullets and get away from the hand dirt cheap with no one being the wiser.

Understand that I don't think it is ever *wrong* to raise with the aces, so even if you decide to raise when the pot is multiway you aren't necessarily misplaying your hand. It's just that there are other strategy considerations. It also isn't wrong to just limp in from late position and see the flop cheaply, as Caro suggests.

Danger Flops. Any two picture cards that fall when you have two aces add up to a dangerous flop for your bullets. Quite often your opponents have flopped two pair, a pair and a straight draw, an open-ended straight draw or even a set. So if you get a lot of action when two face cards are on board, you probably are beat. You have to use good judgment as to whether you're going to proceed, how expensive your opponents are going to make it for you to continue. Sometimes when your treasured ace comes on the turn, it makes a straight for somebody else, so even with a set of aces you have to play cautiously if there are three straight cards on the board. In that case, I may very well shut down. I won't necessarily throw my hand away because I'm hoping to make a full house if there are more cards to come, but nothing says that I have to jam it to the hilt as some players do with three paints on the board and it's obvious that there is a straight out against them.

Now suppose you're in middle position with aces and two people have limped into the pot. In this situation I usually will raise with my pocket rockets to try to force out players behind me, including the two blinds. You probably won't be able to force out the limpers because once someone has voluntarily limped into the pot, he usually is going to call a single raise. Of course, it's a thing of beauty if you raise and someone comes over the top of you because that makes it more likely that other players will be forced out of the pot for the double bet, including the early limpers. If this situation arises, do not immediately reraise with your aces. Wait until fourth street if you get small cards or one face card on the flop. Then raise your opponent at the double-bet level. This is exactly what you would like to see happen — a bunch of dead money in the pot and you're heads-up with the best hand. How much sweeter can it be?

Playing Two Kings

I joke with my students that the first rule of hold'em is that any time you have pocket kings, an ace automatically falls on the flop. Obviously that isn't true, it just seems that when you are the fortunate recipient of two kings some guy who has called two raises with an A-2 offsuit flops an ace and knocks you off. Kings are always vulnerable to the dreaded ace coming on the board — and so many people will play any hand that contains an ace. Therefore I think that you virtually should never slowplay pocket kings. I will play as aggressively as I can before the flop to try to drive as many people out of the pot as possible.

The texture of the flop is very important. (I discuss this concept in great detail in *Tournament Poker*.) When any two high cards from J-10 on up to K-Q hit the board, they also hit a lot of players in several different ways. When you see a flop like that, even if your aces or kings are still good at the moment they can easily be outdrawn. So you have to try to either protect your hand if you think that it's still the best hand, or be prepared to abandon ship if a lot of betting and raising goes on before it gets to you. It's no disgrace to occasionally raise the white flag and live to fight another day. Not doing this is one of the biggest weaknesses that many limit hold'em players have. So seldom do they get a big pair like aces or kings that they become frustrated when they get a bad flop and continue playing the hand — even though they *know* they are beat — when they should fold it. Being able to make important laydowns is what separates the pros from the pretenders.

There are times when even two kings should be passed in limit hold'em ring games. Remember that guy who has the spider webs building up on his chips because he hasn't moved them in so long? Suppose he three-bets two solid players who have already entered the pot for a raise — what hand must he have? There's probably only one hand in the universe that he would be that aggressive with. Since you have two kings in your hand, it's highly unlikely that he has the other two kings, so what does that leave him with, two queens? If he's as rocky as you think he is, would he three-bet two other strong solid players who have raised early with two queens?! Not likely. He might see a flop with a pair of queens, but he probably wouldn't three-bet them. Therefore there is only one hand that he could have — two aces. Now what do you do with your pocket kings?

Playing Two Queens

Queens and jacks are a lot more vulnerable than aces and kings because of the potential for either an ace or a king hitting the board. When an overcard to the queens or jacks hits, the ace is always the most dangerous because more people will play a random hand that contains an ace than one that contains a king. I'm less worried if a king hits the board, especially if it's checked to me. If a king hits and an opponent checks to me, I usually will go ahead and bet my two queens. If I get raised or check-raised, then I will have to decide whether my opponent would have raised without having a king in his hand.

Generally speaking, if you are raised or check-raised when an overcard hits, it's time to abandon ship. You can't afford to be the sheriff at the table, calling people down on the outside chance that they may be trying to run over you or bluffing. If you fold 100 percent of the time when someone either bets into you or raises when an overcard to your pocket pair hits the board, you will be saving money in the long run. Remember too that even if you have the best hand at the moment, they must have something to be betting or raising with, which means that even if you do have the best hand with one or two cards to come, you could easily get drawn out on in a future round (if you aren't already beat). When an overcard comes, it should automatically raise a red flag in your mind — and a double-red flag when someone bets into you or raises.

Playing Two Jacks

Limit hold'em players misplay two jacks quite frequently; it seems to be a very difficult hand for most people to play. If you're the first one in the pot, it is quite correct to raise even under the gun, but if someone has already brought it in for a raise, three-betting the hand is not always the proper play.

Occasionally I might three-bet it, depending on who the raiser is, from what position he raised, and what I know about him. If a very solid player raises from under the gun, he usually has big cards so I probably won't three-bet it with pocket jacks although I will see the flop. If the raise comes from an action player in a late position, I almost certainly will three-bet it to try to isolate and get it heads-up. So what I do with the jacks depends on the action in front of me, what position it came from, and what I know about the player. Is he loose, is he tight, is he somewhere in between, is he an action player?

If more than two limpers are in the pot, I usually will also limp. That way, if the jacks are an overpair to the flop, I can play them strongly. And if an overcard comes, which happens around half the time, I can get away from the hand cheaply.

When to Fold'em. There also are times when I will fold either pocket jacks or queens. For example, when a massive raising war occurs before the flop and before the action gets to me and these are solid aggressive players waging the war. And which hands are they aggressive with? Big pairs and big slick. If they have a big pair, I'm in terrible shape with queens or jacks. I'm not talking about the maniacs, the kamikaze pilots who jam it with suited connectors or small pairs or other hands that don't warrant the action — I'm talking about solid players who don't go to war before the flop unless they have lots of bullets. If they're willing to fire their guns before they see any flop cards, this should be a red flag for you.

Every time that I have ditched pocket jacks or queens before the flop in these circumstances, I have been right. You will be too.

Playing Medium Pairs — Tens Through Sevens

With a pocket pair of tens down through sevens, you have to play more selectively. Tens are very vulnerable to overcards, although they do have added value in that you need either a ten or a five in your hand to complete a straight. If you start with two tens it is less likely that someone else has a ten in his hand, which gives you an edge if connecting straight cards come that require a ten for completion.

If I am the first one in the pot, I generally am willing to raise from middle position on with a pocket pair of tens, nines, or possibly eights. Of course, this is after two or three people already have passed. If I am the first to act (under the gun), I usually will limp in. If all hell breaks out around me — raise, raise, raise — it is a clear pass. If there is only one raise, I will see the flop and then determine how to proceed. If I'm against a loose raiser and have an overpair to the flop with my tens, nines or eights I usually would lead into him (if I think that I have the best hand) hoping that he will raise so I could reraise, or possibly even check-raise.

When I am up against a very solid player who has raised behind me, I will play the hand with genuine caution. If I bet my overpair on the flop and get raised and he keeps taking the lead, he's practically telling me out loud that he has a bigger over-pair than mine, or at least an A-K. Therefore I must decide whether

I want to continue with the hand. If I do, I will shut down and just check-call to the river. If I am convinced that I am beat, I will simply fold.

This is why position is so important in limit hold'em. I think that tens, nines and eights are a little too good to routinely pass, but playing them from an early position is one of the most difficult situations you can find yourself in. If you're in a very loose-passive game, you certainly can play them but if you're in a super-aggressive game in which it's getting jammed up every time, you may be better off in passing at the start. With two tens you are not a favorite to have an overpair to the flop, and if it's going to cost you three or four bets just to see the flop, that's too expensive.

Two sevens also is a medium pair, but don't forget that the bigger the pair the better off you are. So many times overcards to your sevens come on the board and even if they don't, that usually means that there are connecting cards out there that someone could have flopped a straight to or two pair. Remember that in loose games, a lot of players will play the smaller connectors.

In the loose-aggressive California-style hold'em games, a lot more players are coming in from earlier positions with medium and low pairs than what they're "supposed" to do according to standard hand charts. I actually have seen players gamble before the flop by raising from the blinds with hands such as pocket fours, which I think is ridiculous. The result of their raise is simply to build the pot so that other types of hands gain proper pot odds in calling the raise and continuing to play after the flop.

Invariably the raiser will have to flop a set to win the hand. Sometimes too, he will either lead at the pot into a large field or throw in extra bets if someone else bets. Of course, these players sometimes hit a set either on the flop or on a later street — and then they get to cackle and giggle, especially if their opponents have been betting all the way with overcards and bigger pairs.

A Tip from the Top
The cardinal rules of limit hold'em are:
- Hold'em is a big-card game.
- Position, Position, Position

The current style of play, especially in the wild and reckless California-style games, is to play *any* pair including deuces *and* to bring it in for a raise. This is not correct strategy, but it is what you have to contend with in these types of games. This is one reason why bankroll fluctuations are much greater in these games. In the long run, if you're playing a solid, conservative game you'll get the money — but in the short run, these types of games can play havoc with your bankroll and mess up your head. If you start to play with your emotions, losing your reason and logic, you wind up destroying your game plan. A lot of times otherwise reasonable players will start gambling just like their opponents are doing. When they do that, they are playing right into their opponents hands, playing the enemy's style of game.

Playing Little Pairs — Sixes through Deuces

Little pairs should not be played in early position, the first two or three spots in front of the big blind, *unless* you're in a very loose-passive game in which you can see a lot of flops cheaply because nobody's doing any raising. Under these conditions, I may very well limp in with a small pocket pair hoping to get a big flop to my little hand. Just remember that hold'em is a big card game. So when you play little pairs or medium pairs, try to play them cheaply with the idea of flopping a set to them and then making a lot of future bets to increase your implied odds. But if you have to put in a lot of money before the flop they are a losing proposition.

Naturally, the bigger the small or medium pair the better. With a pair of eights or sevens, you can flop an overpair to the board but that's a lot tougher to do when you have sixes or lower. I'm not adverse to gambling in position with these hands for one raise if enough people have already come into the pot and it's unlikely that anyone behind me will reraise. In other words, if a guy raises it up from early position and two or three players have called, I'm not going to throw away two sevens if only the blinds are left to act behind me. Because I will be getting big implied odds, I am willing to risk two bets to see the flop, try to hit the set, and then massacre everybody after the flop.

It is when you routinely play these hands in loose-aggressive games in capped pots that they go down in value. Or when you have two sevens, for example, and only one or two people are in the pot in a relatively tight game, you aren't getting much value for this hand. So what I try to do in a very tight game as opposed to a loose-aggressive game is this: If I'm the first one in I may decide to attack with medium pairs trying to pick up the blinds. If I'm not reraised I probably still have the best hand. And these small to medium pairs can win a fair amount of the time heads-up with no improvement. But once two or more people enter the pot, your chances of winning with a small or medium pair goes way down in value *unless* you flop a set. Therefore, the play of these small and medium pairs must be different in a tight game than in a rammer-jammer loose-aggressive game.

By the way, these rammin'-jammin' games used to be the exclusive province of the low-limit players but that no longer is the case, especially in California, Mississippi, and on the East Coast. A lot of players are being very aggressive in these games and gambling with hands that don't deserve it.

I have always preferred small or medium pairs over suited connectors because the pairs play so easy after the flop. My rule of thumb is "No set, no bet" unless I flop an open-ended straight draw or have an overpair to the flop and everyone defers to me, which means that I probably have the best hand. So long as I think that I have the best hand, I will keep pushing it. So, small and medium pairs play best in multiway pots, especially if you can see the pot cheaply and get good implied odds. This is why I don't like to raise much before the flop unless I'm just trying to pick up the blinds.

Players are making mistakes when they raise from up front with pairs like sixes. They're doing what I call "running the gauntlet," trying to run through the whole field yet to act behind them. Certainly they will occasionally flop a set and win with those hands, but you can say that much for any two cards. Just because any two cards can win doesn't mean that you should play any two cards, or play them aggressively.

Playing Ace-King

I have long felt that in all forms of hold'em, but particularly in limit hold'em, the most misplayed hand is A-K. I can't tell you how many times I've seen players flop absolutely nothing to this hand and continue playing all the way to the river trying to snag an ace or a king. Any time two or more people are in the pot and there's any kind of action to you, your hand is so much toilet paper.

I've seen people call a bet and a raise with A-K after the flop with no draws to it, with nothing except two overcards. This is horrible play, but people also do it with any two *other* overcards, not only with A-K. I'm not just talking about low-limit games here either — I'm talking about $10-$20 and up when someone has a dry ace and keeps coming. Sometimes a player will pair the ace or the king and still lose the pot.

The beauty of the A-K is that if you flop either one of your cards you always have top pair with top kicker. So when you get action from other players who also have flopped top pair, you always have the best of it. Remember that you're going to flop a pair to A-K, or any two unpaired starting cards, about 30 percent of the time, which means that you *won't* flop to it the vast majority of time. This doesn't mean that you shouldn't play the hand, of course, it just means that you're an underdog to flop to it.

Say that you raised with A-K from an early position and got four or five callers. The flop comes something like Q-9-2 rainbow. It is suicide from almost any betting standpoint to lead with this hand. Someone invariably is going to flop something. It's even worse if three connectors fall on the flop, in which case you could be drawing stone cold dead. If you lead into the field, you probably will have to call a raise to stay in the pot. But that's exactly what some kamikaze types will do — lead into the field with no pair, get raised, and continue playing the hand all the way to the river. This is madness.

If you have raised with A-K before the flop and then check it when you don't catch anything to the hand, you not only may get a free card but also may find that your table presence has improved: You are a player who only bets when you have value.

Either-Or Situations. There are times when I may continue to play the A-K even though I haven't flopped to it. Almost invariably that is when I am against only one or, at the most, two players and it looks to me as though it's an "either-or" situation. For example, the flop comes 9-9-2 with two to a suit on board. I'm not at all sure that my opponent(s) has a nine in his hand, although he could have a flush draw. I may decide that the A-K is still the best hand and keep coming with it.

The either-or part of my thinking is that *either* he has flopped a very big hand (or a very big draw) *or* he has flopped nothing. If I think that he has flopped nothing, I will keep playing the hand. Or if I think he is on a draw, I will keep playing. If the third flush card comes, naturally I will be prepared to fold. Occasionally, someone will have a pocket pair that he thinks is the best hand and play to the end because he thinks his pair is good (which it is), but sometimes you will spike an ace or king and beat his pocket pair.

Against more than two players, I am not going to continue playing an A-K after the flop when I flop nothing to it. Even against only two opponents, it must be an either-or situation. If you're up against tricky aggressive players who may or may not have flopped a pair, but who think that you're on A-K, they may be very aggressive with just a small pair or with nothing. Then you're forced to guess. Guessing is what you're trying to make your opponents do by your style of play. If you're the one who's always guessing, you're going to guess wrong. Guessing wrong is exactly what you want *them* to do, not yourself.

Sometimes when I'm heads-up with an A-K against an opponent that I don't think has flopped anything, I may check to him to induce him to bluff-bet just to get some action. Then I will call him down. But this play has to be done against a tricky-aggressive player that you think will bet with zilch. He must be someone who will bet with nothing thinking that you have nothing and hoping that you will lay down whatever you have — except that since your "nothing" is ace-high, it probably is better than his "nothing."

Playing Two Big Connected Cards

Playing A-Q. The big connectors that have the strongest value second to A-K are A-Q. In unraised pots an A-Q goes way up in value, but if the pot is raised by a solid player in an early position, the A-Q goes down in value and sometimes should not be played at all. It all depends on who did the raising, how tight he is. If you're up against a player who has a layer of dust on his chips, who hasn't played a hand in an hour, and he suddenly raises in first position, what do you think he might have? You can take that A-Q suited or not and pitch it in the muck because that's where it belongs.

Suited versus Unsuited Cards. Any two big unpaired cards lower than A-K or A-Q naturally go down in value. Being suited is a bonus, but most people magnify the value of having a suit. It isn't worth nearly as much as they think it is. According to *Super/System* by Doyle Brunson, if you start with A♦ K♦, you will flop two diamonds 10.94 percent of the time, making the odds against 8.14-to-1. You will flop an actual flush less than .85 percent of the time. Having a suit doesn't even come into play most of the time, which means that if two high cards aren't worth playing on the value of their ranks alone they probably shouldn't be played at all.

A Tip from the Top
If two cards are not worth playing
on the value of their ranks alone,
they probably should not be played at all.

For example, suppose you have the Q♣ J♣ in early position. This is a hand that most hold'em players will play under the gun, but they are making a mistake when they do that. A lot of these same players will not play a Q-J offsuit (although some of them will even play that) because they know that it usually is a losing hand. The Q-J suited might be a little bit better, but it still is a losing proposition from first or second position in a full ring game. Playing it is a mistake from a front position unless you're in a loose-passive game, in which case I might consider slipping into the pot with two big face cards. Of course I might raise with that same Q-J suited in a late position if no one has yet entered the pot. But playing it out of position, even for the minimum bet, is not a good play.

A lot of players use suitedness as an excuse to play a hand that they otherwise would not consider playing. Even so-called "good players" who are momentarily stuck or on tilt will enter pots out of position with inferior holdings because they are suited. But unless you have unusual psychic abilities or X-ray vision that allows you to read what's coming off the deck, you can never know if or when your coveted flush cards will hit the flop. Almost all of us have occasionally succumbed to emotions or hunches — "I just knew the flush was going to come" — and sometimes it does come, but usually it does not. Anybody could be a world beater if they always knew what was going to come on the flop, but we don't know that and so we have to abide by sound game theory and solid strategies about which cards to enter the pot with.

Throughout their poker careers most players, even the most successful pros, lose money on *any* hands they enter the pot with from the first three positions. So you have to be very selective about which hands you enter the pot with, and certain big cards (suited or not, connected or not) have to be played with caution, if at all, in the first three positions after the big blind.

When playing suited connectors or even non-connectors, you should realize that if you flop two cards of your suit, you are still an underdog after the flop. You are now committed to call on the flop and usually on fourth street. Thus, if you don't hit the flush you are burning up at least two bets, even more in a raised situation. Also, you might make the flush and still lose to a bigger flush if you're in a multiway pot. Remember that when you are playing a flush draw in a multi-player pot, it had better be the nut-flush draw.

Playing J-10 and Other Big Connectors. When I have two big connectors and will be the first one in the pot, I like to bring it in for a raise. This includes A-K through Q-J. It does not include J-10, which is the favorite hand of a lot of people. Remember that you might get a better hand the next deal, so why burn up money on J-10 with a raise? You can flat-call if you want to, or call a raise after you have limped in but why set yourself up to be reraised and cost yourself three bets instead of one or two?

There used to be a misconception that J-10 suited was the best starting hand in hold'em, but that has proved to be so much hogwash. Two aces is the best starting hand and will always remain that way. Played under the proper circumstances, a J-10 suited or unsuited can be a very profitable hand, however it isn't profitable if you play it under the gun or call multiple raises with it.

Some people call those raises with their beloved J-10 suited, just like they do with their big pairs, and then catch a little piece of the flop and trap themselves for multiple bets, usually with a sorry result. Occasionally they get there with the J-10, just as they might do with any two cards. In fact, any two cards (all the way down to 7-2 offsuit) can be played with profit under the right set of conditions. And any two cards up to and including kings often cannot be played under any conditions. Just about the only hand that you safely can say should be played 100 percent of the time is two aces.

The big connectors are A-K, A-Q, A-J and possibly K-Q and K-J, and I only like K-Q and K-J in unraised pots in late position. I have occasionally violated this principle and called a raise in late position with these two hands — and was justifiably punished. I also have limped in from early position with a K-Q or K-J, called a raise behind me, flopped top pair — and was punished. Does this mean that you should always fold your K-Q or K-J? Of course not. But it does mean that you must be selective about when you enter the pots with these types of hands.

For example, suppose there are two or three limpers in the pot and you have the K♠ J♠ two or three spots in front of the blinds. You don't want to raise with this hand, but you can see the flop with it. Ditto with a hand like A-10 suited. But let me clarify one thing: I also would call with these hands unsuited from a late position in an unraised pot with a couple of limpers already in the pot. But if the pot has been raised, these hands go down so much in value that they usually are not worth playing.

A Tip from the Top
Half the battle is avoiding traps before they snap their jaws on you.

I try to avoid having to make tricky, delicate decisions after the flop. When you play one of these marginal hands in a raised pot, many times you will flop something to it. If there is any kind of action in front of you, you will always be in a precarious situation. Before the flop you're actually looking for a hand that will play itself so that you won't need to make delicate decisions after the flop. Although I think that my personal judgment will be superior to most of the players in the game, that doesn't mean that my judgment is flawless. Half the battle is trying to avoid these traps before they snap their jaws on you.

Don't misunderstand me: I won't *routinely* throw away A-10 in late position, suited or unsuited, in an unraised pot. Sometimes I will slip in with it because my thinking is this: If someone really had a strong hand better than my A-10, he probably would have raised (unless he was sandbagging, which does happen). If I flop to it and there's a lot of strong action in front of me (remember that I entered the pot in late position), I can decide whether I should continue playing or should fold. Nothing is set in stone. Just because I came into the pot with an A-10 and flopped an ace — or better yet, flopped a ten (the biggest card on board) with top kicker — doesn't mean that I must continue playing the hand when there's a bet and a raise before it gets to me. People sometimes forget that.

Even a fair number of higher-limit players (not just low-limit players) will ignore positional considerations and continue playing in this type of situation. They will play 10♣ 9♣ under the gun or two deuces from early position, and with middle or small suited connectors or pairs, they will automatically call a raise. If I choose to gamble a little bit before the flop, I would much rather gamble with medium or small pairs because they play so much easier than connectors after the flop — a lot more judgment is involved with connectors if you catch a piece of the flop. But when I'm gambling with these hands, I want to have position and several limpers in the pot. I don't want to gamble with them from up front.

Playing the Small Connectors

The bigger the connectors, naturally the more value they have. The smaller the connectors the more vulnerable they are to overcards. When you play the bigger connectors and flop to them, you often will have the top pair, sometimes even top pair and big kicker which will hold up. With small connectors you don't have that luxury. You might pair up but have only a mediocre kicker.

For example, suppose you play the 8♣ 7♣ and the flop comes eight high. You have top pair with a weak kicker. You're vulnerable to overpairs and unless you flop a straight draw to go with your top pair, you can't take a lot of heat with your top pair. Remember that there are a lot of players with the any-ace mentality who play those A-8 hands and they will be giving you a run for your money with top pair, top kicker. If people are willing to go to war on the flop, you had better be able to make a fast surrender.

A lot of people always speak of connected hands as "suited connectors" as though they must be suited in order to play them. That is nonsense, of course. Although being suited may add a little more value, it also can get you into a world of trouble when you flop a flush draw and are up against a bigger flush draw.

Say that you have an 8-7 offsuit on the button and five or six people have already entered the pot. I think it's worth seeing the flop for a minimum bet because you have fairly good implied odds and you have position. I certainly would play the hand suited, so why wouldn't I also play it unsuited? Or suppose you're in the small blind with a hand like 5-4 offsuit. It certainly is worth another half-bet to see the flop, and you can defend the big blind with small or medium connectors when there are six or seven people already in the pot because you're getting a pretty good price for one more bet. If you don't flop to it, you can easily get away from the hand. So, there are several situations in which I would play two rather small, unsuited connectors — usually for the minimum bet or for one more raise under the conditions I have described. Very seldom will I come in cold for a raise with these types of hands. With nothing invested in the pot, why would you want to cold call a raise with a hand like 9-8 offsuit *or* suited?

Remember that hold'em is a game of big cards. Hands like 9-8 or 5-4 aren't what I would classify as big cards. I wouldn't even classify the J-10 that so many players fall in love with as big cards.

A Tip from the Top
In poker you must become a situational thinker.

Remember that in poker you have to be a "situational thinker," as my esteemed publisher Dana Smith puts it. At the lower limits it seems that the vast majority of players only know which cards *they* have without having a clue about what their opponents might be holding. They are guided only by hand values. As the limits increase, the sophistication of the players' thinking processes usually also increases. The best pros are players who can think on their feet, who can improvise and quickly adapt to changing game conditions or whatever has happened on the flop. Anybody who thinks that he has seen it all in poker (including the pros who have been around since Pearl Harbor) is forgetting that there is always something new under the sun, there's always some new wrinkle or new situation. The best pros can adapt to these changing conditions — they can figure out when someone is making a move at the pot and respond with a re-move with medium strength hands. This is where they make their bread and butter. They know when to play the marginal hands, when to continue with them, when to get loose from them — how to win with them.

The big hands such as the big pairs and big connectors usually play themselves, especially when you flop to them. The trash hands also play themselves because you usually aren't involved with them to start with unless you're in the blind in an unraised pot. It is all of the in-between hands — the connectors, the small pairs, the big connectors other than A-K — that require so much judgment. These are the "trouble" hands that require expert judgement in knowing when they can be played for profit.

Hold'em is deceptively simple. There is no memory work, all five community cards can easily be seen, and you don't have to remember any upcards (as you do in seven-card stud). Therefore some people think that they have mastered hold'em after a few initial successes at it. Or maybe they are the best players in their home games or local casino games and they think that they have mastered the game because they have beat their small group of opponents. But hold'em requires a lifetime of learning — no one is ever going to learn everything there is to know about it because something new is always coming up that changes the face of the game.

Adapting to Change. With the advent of the aggressive California-style of play, hold'em has evolved tremendously over the past ten years. Some of the super-aggressive players have risen to the top of the hold'em ranks. They have opened up their games and achieved highly successful results with a totally different style of play from more traditional hold'em players. What you hear from some of the more conservative players is, "These new guys just don't know how to play." Many of the older players who are so accustomed to a certain style of play that has been successful for them in the past may need to adjust their games to adapt to the changing style of hold'em. Some of them need to open up their games a bit more, as the new breed of player has done. Perhaps they have become too predictable, too stuck in the status quo, and are not adapting properly to today's faster style of play.

You must be willing to mix it up from time to time, not always waiting for two aces or two kings to enter the pot. Do I mean that you should start tossing in your chips on small connectors and pairs with reckless abandon? No, not at all. I am simply saying that when you are playing against loose-aggressive players, you cannot always fold just because they're doing a lot of raising. Sometimes you have to hang tough. For example, suppose you have A-K and the flop comes K-J-5 with two to a suit. The new breed of player might be raising, even capping the pot, with his flush draw but that doesn't mean that you should fold your A-K against him.

Of course, sometimes it does mean that you should fold — if the guy with the cobwebs on his chips comes out raising. The rock's raises mean a lot more than the loose-aggressive players who are pushing top pair with a weak kicker to the hilt. You have to understand the new breed of player's modus operandi, and the only way to know it is to study your opponents, get a line on what they're doing, see what types of hands they're turning over, and make appropriate adjustments. Never forget that poker is a people game played with cards, not a card game played with people.

Playing Ace-Anything

You will find a lot of players in loose-aggressive games who have the any-ace mentality, both in the low-limit and the bigger games. It's an ace and a race. These players are ultimately doomed to failure. There are times, however, when I will play a raggedy ace — usually when I am in late position and attacking the blinds and I think that my ace is good. Playing that ragged ace is one time when I give more credence to being suited, because when I am drawing to a flush at least I'm drawing to the nut flush.

If the pot is raised by an early player, you should pitch any ace that doesn't have a big card along with it. There may be one exception to this, and that is when it is a raised multi-way pot and you are on the button and will be getting a huge price for the hand. In that case, you might call the single raise hoping to hit your suit or lucky straight (if you have a wheel card with the ace). But be prepared to abandon ship immediately if all you flop is an ace and there is any kind of action in front of you.

Now suppose you're against only one or two players and you decide to play an A-9 because you don't think that your opponents have anything better than that. An ace comes on the flop and it is checked to you. Now you can be aggressive with this hand and continue betting until you have reason to believe that someone may have you beat. Just be very selective about when you play these types of hands.

If I'm up against one of those loose-passive guys who plays a lot of hands and I'm on or next to the button, I may raise with a rag ace to try to force the blinds out and play it heads-up against the weak-passive player who will spend most of his time checking. These are the types of players who will check-pass if they have nothing, and will only check-call if they have flopped something. Usually, they will not lead at you unless they have a big hand, although you can read that pretty easily.

Of course, these also are the types of players who might check-call through the entire hand with a better rag ace than I have, so if my opponent check-calls me on the flop and I can detect no possible draw that he could be on, I probably would also check after him on the turn and river. If I do decide to bet the turn and again he calls, I would not bet at the river because that would be a negative expectation bet. He would call me *only* if he could beat me, so there is no reason for me to bet.

Hands like A-9 or A-4 do have some value, then, against one loose-passive opponent when you have position on him. But anytime the pot is multiway, you usually don't want to play that type of hand. What do you want to flop to it? If you did catch a piece of the flop, you would wind up guessing about what to do with it.

I might play a rag ace in the small blind in an unraised multiway pot for a half a bet. On the flop I can check from first position and see what my opponents do and develop a pretty good idea of where I stand. You could say the same thing if you're on the button with an ace-rag, but over the years I have found that when I limp in with ace-rag on the button in multiway pots, I never know what I want to flop to it. Occasionally I will get two pair or flop a straight with my wheel-card kicker, but overall I have found that I have lost bets by getting involved with this type of hand.

Just be aware that a lot of people play any-ace so that you can be on the defense against that type of warped mentality. In fact, if your opponents are playing weak aces and you aren't, this can be one of your best sources of profit because you know that they will always give you action when you have the better kicker. A lot of these players know better than to play weak aces, but they just can't restrain themselves. Then when they flop an ace they just can't quite bring themselves to lay it down after the flop.

The ace-anything mentality is pervasive in hold'em games up to $10-$20, often $15-$30 and sometimes even $20-$40, but in games higher than that you very seldom run into it because the players in $30-$60 games and higher usually are far more sophisticated. In today's economy the $20-$40 game isn't quite as big a game as it used to be and you will see a fair amount of very liberal play at that level. For example, our publisher and editor Dana Smith was watching a $20-$40 hold'em side game during a tournament in a Southern California cardroom when this scenario came down: A player in middle position called the blind with the J♣ 5♣ and another player called with A♥ 4♦ two spots off the button. The flop came with the 8♣ 4♥ 3♠. The J-5 checked, the A-4 bet, the blind folded, and the J-5 called. On the turn came the 5♦. The J-5 checked, the A-4 bet, and the J-5 called. The river card was the 5♠. The J-5 bet and the A-4 called saying "OK, I'll pay you off," and later complained about the bad beat he had taken!

Is there ever a time when you will play total trash? For example, suppose eight out of ten players are in a pot and you're on the button with a low two-gapper such as 7-4. Do you play it? No, although you might occasionally play a one-gap hand such as 7-5 or 8-6. You certainly will not play something like Q-8 offsuit, although you might play a K-6 suited for a single bet (remember, only in late position in a multiway unraised pot). This is one of the only times that you might play this type of big-little suited hand. (Some players, especially in the very low-limit games, have the any-king mentality, which is even worse than the any-ace mind set.) However, you lose virtually nothing by passing these types of hand every time.

I might play a K-X suited when I am the first one in the pot in a very late position and several people already have passed. In this situation I might decide to make a play at the blinds, especially if they are not liberal blind defenders. You see, you can make a profit in hold'em with any two starting cards — under the right conditions. If you're playing in a fairly tight game and are in late position, you sometimes can pick up a tell from the blinds that they don't have much, and you can raise with even 7-2 offsuit. You aren't raising on the strength of your hand, you're simply making a positional play at the pot. Of course, in a loose-aggressive game you wouldn't even consider such a play. And you wouldn't make this play in loose-passive games because most of your opponents are calling stations. It makes no sense to raise a calling station or a liberal blind protector with 7-2.

The Nature of Your Opponents

Loose-Aggressive Players (Maniacs)

Loose-aggressive opponents are the most difficult opponents to play against because a lot of times you cannot put them on a specific hand. They will give action, make a lot of aggressive plays at you, and if they think you're weak they will come flying at the pot with a barrage of bets. Then it's up to you to decide whether they have a real hand or are just trying to take the pot from you because they think that you're weak. Sometimes they will come into the pot weak, but get a big flop to their bad hand. When this happens, it is very tough to put them on anything. I've seen loose-aggressive players raise the pot with 5♣ 3♣ from early position and the flop comes 6-4-2 — and if I have an overpair they're going to barbecue me. I'm going to lose some bets until I figure out what has happened to me.

Although the loose-aggressive players that you so often meet up with in the California-style games are difficult to play against, they can be your greatest source of profit. They are in so many pots with hands that don't warrant their action and they will often come chasing after you when you have the goods so that you will win some of your biggest pots against them. Sometimes they will force you to win a much bigger pot than you had planned to play because they put in so many extra bets with inferior hands or draws that didn't get there at the river.

They also can herd you right into the nuts. A maniac may not have the best hand, and you may have him beat, but another opponent may be sandbagging behind you with the best hand. This is one reason why playing against loose-aggressive players can cause such big fluctuations in your bankroll.

However, some of the best players in California are loose-aggressive. Men Nguyen falls into this category as does Kevin

Song. Although they usually play this style, they also are capable of changing gears and playing more conservatively. One of the problems with playing against these players is that it is hard to know when to give them credit for having a hand. They can be your most dangerous opponents if they really know where they are in a hand. When they have a pretty good read on you, but you don't really know where they're at, they can manipulate you in certain situations — *if* they are crafty and smart, and *if* they really have a good grasp on what they're doing. But if they are just the rammin'-jammin' type who might show you any two cards, they may be lost and not really know where they're at in the hand. Or they may be trying to just bulldoze their way through the hand by bluffing. You have to decide whether your aggressive opponent is a smart strong-aggressive type, the loose-aggressive marginal-hand type of action player, or simply a rammin'-jammin' gambler who will play anything.

Strong Opponents

A strong opponent usually plays pretty solid hold'em, makes the correct positional plays, has a good grasp of where he's at in a hand, plays good hand values and knows the value of position. These are usually the professional players, the ones you least want to play against. If you cannot avoid playing with them, always try to have position on them keeping them to your right as often as you can. If you yourself are a top player, you can understand the mentality of other top players better than others understand them, but still you would rather have them playing on your right than your left.

Weak Players

Weak opponents fall into several categories: They are either weak-passive, weak-tight or loose-aggressive players. The loose-aggressive player plays a lot of hands and frequently raises. The weak-tight player often will allow you to run over him, giving up his hand against your more aggressive play. The weak-passives are your ideal opponents, the most perfect people to play against. They don't push their strong hands, they allow you to dictate and dominate the action. They are the classic calling stations who won't bet their own hands but will call a lot of your bets, consequently they don't get full value from their winning hands. They also don't bluff often enough and usually wind up donating their money to their opponents.

Calling stations may pay you off at the end knowing that they can't win just because they are curious about what you were betting with. Sometimes it's worth it to them to call an extra bet on the end just to prove that they were right, that you did indeed have a better hand. If you are ever tempted to do this, just remember that curiosity killed the cat.

Of course, everybody knows that you never try to bluff a calling station, not once not ever. But you can value bet a lot of hands against them. You don't need to have a giant hand, just the best hand, and keep betting it trying to extract the most money from the calling station. You have to be sure enough in your mind that you have the best hand because the calling station will call you down with a lot of different holdings (third-best pair, two overcards).

The higher you go in the limits the fewer of these types of players you encounter. The higher a player progresses in the limits he plays, usually the stronger and more aggressive he becomes.

Tight Players

In the lower-limit games tight players usually will wind up making an overall profit, although not a huge profit since they don't play very many hands. When they are in the pot, they will always have stronger starting hands than most of their opponents.

At the higher limits against strong-aggressive players, tight players don't fare very well. The nit will not get enough premium hands to start with, and when he does get one he won't get much action on it anyway because the stronger players will read him for a strong hand and duck him so that he will end up winning smaller pots.

This is not the best way to be successful at the higher limits, although it is successful at the lower limits. You would be surprised how many low-limit players who have not been observing their opponents will call a raise against a super-nit who hasn't played a pot in an hour. You should not be giving this type of player any action. Once in a while, a rock will make a play at the pot but it happens so seldom it isn't worth trying to keep him honest. Even if you think that he might be taking advantage of his tight image by bluffing, it usually is a losing proposition to call down a tight player.

Deceptive Players

Deception is mandatory to achieve long-term success in any type of poker, particularly in limit hold'em. You cannot routinely play in a predictable fashion and hope to make a profit. Some other poker authors have suggested occasionally raising with hands such as 9-8 suited or a pair of fours from early position. The problem is that some people try this far too often, perhaps because they have the false idea that they should "advertise." However, they sometimes put too much money in their advertising budgets and wind up with only bad habits as pay for their efforts.

The deceptive players will occasionally bet strong hands, sometimes sandbag them looking for a check-raise, and occasionally check-call on third street waiting until fourth street to put in a raise, or even check-call to the river and then raise. They may even raise on come hands. In other words, they are always doing something a little bit tricky, mixing up their play to create confusion in their opponents' minds.

Of course, the more confusion you can create in the minds of your opponents the more likely they are going to make incorrect choices. When you put them to the guess, they usually guess wrong.

Game Conditions

It isn't so much the texture of the game as it is the *people mix* that I'm talking about here. Every game is made up of people, therefore if you know the kinds of players in your game you can better determine whether the game conditions are favorable to you. For example, if you realize that most players at your table are playing the "California-style" hold'em, you can make an adjustment to that faster style of game. Or if they're playing "by the book," you can adjust to the more traditional type of hold'em game.

A lot of players at your table may be playing the more traditional type of hold'em, but at the same table you may find two or three of the new breed of players, the rammin'-jammin' loose-aggressive guys. If you live in Southern California, one or two "freeway" players might also drop into your game on their way home from work or on their lunch hour. (In Las Vegas, they're called "tourists.") These freeway players aren't just sitting down in the lowest limit games, they're also playing $20-$40 — they have disposable income and like to play poker with it.

If most of the players at your table are playing "by the book," they are playing in a more predictable fashion. They have studied the Sklansky and Krieger hand-value charts and are pretty much playing according to those standards. Since these players are fairly predictable, you probably will know where they are in most hands and therefore, you should not lose any money to them unnecessarily.

The California-style hold'em players are more difficult to play against. These are tough players who are selectively aggressive and will make plays at the pot with a good sense of timing. It is difficult to always know where they're at in a hand. You want these guys to your right as often as possible.

The freeway players usually are playing what I jokingly call the "SOP" method, playing by the seat of their pants. They are in the game for a short time, they're there to play and just have a good time. They will play a lot of different types of hands, some of which are rather strange. Tourist types in Las Vegas have the same mentality. When a lot of them are at the table, there usually will be a lot more action in the games.

So you judge the game conditions by the types of players at your table and adjust your play accordingly.

Show 'n Tell Hold'em. Another name for these games is no fold'em hold'em. They usually are played at the lower limits and sometimes in the $10-$20 games where you will find five or six players contesting each pot. Occasionally you'll even find show 'n tell players at the $20-$40 level, although not very often.

If you're in one of these multiway-pot, rammer jammer games where every pot is raised and reraised with five or six players contesting most pots, I personally believe that it is suicidal to try to run over players. They are not going to be run over, so you're going to have to show them a hand. This means that you should try to save bets as often as you can. Or if you have a marginal holding that can develop into the best hand or already is the best hand, try to play it aggressively enough to force players out. If you can't do that, try to play it as cheaply as you can, looking for a cheap showdown. It is virtually never correct to bluff under these game conditions because these players are not going to fold, they're going to call you.

Tight Games. If the game is basically tight, you can bluff more frequently and run over your opponents a little more often. Just be ready to slam on the brakes when they start playing with you. If they're prepared to play with you, they have a hand and if you don't have one of equal or greater strength, watch out.

How Many Players Are or Will Be In the Pot?

Your estimation of how many people are likely to be in a pot with you — how loose-aggressive, loose-passive, or tight the game is — will affect the hands that you consider entering the pot with. The perfect game is loose-passive, so if I'm in one of these types of games I might slip into the pot with a few more hands than I normally would play — in particular, small pairs and suited connectors even if I'm out of position with them. I will do this because they go up in value in multiway pots and conversely, they go down in value in shorthanded pots. Therefore, the type of game that I'm in will affect how many of these hands I decide to play.

The Two-Limper Rule. The two-limper rule says that once two people have voluntarily entered the pot for the minimum bet, the pot already has shaped up to be multiway. (I first coined this rule in *Tournament Poker*, where I discuss the concept in detail.) Counting the two blinds, there already are four people in the pot before the action gets around to the next player. Therefore, once two limpers are in there I will be more willing to slip in from middle position onward with a few more hands that I might have passed if I had been the first one in the pot.

For example, suppose I have two fours in middle position. This is a hand that I ordinarily would pass under normal game conditions in which 40 percent to 60 percent of the hands are raised before the flop. However, once two people have limped in making it a multiway pot, even if it gets raised behind me I know that I am getting a good price to the hand. I also may cold-call a raise with a pair of fours when four or five players to my right are already in the pot. What I don't want to have happen is to call a raise from an early position with four or five people yet to act behind me, anyone of whom could reraise and make it too expensive to play.

To summarize, the conditions under which I will cold-call a raise with a small pocket pair or small connectors are when several limpers are already in the pot and I am in very late position next to or on the button so that it is unlikely that I will get reraised. Usually, the limpers will not reraise (although they occasionally will violate that rule of thumb). If you're in the type of game where a raise lights a fire under the chairs of the limpers and they all go crazy with reraises, that's a different story — you're better off ducking the hand to start with. Of course, that's something that you should know as the result of your observations of your opponents.

You must play according to the existing game conditions. The more people in the pot, particularly a raised pot, the greater the pot odds which means that you have more incentive after the flop to continue playing if you catch any part of it. This is why some of the worst drawouts occur when you have a premium starting hand. Someone will flop bottom pair or a three-flush and will keep coming because there are 14 or 15 bets in the pot. They may not even be sure what the correct pot odds are, but in their minds at least they have enough of the flop to continue playing — and sometimes they put a terrible beat on you. A typical example is when someone enters the pot with

A-3 suited and the lowest card on the flop is a three. With bottom pair they keep coming, or with an inside straight draw, or with as little as a three-flush.

Manipulating the size of the pot and thereby influencing the pot odds is sometimes a way to protect your hand. Suppose that you have two aces, you're in late position and six people have already entered the pot. (Caro advocates just limping in, which is not all that bad a strategy.) It's never necessarily wrong to raise with two aces, but think about what happens when you raise. When you make the pot much bigger, the five or six people already in the pot are very likely to call your single raise. They will be getting a much bigger price to draw to virtually anything, therefore you are giving your opponents a good excuse to continue playing. If five people are contesting the pot and individually they are underdogs to you, you are the underdog to them collectively. One of them is liable to get there by hitting a lucky second pair, a backdoor flush, or a gutshot straight.

What Will It Cost You to Enter the Pot?

How much a hand will cost you to play definitely affects what you enter the pot with. The earlier your position the less information you have, therefore the more likely it is that you will be subjected to raises and reraises. This is why position is so important. The later your position the more information you have. You've seen the action in front of you, therefore you can come in with more hands on the button because you know that you're less likely to be subjected to a raise or reraise behind you.

As T. J. has so eloquently stated, never forget that limit hold'em is a big-card game. This doesn't mean that you can never play middle connectors but it does mean that they should be played for minimum bets in late position, as a general rule. If it's going to cost you more than a single raise, they simply are not playable.

If you know your opponents, you often can determine how much a pot is going to cost you. By simply looking to your left you also can pick up little tells on the enemy — you sometimes can determine who is probably going to play the hand and who is going to pitch his hand. You also may be able to tell whether someone is getting ready to raise because you see him loading up on chips. As Caro has written, chips flow in a clockwise motion around the table, meaning that you will win chips from people on your right and lose chips to those on your left. You have position over people to your right and the players to your left have position over you. This is why you're supposed to make friends with people on your left and make war with the bandits lurking on your right.

I know that a lot of this information is old hat to many of you, so I am hoping that it will act as a refresher course for you. Players at all levels tend to get lazy in their playing habits after a while. When I say "lazy" I mean that they become very predictable, playing the same hands in the same way all the time. This is why other authors have suggested mixing up your play by occasionally raising out of position with hands such as 7-6 suited or a pair of fives. If you happen to hit the flop, you not only win but your unpredictable play keeps your opponents off guard so that when you have a legitimate hand they will give you action. You might even show the hand that you raised with just to inspire later action. Some exceptionally clever players will do this with the idea of trying to plant that thought in their opponents' minds, and then they will pull the same trick again (raise with mediocre cards). But they have to be up against sophisticated players who think that deep, whereas most players don't.

A lot of players who have been beating the game begin to feel a little overconfident and think that they can play more hands, so they start slipping into the pot earlier and weaker, believing that they can outplay their opponents after the flop. They get sloppy, lose their discipline, and eventually it catches up with them.

Sometimes a player will deliberately stall his move or make a false move at the pot trying to get a fix on what the people behind him are going to do. Be wary of this angle shot and others. Also, don't make your move until the action gets to you so that you don't give off a tell about what you're planning to do, especially to players on your right. You want them to act the way they would if they had no knowledge of your intended action. For example, suppose I am in middle position with a hand like A-7 offsuit (which I normally wouldn't play) and there are no limpers in the pot. Even though I have a substandard hand, if I can tell that everyone behind me is getting ready to pitch their hands, I will bring it in for a raise because it probably will be a favorite with position against the random blind hands. ♠

Tom McEvoy wins the trophy (and the girl?) in Limit Hold'em at the 1994 Diamond Jim Brady tournament at the Bicycle Club.

4

Things to Think About ...
ON THE FLOP

Tom McEvoy & T. J. Cloutier

The heart and soul of limit hold'em is the flop. With your two hole cards and the three community cards, you now know five-sevenths of the hand. The flop defines the value of your hand — more hands will be determined by the flop than at any other time in the game. How well you play from there onward will pretty much dictate your success or failure as a hold'em player. Here are some questions that T. J. and I address in this chapter:

• **What if you raised before the flop with A-K and get no help on the flop?**

• **Do you ever continue with the hand when you flop bottom pair? What about middle pair?**

• **What if you flop top pair but have a bad kicker?**

• **When is it correct to draw to an inside straight?**

• **What do you do with a hand like K-Q when an ace hits on the flop?**

• **What is the primary reason why most players raise in limit hold'em?**

Obviously a lot of people will make hands on fourth and fifth streets, but if your hand doesn't mesh with the first three community cards you won't be there anyway. If you hit a lot of flops, you're going to be a winner in the game because the best hand on the flop holds up often enough to put you ahead, even though you would sometimes swear that it doesn't.

There are a few professional, aggressive players who will play somewhat weaker before the flop, play a few more hands than perhaps they should, but they have a great feel for where they're at and play superbly from the flop onward. They can get away with this style of play and still be highly successful whereas most players cannot. Therefore most of us need to start with good, solid hand values and know how to play position properly.

TJ: I'll give you a good example of this type of player. If you watch "Miami" John Cernuto play Omaha high-low, you will see him occasionally start with hands that are rather strange. But from the flop on, he plays absolutely perfect poker — and that's why he is a step above most Omaha high-low players. He has transferred this discipline and style to hold'em and has won several major hold'em tournaments. Now let's took a look at how Tom and I play various types of hands on the flop.

Top Pair-Top Kicker

Tom: This is a hand that I will play strongly and aggressively. The more players in the pot the less reason to try to slowplay, although I occasionally will slowplay against one or two opponents particularly against someone whom I think will take the aggressive lead in the betting. If I'm first to act I can possibly check-raise on the flop or wait until fourth street to check raise. But if I'm first to act in a multiway pot I will lead at it. I'm actually hoping that I will get raised so that the field will get thinned out.

TJ: But what if it's a broken board and you get raised? If the raiser is a good player, you probably would call but you would not lead again unless you improve.

Tom. Right. And of course, top pair-top kicker goes way down in value if there are three connecting cards on board (although it sometimes will give you some type of straight possibility). And it goes down in value if there are three suited cards on board and you don't have a card in that suit. You have to be wary of either a flopped flush or a strong flush draw out against you, and be very leery if a fourth card in that suit hits on the turn. The more people in the pot the more likely it is that someone either has you beat or is drawing to a strong hand.

Being last to act also affects my play when I have top pair-top kicker. Depending upon how many people are in the pot, I have several options. One option is to just smooth-call if there are one or two other people in the pot with me and someone has bet in front of me. My second option is to raise to try to thin the field. I like to raise if several people are in the pot with me.

TJ: I will only raise with this hand if I have one or two other players in the pot with me. More players means more possibilities for two pair or a set.

Tom: A lot of times I will wait until fourth street to put in the raise. Or if I have a single opponent who is extremely aggressive, I may wait until the river to raise so long as I am reasonably sure of two things: (1) That he will bet; and (2) That I still have the best hand. He must be this type of aggressive player because any real player will only call the raise if he has me beat. When a good player isn't sure that he has you beat, he will shut down.

This is another case when knowing the nature of your opponent is valuable. Some players will bet on fourth street but if they get called, they will shut down at the river. For example, if they have been betting A-Q when an ace is on the board and you (the preflop raiser) have just been calling with A-K, they may be fearful that you have an A-K and will decide to just check-call at the river rather than bet into you again. Sometimes players will be aggressive but if you raise them, they will fold. Other players will just keep on firing. The point is that you can get an extra bet from your opponent if you read him correctly. Your goal is to squeeze the maximum profit out of your one-pair hand.

TJ: The only time that I would raise on fourth street is when I am sure that my opponents have inferior hands. A lot of times fourth street gives opponents their second pair.

If there are several people yet to act behind me and someone bets into me, I would rather raise on the flop to thin out the field. Don't forget that I only have a one-pair hand and one-pair hands are very vulnerable so you have to protect them. One way to do that is to raise to try to thin the field. People with strong draws, open-end straight draws, flush draws and so on won't necessarily fold their hands but at least you're going to make them pay to try to draw out on you.

Remember that if someone has A-K, A-Q or A-J and the top pair is there, it's probably been a raised pot since players normally will bring it in for a raise with these types of hands. When you have top pair-top kicker, it always involves an ace, of course, or you wouldn't have top kicker.

Now what if you're in the pot in a freeroll situation with something like A-8 suited and the flop comes eight-high? This is a very dangerous flop because there are a lot of hold'em players who don't raise with pocket tens or nines, for example.

Tom: Also, it's almost a cinch that there are a couple of connecting cards on board if the flop comes eight-high. Since people play connectors, you could already be up against a made straight, a straight draw or two pair. Even though you have top pair-top kicker in an unraised pot with your A-8, you easily could be in trouble.

TJ: This is one of the reasons why I don't raise in a multiway pot when I make this type of hand on the flop.

Tom: If the pot was raised before the flop, more strength usually is out. Say that you had an A-J and decided to raise from late position and got called. The flop comes jack-high so you have top pair-top kicker. Even if two or three people are in the pot, I will lead at it because I don't think that an overpair is out since it didn't get reraised before the flop. As you can see, I will play this type of top pair-top kicker differently than I will play the A-8 type of hand we discussed above.

TJ: And you won't have to worry nearly as much if you get raised because quite often, the raise is coming from somebody with a K-J or Q-J, even a J-10. People will call a raise with those types of hands when you raise from a middle to late position because they don't think that you're that strong.

Tom: Yes and some players just like to gamble with those types of hands. Some people simply cannot lay down a K-J, Q-J or J-10.

TJ: As the hand develops after the flop, you have to play the way that the action dictates from there onward. Say that you have raised preflop with that A-J and the flop comes with J-9-4. One guy leads off with a bet, the next one folds and now it's up to you. What do you do with the hand? You're supposed to raise it in limit hold'em. If the original bettor comes back over the top of you, there's a chance that he might have two pair, a set or a draw: He could have J-9, trip nines, or Q-10. At that point, you have to decide how to proceed.

Tom: If I get three-bet in this spot, many times I will shut down with my one-pair hand, even with top kicker. I'm not going to throw my hand away, but I won't necessarily play back at my opponent. Of course, If I hit my kicker that's a different story.

TJ: Suppose the first guy bets, you raise and the man behind you puts in the third bet. A lot of times a good player will put in a raise in that spot when he has a draw to try to get you to check to him on the turn so that he can get a free card. The good player who raises in this spot probably does not have an overpair because the pot was raised before the flop. If it gets raised before the flop, most hold'em players will reraise with a pair of queens or higher. (Bad players aren't trying for free cards when they raise in this scenario, they're just trying to build a pot.) Whether the pot was raised or unraised pre-flop makes a big difference in how you play top pair-top kicker on the flop.

Tom. Absolutely. Suppose you raise up front with A-K or A-Q and get played with. On the flop you're up against a good player to act behind you. If the flop comes somewhat ragged — A-9-4, for example — I will certainly lead at the pot. If I get raised by the good player sitting behind me, I have to decide whether he would raise with a better hand than my A-K or whether he is testing me because he called my preflop raise with A-Q or A-J suited. Or would he put a play on me?

Based on the texture of the flop, if I suspect that he raised looking for a free card on the turn I will reraise him. Then if he pops it again, I will slam on the brakes. He has succeeded. Since he has put in four bets on the flop, he may have hit a set. It is doubtful that he holds an A-9 or A-4 because a good player normally will not play that type of hand. However he certainly would play two nines and he might even play a small pocket pair, so I have to shut down on the flop.

TJ: The best advice that we can give in this situation is to play your instincts. There is no cut and dried rule to cover it.

A Tip from the Top
There are no cut and dried rules
that cover everything. Sometimes
you must follow your instincts.

Tom: Many times I will simply check-call on fourth street and check-call at the river.

TJ: There also are times when you might check-call on the turn and by the time it gets to the river just say "I'm beat" and throw it away. It depends on how you feel about the hand.

One of the hardest hands to play on the flop is when you have an A-K and the flop comes K-Q-rag, K-J-rag or K-10 rag — these all are hands that people call raises with in limit hold'em. How do you proceed on this type of flop?

Tom: My normal response is to lead at it. If someone raises I know that he could have a variety of draws or two pair. So I may slow down and see what the turn card brings. If my opponent is very aggressive, I will reraise him and bet out on fourth street if a rag comes. If it's another threatening connecting card that doesn't help me, I will consider either folding or check-calling. If a rag comes I might check-call, or I might lead at it again if I think that my opponent is on a draw. Let's say that the flop comes K-Q-8, I bet and someone raises. People will raise with a king and a weak kicker, a draw, or sometimes even second pair. If I think that is the case, I will bet again on fourth street.

TJ: Now suppose that you're in a multiway pot. You bet your A-K, you get raised, and a player cold-calls the raise before the action gets back to you. How good is your A-K now? Obviously it goes way down in value. There are a lot of situations in which you simply throw it away on the flop and lose only one bet to it. You have to evaluate the quality of your opponents: Who is making the plays?

Tom: If they are rather wild players, you usually should still shut down but not necessarily throw the hand away.

TJ: Look at this scenario: You have the A-K and you're up against K-Q in one spot and J-10 in the other spot. With the K-Q-8 flop you lose the pot to the J-10 if you double-pair. And if you *trip* up, the K-Q *fills* up! You're in such a bad spot, it's pathetic. You started with the best hand, but on the flop you're so bad off it isn't even worth your calling.

Tom: You have to be able to read the situation and the players correctly to be able to make that laydown. And that really depends on your ability to read what the other players hold and your feel for the game. This is a talent that cannot always be taught. We can give you some scenarios to work with, but we cannot show you exactly how to do it.

Top Pair-No Kicker

This type of hand presents an entirely different problem. Say that you have an ace with a weak kicker and an ace flops. If there are several people left to act behind you, your best strategy is to check and see what happens. If it gets checked all the way around or if a very loose-aggressive player who is last to act bets, you might put in a check-raise against him if you don't think that he has an ace in his hand. You're trying to get everybody else out to get it heads-up with him. However if a solid player bets, your best play usually is to check-pass. Unless you have a straight or flush possibility, you have very few outs with only three cards that will hit your kicker.

Now suppose you're last to act and the two or three other people who are in the pot check around to you. With top pair-no kicker you can bet. If you get check-raised you are put to the decision as to whether your opponent would check-raise you with either a draw or with a hand that is worse than yours. Some players get very aggressive with second pair, for example, and will check-raise whoever bets last because they think that he doesn't have anything and is just trying to steal the pot. If that's the case, I might just flat-call the raise and then simply call him down. If he happens to have me beat, that's my misfortune. This is a situation in which you must read your opponent correctly.

Naturally I wouldn't call a check-raise and then proceed past fourth street if I were up against a solid player who probably has a hand. At best I have a marginal call on the flop trying to hit my kicker to make two pair. If I don't hit it on fourth street and he bets into me again, I will pass. In a multiway pot with so many bets in it, it usually is correct to call a check-raise and peel a card off as long as you're reasonably certain that if you hit your kicker you will have the best hand. Or if you're drawing to a straight or flush possibility and you also have top pair.

Another strategy that you might use when you have top pair-no kicker in a multiway pot was recommended to me by a professional player whose play I highly respect: "In this situation, my current line of play in a multiway pot is to check. This eliminates the check-raise and establishes the possibility of my raising on the turn if the action makes it look like I have the only ace or one of the two aces in play. After raising the turn, I favor checking at the river and hope for a favorable showdown." Certainly this is a viable way to handle top pair-no kicker in multiway pots.

But what if it's shorthanded? When you're in shorthanded situations you have a big decision to make. If you're up against only one player who either bets into you or check-raises you, you have to decide whether it is possible that he could have a weaker hand than yours. It doesn't matter if you have no kicker to the top pair *if* your opponent doesn't even have top pair. This is where your judgment comes in: Does he have the hand that he is representing? Again, your decision depends on knowledge of your opponent based on your observations of his play. Remember also that in shorthanded situations there's nothing wrong with check-calling through the showdown.

Top Pair With a Draw

Top pair with a flush or straight draw is a much stronger hand than top pair-no kicker. If there are lots of people in the pot when you have this type of draw and you can't drive them out with a raise, you are usually better off just calling and luring them into the pot hoping that they will stay in and that you complete your flush or straight.

If you have top pair with top kicker and *also* have a flush and straight draw to go with it, I think it's OK to be more aggressive with the hand. But what if your kicker is somewhat weaker? Suppose you have a Q-10 suited and you flop a queen along with two of your suit. You have top pair, but your kicker is only so-so. Anyone with A-Q, K-Q or Q-J has you beat on the flop. If a very aggressive player bets into you, this may be a good time to just flat-call and let anybody who wants to enter the pot behind you get in cheaply. There's a good chance that you will have to improve the hand to win anyway, so rather than trying to drive everybody out when you have a decent draw, let them come in.

On the other hand, if you think that you have the best hand with a flush or straight draw to go with it, you may want to raise the original bettor to try to drive everyone else out so that you will have a better chance of winning with top pair alone. Your strategy will depend upon whether you think that you have the best hand with top pair-mediocre kicker. If you think that you have the original bettor beat with the top pair, it's OK to be aggressive and raise with it to try to get it heads-up with position. However, if you think that you are beat at the moment, your best strategy is to just call, let others enter the pot cheaply, and get a better price to draw to the hand.

If it has been bet, two or three players have called, and nobody is left to act behind you, I think it's OK to go ahead and raise with top pair-mediocre kicker, assuming that you have a strong draw to go with it. First of all, you may drive out some of the other players, leaving some dead money in the pot. Secondly, you still have a reasonable draw to the hand. Also, your opponents often will just call and then check to you on fourth street, giving you the option of taking a free card if you haven't improved the hand.

As you can see, the play of top pair with a draw differs according to your table position and whether you think you have the best hand.

Playing Top Set

There is little difference in the way that you play top set, middle set or bottom set because it is so seldom that you will run into set over set (two competing sets). Although it doesn't happen very often, when it does happen you're simply going to lose a lot of bets if you have the weaker set. I wouldn't play middle set much differently from how I would play top set, nor would I play bottom set very differently from how I would play middle set — unless the action is so great that I have reason to believe that either a bigger set, a made flush or a made straight is out against my set. In that case, I would have to put on the brakes.

When you have top set and no made straight or flush is possible at the moment, your main strategy consideration is to build the biggest pot that you can build. You have a very strong hand with which you will win more than 80 percent of the time.

Occasionally a set may be connected to a very dangerous flop. For example, suppose it comes Q-J-10 and you hold 10-10. If someone has raised before the flop in early position, they easily could have raised with A-K, as most players would. In this case, you have to play more cautiously, especially if a lot of players are contesting the pot. There could even be pocket queens or jacks out against you. This doesn't mean that you should dump the hand, but if there is substantial action before it gets to you — it is bet, raised and reraised — you have to slam on the brakes. Based on the preflop action, if I think that a bigger set is out against me, I will pass. Laying down a set is one of the most difficult plays in limit hold'em.

If you're up against what you believe to be either a made flush or straight in a multiway pot, there usually is enough money in the pot to continue playing in the hope of filling up. In this case I usually will play the hand passively, just check-calling with it or flat-calling in late position.

The only exception might be if there was a lot of preflop raising and the pot is a substantial size so that I am getting a big price for drawing to a full house. Since I know that I will have to fill to win, I have to be getting a pretty big price to allow myself to get caught in the middle of a jammed pot if I truly believe that I'm beat at the moment. The worst situation to be in is having a one-out hand against a bigger set, whereas if you're up against a flush or a straight you have a reasonable chance to draw out.

If you are last to act and a flush or straight card hits on the turn and it is checked to you, your action will depend on how many players are in the pot. The fewer the players the more likely you should be to bet. If you get check-raised, you usually should just call trying to fill up at the river. If you don't fill at the river, you have to make a decision as to whether your opponent would have check-raised with less than a made flush or straight. If you're up against a conservative player who wouldn't bet or check-raise it with less than a pat hand, you have to lay it down. But if you're up against an Action Joe who makes a lot of aggressive plays, you probably should call him down. Against players who are new to the game, ones that you don't have a definite line on as yet, you might have a greater tendency to call them down because you just aren't sure yet about how they play.

When a scare card comes on fourth street and it's checked to me, if only one or two other people are in the pot I will go ahead and bet most of the time. But if I'm up against a notorious check-raiser who frequently sandbags, then I will have to make a close decision as to whether I have the best hand and should bet or check. If I'm in a multiway pot and it is checked to me when a flush card hits on the turn, I am in a somewhat greater dilemma about what to do. I like to be as aggressive as I can be as often as I can be. The more passive my opponents the more likely I am to bet. The more aggressive and deceptive they are the more likely I am to also check if a scare card comes on fourth street.

If I decide to just check on fourth street, a lot of players will automatically decide to fire out at the river no matter what comes. So long as a fourth straight or flush card doesn't hit, I most likely will pay off the hand.

T. J. Cloutier autographs a book at the Gamblers Book Club in Las Vegas during a book signing for *Championship Omaha*.

Playing An Overpair

An overpair to the flop is played somewhat similarly to top pair-top kicker. In other words, an overpair is a one-pair hand that must be protected. When I flop an overpair, I usually feel more confident if it is aces or kings. The smaller the overpair the more vulnerable it is, of course, and the bigger the overpair the greater the value that I put on it.

This is a hand that I will play aggressively on the flop because I am hoping to eliminate players in order to give my hand a better chance to hold up. This might mean checking in early to middle position hoping that someone will bet behind me so that I can check-raise and force people out, or it might mean leading into an aggressive player in the hope that he will raise and drive people out.

Suppose I raised with a pair of jacks before the flop, for example, and someone reraised. Then the flop comes something like 10-4-2. Now I will lead into the raiser who is on my left, hoping that he will raise so that I can thin out the field. Hopefully, he doesn't have a bigger pair than mine — if he does, I obviously have a bit of a problem. This is not the type of play that you want to make against Mr. Spider Web, the guy with the dust on his chips. You may bet once against the rock but if he raises, it's time to just call or even fold if you think that he has a bigger pair than you have.

You can occasionally slowplay an overpair if you're up against only one or two players. If I am the first to act against a very aggressive player, I like to check so that I can either check-raise on the flop or wait to check-raise on the turn. In this respect playing an overpair is quite similar to playing top pair-top kicker.

Playing a Middle Pair

Middle pair is one of the trickiest hands to play in hold'em. Sometimes it's good, sometimes it isn't good and trying to decide which is which is one of the most difficult decisions you have to make. Once again we get back to position and table image in limit hold'em.

Certain aggressive players play middle pair totally differently from the more traditional play of the past. They may play very aggressively with middle pair if they think it is the best hand, including check-raising on the flop. Sometimes they will lead with it and other times they will check-raise. Or if they think that they might be up against top pair, they sometimes will raise with middle pair hoping to get a free card.

What separates the men from the boys, the women from the girls, in limit hold'em games is being able to make proper judgements as to when that middle pair is the best hand and when it is not — when to get away from it and when to either be aggressive or call your opponent down with it. Suppose you're up against an aggressive player who bets a lot of drawing hands, or who is last to act and will bet when it is checked to him — or like so many players, if it is checked to him *twice* will bet the second time no matter what his hand is. If you're up against this type of player, then you have more reason to continue playing the hand. You may even want to raise him if you think that you have the best hand.

It's pretty sweet when you've put the guy on a bluff or semibluff, check-raise him with middle pair, and a player with a better pair or top pair folds — because you have made the right read at the right time. Again, knowledge of your opponents comes into play. If you have a really big kicker such as an ace or king, that helps too — the only catch is that someone else may have top pair with the same ace kicker and you can get in a world of hurt if an ace comes on the turn. So you have to be reasonably sure that you will have the best hand if you improve by hitting your kicker.

For example, suppose the flop comes K-J-4 and you have A-J. If you hit your kicker ace on the turn, one of your opponents may have an A-K and another might have a Q-10. Generally, most players will raise with an A-K before the flop whereas they won't raise with something like Q-10. Therefore if the pot was *not* raised before the flop, there is a greater danger that a Q-10 is out whereas if it was raised before the flop, you have a greater danger of being against an A-K than a Q-10. This is why the preflop action often determines what you do from the flop onward.

When You Have Bottom Pair

Bottom pair, of course, is an even worse hand than middle pair. Although it occasionally will be the best hand, it is not a hand that you can play with any degree of confidence against even one opponent. If I have bottom pair and no more than two people are in the pot, I will go ahead and bet if it is checked to me. The same goes for any pocket pair that I might have when there are three overcards on the board. For example, suppose I have a pair of threes and the board comes 9-7-4. If it's checked to me, I will bet *if* no more than two other players are in the pot. Bottom pair has to be played with caution and if you're first to act, it is almost a certainty that you will have to check, hope to get a free card, and make two pair or trips on the turn. If you are in a multiway pot, naturally you will check and then fold against any action.

Playing a Flush Draw

Flush draws are semibluffing hands. If you have overcards to the flop, so much the better because you have a chance to pair up and win the pot as well as hit your flush and win. The way that you play the flush draw depends on your position, how many people are in the pot, and what a raise might accomplish. If I am hoping to drive out potential callers with a hand that I know that I will have to hit the flush to win, it isn't correct to raise.

If I am heads-up with a flush draw and overcards, especially against a player who represents a lot of hands, it may very well be correct to raise and continue taking the lead, perhaps getting him to fold a slightly better hand. And of course, I can always improve by hitting the flush or pairing one of my overcards if he calls.

The Aggressive Approach. Suppose I am either last to act or next to last to act. Someone has bet and there are several callers between me and the bettor. In this situation I like to gamble with this type of hand (the nut-flush draw and two overcards to the flop) because I have a reasonable chance of winning by either hitting the flush or pairing one of my overcards. With two cards to come, I will make the flush approximately one time in three and if I have two or three other opponents in the pot, I'm getting the right price to raise with this hand. Even if I am reraised I still am getting the right price — in fact, I might even cap the pot and then if I don't get any improvement on fourth street I might get a free card, which I will gladly take.

Sophisticated players will read you for a potential semibluff when you make this play, and if a flush card doesn't come on fourth street they will lead into you. In fact I recommend making this type of play. If I think that an opponent is jamming it on just a draw and that draw doesn't hit on the turn card, I will fire right back into him so that he doesn't get a free card from me. He will have to pay to make his hand, even though there is enough money in the pot to justify his continuing to draw to it. By betting I know that I will have the best of it because he is not a favorite with one card to come.

TJ: Remember that a lot of times a raise on the flop is made by a drawing hand to get a free card. His raise is made in position: You're betting, he's raising behind you. He may be putting you on one pair and he raises so that you will check on the turn card. But good players recognize that move and so if no flush card or other scare card hits, they fire into the raiser again. Usually, only the better players make this play (raise in position with a drawing hand). Weak players seldom consider it — if they raise, it may be because they have a big draw but chances are that they aren't thinking, "If I raise, I'm gonna get two free cards as the result." They're just raising to build the pot and make their hand so that they can win a big pot, whereas the professional is making the raise to get cards for nothing at the higher level.

Tom: The pros understand this move and recognize it when other players make it. Usually they will make fewer moves if they think that their opponents understand what they're doing. They make these plays against weaker players who can't figure it out as easily. This is not to say that "players" don't make moves against other "players" — it's just that their thinking is at a different level.

TJ: If you're going to make this play, you had better be drawing at the nuts. You don't want to be drawing to a jack-high flush and raise to get a free card in a multiway pot where somebody else could be drawing to a higher flush.

Tom: A weak player also will find more excuses to play weak hands. Suppose a bad player has suited cards such as Q♠ 8♠. He wouldn't play this hand offsuit, but because the cards are suited he finds an excuse to enter the pot. This also is where a good player's edge lies: If you don't do what they do, you're ahead of the game. The biggest fault of most poker players is putting someone on a hand that they can beat in order to justify their call. The truly bad players are the ones who will make the overcall with two pair when, for example, another flush card falls on the end and there's a bet and a call before it gets to them. At that point, their two-pair is worthless but often, they still will make the overcall.

Position is not nearly as important to this type of (loose) player. He will play any hand from any position. If the action is three-bet to him and the maximum is four bets, he won't throw away a hand like 9♠ 8♠, he'll cap it. But as T. J. points out, when they're capping pots with hands like 9♠ 8♠, they usually have one of two reasons for doing it: (1) Either they're big winners in the game and have been racking up the game by catching hands and ramming and jamming, or (2) They're big losers in the game desperately trying to win a big pot to recoup their losses.

An Open-End Straight Draw

An open-end straight draw is played somewhat similarly to a flush draw. You can be aggressive with it on the come when you also have overcards. Otherwise it is more of a calling hand where you are hoping to make the hand as cheaply as possible and keep other people in the pot.

Suppose I have a K-Q in my hand and the flop comes with J-10-4. Many times, pairing up my king or queen will only get me in trouble, so I will be less aggressive with a straight draw than a flush draw. And if two suited cards are on board, I may have only six cards instead of eight to improve to the best hand. So you must be a little more careful with a straight draw than you would be with a flush draw.

However if I'm heads-up against an aggressive opponent who may not have the hand that he is representing, I might test him with a raise. Or if I'm against a timid player who I might be able to run over, I will do the same thing. The point is that you sometimes can take an aggressive posture with this type of hand against a single opponent.

I will gamble with an open-ended straight draw when I am last to act, the pot has been bet and several players have called, and either end of the straight will be the absolute nuts if I hit it. I'm getting around the same price with two cards to come (about 2-to-1 against) as I would be getting with a flush draw. I like to bet come hands aggressively in the right set of circumstances because I want to guarantee action when I have made hands. I want my opponents to know that I occasionally will raise with come hands in order to entice future action on hands that are not come hands.

An Inside Straight Draw

Try to play an inside-straight draw cheaply if you can. You might also semibluff with it if you're last to act, especially if you have overcards to the flop. For example, the flop comes 7-6-3 and your have 10-9 in late position. If it is checked to you, you might fire in a bet to try to pick up the pot. If you're called, at least you have some outs — you may hit an eight to make the nut straight or you might even pair up with a ten or nine to make the best hand.

However it is not a good idea to lead into the pot if you're first to act and there is an overcard on board — for example, if the flop comes with cards such as A-7-6. Although there are authors who have recommended betting into the field when there is an ace on board ("to drive out hands such as K-J"), I do not believe that this is a viable play.

The K-J types of hands probably are already beat when there's an ace on board so betting into the field doesn't accomplish that much. The bet may slightly increase your chances of winning that particular pot by getting players who have overcards to your hand to pass, but that will most likely be offset by the fact that it will cost you more to draw to the hand because you probably are going to be raised. This is where the reasoning breaks down, where the proponents of this type of play totally miss the boat.

Anybody who has an ace with a good kicker, the loose geese who are playing ace-rags, and even players with drawing hands are likely to raise and possibly reraise. So although you might slightly increase your chances of winning the pot by betting at it, you greatly increase the number of chips you probably will have to expend to draw to the hand. Drawing to it as cheaply as possible makes a lot more sense than drawing to it more expensively. Remember that your win at the end of a session often amounts to the bets that you have saved.

However if you are the last to act and it has been checked to you, it may be correct to bet one time because no one may have an ace in his hand and therefore may be afraid to contest the pot. You also might call a single bet when you are last to act and someone has bet in front of you. But when there is an ace on the board and you are first to act with an inside straight draw, it clearly is wrong to lead into several opponents. So many players play ace-anything that you are very likely to be subjected to one or more raises, especially in the loose California-types of hold'em games that we discussed earlier.

When I am either the first to act or am very early to act, I try to play an inside-straight draw as cheaply as possible in the hope of getting a free card to try to hit my hand (I am about an 11-to-1 underdog to hit it). If four or five people came into the pot for a raise before the flop, and I decided to call the raise from the big blind (which often is a reasonable thing to do), there now are 10 or 11 bets in the pot.

Now suppose that I check on the flop and somebody bets. It gets all the way around to me and either no one or only one player has called the bet. If there are only one or two people between me and the bettor, I think it is reasonable to call the bet and take off a card. The pot is now laying me approximately the right price, plus I am getting the implied odds (the future bets that I can expect to win if I hit the straight), so it is quite correct in this spot to call. But to subject myself to one or more raises by leading at the pot with only an inside-straight draw when there is a big overcard on board is sheer folly.

A Straight Draw with a Pair

Having a pair to go along with your straight draw is similar to having a flush draw with a pair. The pair gives you more outs, added strength. How aggressively you can play depends on how high your pair is. Suppose you have a K-Q and the flop comes Q-J-10. You have top pair with a good kicker, plus the open-end straight draw. This is a hand with which you can be reasonably aggressive. Even if someone has flopped two pair, you still have a reasonable number of wins against him. Or if an opponent has flopped a straight, you have the possibility of tying him or beating him if he has a 9-8. Now suppose that you have a slightly different hand, an A-Q, with the Q-J-10 flop. I like this scenario even better because if a king comes you have the nut straight whereas with a K-Q you make top two-pair but you don't make the straight.

These are the types of hands that I will play reasonably aggressively. If I am the first to act, I have no problem with leading into several opponents. However if the pot was jammed before the flop, I would be more reluctant to lead into it (I shouldn't be in it anyway with a K-Q or A-Q). Or if Mr. Spider Web raised before the flop, I would be concerned that he has a big pair and I would want to play the hand more cheaply. I wouldn't throw it away, but I also would not lead into a solid, aggressive raiser. I would play it more defensively, check to see what the action is, and continue to play against a single bet hoping that I would improve enough to win.

If I am last to act with top pair and a straight draw and everyone checks to me, I will bet 100 percent of the time against two or more people. If I am up against only one opponent and he is someone that I think is tricky and aggressive, a guy who will go after me if I check to him on a subsequent betting round, then I think it is OK to slowplay. But against two or more opponents, I want to protect the hand by betting it. On the flop I have only a one-pair hand and I don't like to give free cards with one-pair hands.

Free cards are the death knell in limit hold'em. So many times people will backdoor a hand that they would not have played if someone had bet on the flop. If several players are still in the pot with you after the flop, the chances are that one of them will get there. Therefore anytime I have a hand as good as top pair (even if I don't have top kicker) or if I have top pair with a good draw to go with it, I will bet the hand if it is checked to me. If I get check-raised I can always slow down and decide whether I want to continue playing the hand past fourth street when the bets double.

Playing Two Overcards

With the exception of A-K, two overcards to the flop may be the most misplayed hand in hold'em. I cannot tell you how many times I have seen players blunder when all they have is two overcards. They raise the pot going in with hands such as A-K, A-Q, A-J or K-Q. The flop comes nine high with three connecting lower cards and they keep coming in the hope of pairing one of their overcards. A fair number of times they still get beat even when they hit one of their big cards, but this type of player wins just often enough to encourage him to continue playing that way.

There are times when I will continue playing overcards, usually when I have an ace working in my hand, I'm up against an aggressive player, and the flop comes with something like 9-6-2. The aggressor may not have flopped anything but if he thinks that I haven't flopped anything either, he will try to take the pot away from me.

One of the weakest plays that I frequently see goes something like this: A player has the wonderful A-K that so many people fall in love with, three people limp into the pot before the flop, he raises it, and the big blind and all three limpers call. The flop comes with ragged cards and all four players check to him. With no pair and no draw, he bets into four other people. No matter how many trash cards are on board, almost inevitably someone has caught a piece of the flop. A fair amount of the time, the bettor will get check-raised or at the least, get called when he could have simply taken a free card. This scenario worsens from there on out: He gets check-raised and continues playing the hand, sometimes all the way to the river. He has lost all those extra bets with a hand that he could have checked on the flop and gotten away from cheaply on fourth street when someone bet into him. Again, bets saved are bets earned. People who habitually take a card off with only overcards to the board will be losers to limit hold'em in the long run.

Of course, there are times when you can continue with just overcards to the flop. Naturally, if you have a draw to your overcards you most likely will continue playing unless you get caught in the middle in a jammed pot, in which case it may not be worth it to draw to whatever you are trying to hit. And you might continue in the previous scenario that I described — that is, when you are heads-up against an aggressive opponent who is willing to represent a hand and come after you.

You also might continue if you get an "either-or" flop. For example the flop comes 9-9-2 rainbow. With a flop like that a player *either* has a very big hand *or* he has nothing. Occasionally, an opponent may have an in-between hand such as a pocket pair that may be good. With this type of flop I am far more likely to continue playing my A-K (for example) against an aggressive player, but I am not as willing to continue playing it against a tight player who check-raises me. Once again, knowledge of your opponents is important.

The overcards, particularly A-K, can be good a fair number of times against an either-or flop. But when multiple players are in the pot with you, that is far less likely to be true, so in a multiway pot you usually are better off just taking a free card if you can. I have to admit however, that I sometimes violate this rule. If I think that I still have the best hand with A-K, it isn't terrible to bet it realizing that I am subjecting myself to a possible check-raise. If that happens I will have to decide whether I want to continue with the hand — if a player indeed has tripped up on the flop, I may be drawing dead unless I catch runner-runner aces or kings. Therefore it usually is better to either fold when several people are in the pot and one of them bets into you, or take a free card if you can.

When You Flop Nothing, Zero

To quote Cool Hand Luke, "Sometimes nothing is a pretty good hand." For example, nothing might be a pretty good hand if you're up against a very tight player who will just give it up if you bet. Or if you're against a loose-passive player who will just call before the flop and fold on the flop if he doesn't have anything. Occasionally, you can run over this type of player, but you cannot run over an aggressive Mr. Loose Goose nor should you try.

Now suppose you're on a come hand that doesn't arrive and you have nothing at the river. I have seen people bet on the end with something like a jack-high hand with which they couldn't win in a showdown. Invariably they will be called and then say, "Well, I couldn't win the pot any other way." When several people are in the pot and you have nothing, you usually cannot win with a bet. In fact, betting will only cost you more money in the long run because you usually cannot steal the pot.

Occasionally you can steal it against a single passive opponent who you think was on a drawing hand. Maybe you can't beat his drawing hand, but you may be able to get him to lay it down. Or maybe you've put him on just an ace-high hand. You can't beat the ace but you don't think that he has paired up and probably will fold if you bet. But even though they are loose-passive, some of these timid players will call you down. So always remember the "loose" part and expect them to occasionally call.

A Tip from the Top
All forms of limit poker are designed
to have a showdown at the end.

Betting with nothing is one form of bluffing. Many limit hold'em players highly overrate the bluff and try it far too often. The element of the big bluff frequently comes into play in big-bet poker, in pot-limit and no-limit games, but all forms of limit poker are *designed* to have a showdown.

Remember that in limit games the pot may have 20 bets in it and it is only going to cost an opponent one more bet to call. He's going to make that call a fair number of times if he has any kind of hand at all. Therefore you simply cannot steal that many pots by bluffing in limit hold'em. I'm not saying that you can never steal, just remember that the bigger the pot the more likely it is that someone will call you. And the more players in the pot the more likely you will get called. These are good reasons to be very selective about attempting to bluff.

It is much easier to be successful bluffing at a small pot than a big pot because players don't have much investment in a small pot and are more likely to give it up. In fact, you can develop a loose rammer-jammer image by constantly betting at small pots. Your opponents will suspect that you're always stealing and so they will give you action in the big pots when you are not stealing. This is a very viable strategy: Get them to think that you're a bluffer when in reality you are only trying to steal when you have a much higher likelihood of getting away with it (that is, when the pots are small and you have only one or two opponents). If they are not fully observant, they will not recognize that this is what you are doing. Of course, image plays don't make much sense if your opponents are not observant enough to notice what you're doing.

Reasons to Raise

Obviously there are many reasons to raise in limit hold'em. We realize that most of you already know them, so we're including them here as just a sort of refresher course. One reason to raise is to get more money into the pot because you have the best hand. Another is to thin out the field so that your hand has a better chance of holding up. Occasionally you raise on a semibluff to get a free card when you have a strong draw and overcards, and you know that your opponent is likely to check to you on fourth street when the bets double.

TJ: But the main reason you raise is because you have a good hand and you want to start building the pot early. Building the pot isn't the only reason, but it is the main reason.

Tom: Ditto for reraising. In most of the loose-aggressive games, raising and reraising are done to build a monster pot.

TJ: Before you decide to reraise before the flop, there are some things that you should think about. For example, do you want your opponents to know the strength of your hand? Most preflop reraisers tip off the value of their hands. Of course some players will cap it with hands like 8-7 suited in rammin'-jammin' games, although not that often. There are players who like to have the privilege in putting in the last raise, sometimes with a piece of cheese they shouldn't have played to start with.

Usually you aren't going to be able to thin the field because the people who really want to play are going to play anyway. Say that you're sitting around back and a player raises from first position. The guy in seat four calls, the man in seat five calls, seat seven calls and now you decide to reraise. Don't plan to limit the field with this raise: In limit hold'em, they're all going to call you anyway. But say that you are sitting right behind the original raiser. Now you might reraise to thin out the field behind you. But in other situations, you're simply tipping your hand.

Tom: Sometimes you don't care if you tip your hand. Suppose you have two aces or two kings — you know that you're tipping your hand with a reraise and you know that they're going to call you anyway, but you're building the pot when you clearly have the best of it.

However if you're up against very sophisticated players who know that your reraise means a big pair, you may want to just smooth-call and try to nail them after the flop. Again you're playing the players and the situation. None of this is set in cement: You have to adjust to the conditions of the moment, to what's going on in your game.

When to Check-Raise

Tom: The purpose of the check-raise is almost always to get more money in the pot because you think it's the best way to build a pot when you believe that you have the best hand.

It makes very little sense to check-raise on a draw. I occasionally will do it against one opponent who is super-aggressive and might be out of line, especially if my drawing hand is headed by an ace and might be the best hand all by itself. I might make this play against a very aggressive player who bets all the time with the intention of restealing from him on a semibluff. I also might make this play against a very timid player whom I think might lay down his hand. But generally speaking, I check-raise because I think that I have the best hand and I'm trying to put more money in the pot and believe that the check-raise is the best way to get the job done.

TJ: A hand came up a while ago in a limit-hold'em tournament that illustrates the use of the check-raise. I was dealt the A♦ 5♦ in the little blind. I called in an unraised pot. The flop came 5♥ 4♦ 2♦. I checked on the flop. The man sitting next to me bet it and got two callers. I popped it with my top pair-top kicker, nut-flush draw, inside-straight draw, and straight-flush draw. (*This* is a strong enough hand for me to play aggressively in limit hold'em!) The original bettor called and the other guys threw their hands away leaving us heads-up. Off came the 10♠ on fourth street. I checked, he took the lead, and I just flat-called him. At the river came a rag. He showed me the K♦ 10♦ and took the pot.

But the point is that this is the type of situation in which you can check-raise. I thought that my opponents would call for a single raise unless the guy on my left reraised it. Of course I also thought that my two fives were good, which they were at the moment.

When to Bluff

Tom: The smaller the pot, the more likely a bluff will be successful. The bigger the pot, forget it in limit hold'em because it's almost never going to work. We mentioned earlier that people try to bluff far too often in limit poker. Limit hold'em was designed to show down a hand, so you'd better be prepared to do that most of the time.

TJ: You can bluff at small pots once in a while, yes, and there is another situation where you can bluff. Suppose it's early in the game (you haven't been in it very long) and a small pot comes up. Now you can make a bluff on purpose, knowing that you're probably going to get called. Then you show the bluff hand so that your opponents can see that you have the bluff in your arsenal. As the game progresses, you can use this (their perception that you will bluff) in your favor.

But as I've already said, if you bluff too often in limit hold'em you may as well give them your wallet and try to win it back because your chances are slim to none. For every bluff that goes through, you're going to lose about ten and maybe even more than that. The bluff is far overrated in limit hold'em whereas it is far underrated in no-limit hold'em if you know how to pick your spots.

Tom: If you do decide to bluff, remember that your bluff should always make sense to your opponents. For example, suppose the flop comes A-9-5 and everyone checks on the flop. Another nine comes on the turn and again everyone checks, including you. Then a deuce shows up at the river. If you decide to bluff-bet at the pot at this point, who is going to believe that you have a hand? You are far better off letting the hand show itself down than trying a senseless bluff.

When to Semibluff

Tom: You can semibluff when you don't have a made hand but you easily could improve to the best hand. You occasionally look for a situation where you can bet with a chance that you won't get called and will win the pot, knowing that you have outs to improve the hand if you do get called.

TJ: A semibluff is when you're on a draw and either lead at it or raise with it. For example, suppose you have Q-J and a 10-9 flops. You have two overcards and a straight draw, but you still don't have a pair. If you bet or raise when you have position, you might get a free card to your draw. You might get two cards for the price of a raise at the lower betting level.

Tom: And if you have a strong enough semibluffing hand against opponents who are not likely to reraise, that's a good time to put in a raise on the flop in the hope of getting a free card on the turn. This almost always happens when you're last to act. If you're on a draw, you aren't hoping to knock players out, you're hoping to keep players in and build the pot in the event that you complete your hand. Actually, you won't be getting a totally free card on the turn if they check, you are getting a half-price card with the chance of getting a totally free card at the river if the turn doesn't do you any good.

Semibluffs are almost always done on the flop, although people occasionally will pick up a draw on fourth street and raise with it. With one card to come, this is a horrible play.

TJ: Sure it is. Somebody raises on fourth street on a semibluff and an opponent comes back over the top and three-bets it. Now it's going to cost the guy three bets instead of one bet to make the draw with one card to come. Doesn't make much sense, does it?

When to Fold

TJ: No matter what you're holding, the number one reason to fold is when you think you're beat. It's that simple. Any time your mind tells you that you have the worst hand, fold. What your mind tells you has been taught to you from playing poker over the years — listen to it.

Suppose you have the A♠ 9♠ in the big blind, the pot gets raised by a solid player, and you call for the extra single bet. The flop comes with 9♣ 5♦ 2♠ and you bet it. The preflop raiser raises behind you. Since the pot was raised before the flop, the preflop raiser sometimes has an overpair. Against an action player, not a super-solid player, you would shut down but continue to play. Against a solid or tight player, consider folding if he continues betting.

Now suppose you have second pair and a flush draw on the flop. Even though you don't have the top pair, your hand is about even against one pair because you have several ways to win. An even hand is 28 wins, which is what you have. You can double-pair (three wins); you can make a set (two wins); and you can make the flush (nine wins). This combination of outs gives you 14 pure wins twice for 28 wins, so you're about even money against one bigger pair.

So you play these kinds of hands, you don't fold them. It's the same situation as when you have Q-J and the flop comes with a 10-9 or K-Q when it comes J-10. If your opponent(s) has top pair, you still have two overcards and a straight draw. So you have six outs plus eight outs, or 14 outs times two, which gives you an even hand assuming that you're against a one-pair hand (obviously you don't automatically make the assumption that it *isn't* a one-pair hand that you're against). So, you continue with the draw in this situation.

Let me reiterate that after you've been playing for a while, everything you do in poker is because your mind has trained you to play that way. So if your instincts tell you to fold, do it. It might be the toughest fold you've ever made in your life, but fold anyway. This is just one hand, cards will be dealt out the very next hand. Even if you fold wrong once in a while, it will pay off for you in the long run. Remember the old adage: Any player who cannot lay down a winner once in a while cannot win.

In 1985, the year that I placed second in the World Series championship event, I laid down pocket kings on two different hands. Both times I made a little raise and my opponent (the same guy both times) made a reraise, though not a substantial one. Both times I showed the two kings and threw them away and both times Ronnie Allen from Kansas City showed me his two aces. This was in the first two hours of the tournament! But if I know I'm beat, I'm beat and that's all there is to it.

Tom: Obviously you have to know your man and your situation. These examples happen to be from tournaments, and I admit that in limit hold'em cash games it's tougher to lay down a good hand. However I should've done just that a while ago in a $15-$30 game I was playing. I was up against a fairly loose player who had been raising constantly. In this particular hand, he raised going in and I reraised from the big blind. He popped it again so I slowed down.

The flop came Q-rag-rag. I check-called him all the way but I really didn't like my kings at any point of the betting. Naturally this was the time when he had a hand — he showed me aces and took the pot. I shut down, yes, but in hindsight I think that I misplayed the hand because innately, I thought that I was beat. Although he had been raising a lot of pots and might have been out of line on some other hands, I should not have assumed that he also was out of line on this hand.

TJ: Remember that in a multiway jammed pot, a one-pair hand probably is not going to hold up. Whether it is even good on the flop is debatable in some situations, so what you're really looking for is a draw to the nuts when you're playing in a heavily contested multiway pot. Even an overpair is a one-pair hand that probably is already beat or is in severe jeopardy. You have to be able to get away from an overpair when the circumstances absolutely dictate that you're beat.

Tom: With so many people actively contesting the pot, it's almost a cinch that someone is going to draw out on you — for example, when two suited connectors are on board and three or four people are fighting for the pot. Someone could have two pair or virtually each end of the deck plus the suit could beat you. So you're not a favorite although you might have the best hand on the flop.

Please understand that we aren't telling you to routinely lay down top pair for one bet just because a solid player bets. You have to have substantial reason to believe that you are beat and not have enough redraws to justify continuing. Sometimes the pot is giving you a big enough price that even if you know you're beat at the moment, you can continue playing if you have enough outs to redraw.

TJ: Any time you have a big pair and don't flop a set to it, the ideal flop is always a broken board with no suits. If it comes with connecting cards or suited cards, a big red danger sign should jump up in your mind. If you get played with when the board comes broken — maybe somebody has flopped a set — there's nothing you can do about it.

Usually when the board comes broken, there aren't that many people contesting the pot after the flop. A lot of them will surrender because they don't have either a pair or a draw. Of course you want guys with three-flushes or three-straights in the pot with you — you want them to be calling you with those bad hands. If they're lucky enough to catch runner-runner to make a hand, more power to them. It is when a connecting or suited board comes that you are in extreme danger with only an overpair.

A Tip from the Top
Think out your hand two or three moves ahead of the play.

We emphasize situational thinking throughout this book. Nothing is cut and dried. You should study enough that when the situation arises, this information will be there for you and you won't have to wonder, "Well, what am I going to do if he does *this*? What can I do if he does *that*?"

Think ahead of the plane as though you were a pilot. Think out your hand two or three moves ahead of the play. "If such and such hits the board, what will I do?" When you're making your play on the flop this thought should be in your mind so that you know where you are all the time. Then when a card hits on fourth street, you already know exactly what you're going to do. This type of thinking doesn't give any tells away either. If you can think ahead and make all your moves at the same speed every time, nobody is able to put a tell on you. ♠

5

Things to Think about ...
ON THE TURN

T. J. Cloutier & Tom McEvoy

Very seldom do you make the stone nuts on the turn, although it does happen sometimes. When you do make the nut hand on fourth street, your main concern is how to get the most money into the pot for a maximum payoff on the hand. Be thinking about the answers to these questions as you study this chapter:

- **Is there ever a time when you might bet with the idiot end of a straight?**

- **How does the size of the pot affect your strategy on the turn?**

- **Should you ever continue with a drawing hand even though you know that you're beat on the turn?**

- **How do you play bottom two pair?**

- **When do you check-raise on the turn?**

- **What do you do when you make your hand on the turn but a better hand is possible?**

- **What should you do when you have top pair but the turn card pairs the second-best card on the board?**

When You Make The Nuts on the Turn

TJ: How you play when you make the nuts on the turn depends on the game and on the players. If you have players in the hand who are betting it all the way through, you might play for a check-raise. In other games where your opponents are super aggressive, you might bet knowing that somebody will raise you.

Tom: If I think that I can get three bets out of it, I will lead at the pot. If I think that I will do better with a check-raise, I will do that. Do whatever you think will get the most money in the pot. Sometimes you'll check and not get any action, but they might not have called a bet anyway. Then if you fire out at the river, your opponents will call you if they think that you're bluffing, so at least you will get some action on the hand by delaying your bet until the river.

Drawing to a Straight

Tom: When you make the nut straight, you lead at the pot if you think that someone will raise so that you can get in the third bet. If you're up against a player who will bet if you check, you check so that you can check-raise him. Or if you think that nobody will bet it themselves but they will call, you lead at the pot because you don't want to lose a bet at the double level. But if you think that the board is so scary that your opponents will fold if you bet, check on the turn and wait to bet at the river where you may get some action.

TJ: If you are still on a draw to the straight, let me repeat one of the beginning maxims of hold'em: Don't draw at the idiot end of the straight. This is a basic mistake that low-limit players make, yet I see even higher-limit players doing it in the loose California-type games.

And middle-buster straight draws? Look at how many players you see drawing to them even when, if they make the hand, they won't make the nuts! The reason I mention this is so that you will be aware that these types of players are out there at all limits, and to remind you to stick to your own standards even when you're playing in wild and woolly games. Just because you see players occasionally being successful making these loose plays doesn't mean that playing that way is correct. Ignore it when you see a loose-aggressive player walking to the cage with racks and racks of chips — he doesn't do it very often.

I think I've told you about the hand in which I had two aces in a $100-$200 game in San Jose. When the board came with an A-Q-9, I bet and got called by an Asian businessman. On the turn came a five. I bet again at the double level and he called. Off came a four at the river. My opponent showed me a 3-2 in the hole. Now I ask you: How many banks would you rob to get a bankroll to play this man? And how many around-the-world cruise ships would you board to play against him?

But if you ever squawk at a player like this when he beats you in a pot, they oughta take you out and hang you by your toes. If a man is making those kinds of plays in poker, he has absolutely no chance in the game. Why would you want to squawk at him and drive him out of the game or smarten him up? Who's the bigger fool — some of these so-called professional players who drive weak players out of the game by making sarcastic comments or the guy raking in the pot?

Tom: I played with a maniac recently who was playing almost every hand, drinking and having a good time. He wasn't accustomed to playing as high as $20-$40 and he was playing any king-rag or queen-rag, raised pot or not. He was taking cards off against ridiculous flops. Here was a typical situation: The flop 7-4-3, his hand was Q-2 offsuit. I had an A-Q and bet the flop heads-up. He called. When another straight card came on fourth street, he checked and so did I.

At the river came a queen. He checked again. I knew that he didn't have a straight or he would have bet it, because that's what he had done in an earlier round. So I value-bet my queen and he called. That was the only hand that I beat him all night long — he cashed out three racks of chips! You see maniacs playing like that all the time in California-type games.

TJ: So where are we going with this discussion? The point is that these are things that you should *not* do. In today's games, people are playing all types of hands, hands that *you* should *not* be playing. The percentage of times that players will lose with these types of hands or making these bad draws will overcome any type of win that they've ever made from them. Just always be aware that you are playing against these types of weak players, loose geese and maniacs.

Drawing to a Flush

TJ: When you have a flush draw, ask yourself whether it's worth drawing to. What kind of player(s) are you playing this pot against? If a flush card comes, is he likely to pay you off if you bet it? In other words, is it worth putting money into the pot to try to make a hand that you may not get paid for?

Tom: Of course, if there are several players in the pot, you're usually getting the right price to draw. And even if you're heads-up and it is unlikely that you will get paid off (you know that your single opponent will fold), you're more likely to continue with a draw to the best hand when there is enough preflop money in the pot from other callers who may have dropped out during the betting after the flop.

But say that there isn't much money in the pot and you're heads-up against a conservative player who perhaps is betting with top pair while you have a flush draw only. In this case, there is little reason to continue playing.

Drawing to a Flush w/Two Overcards:
A Difference of Opinion

TJ: I think that the biggest difference between limit hold'em and no-limit hold'em in playing on the turn revolves around the free-card concept. Say that it is passed to you on fourth street and you have a big flush draw — two overcards and a flush draw. In no-limit hold'em you would never bet the hand because somebody might come over the top of you and then you would lose all that money. You're not going to put in a ton of money on a draw with one card to come in no-limit.

However in limit hold'em you might bet this hand because you know that if someone raises, he can only raise the amount of the limit. Plus, the raise is building the pot so that if either your flush comes in, or if you hit one of your overcards, you stand to win a big pot. This is a major difference in strategy between no-limit and limit hold'em: Hands that you wouldn't dare bet in no-limit hold'em on fourth street, you might bet in limit games because you cannot get shut out by a raise.

With only one or two opponents in the pot, you might even bet a flush draw from up front. I have a rule for that — say that the board comes 9-high with two clubs and you have the A♣ J♣ (a draw to the nut flush and two overcards). There is a chance that you don't need to hit the flush to win, you might win it by hitting either one of your two overcards. With 15 outs, I will bet this hand because I have multiple ways to win the pot: I might win it outright with a bet; I might win if an ace or jack hits the board; and I might win if any club hits the board. If I get called or raised, it is only going to cost me one or maybe two extra bets. I am building a pot at a much smaller personal expense than I could in no-limit, and if I win the pot it will be a big one.

Tom: If you are last to act, I think that it is a mistake to bet a big draw on fourth street if there are multiple people in the pot when you can take a free card without any expense to yourself — especially if you're up against tricky players who might check-raise you. This is a situation in which I favor the more conservative approach, the one that we discussed in the previous chapter when you have a big draw on the flop and also check when it is checked all the way around to you.

TJ: Here's where we disagree. If you have two overcards and a big draw, I think that you should bet even when you are the last to act and could take a free card instead. The more callers the better — if there are three to five players in the pot with you and you bet your draw on the turn, there's that much more money that you can win if you make your hand, which will be the nut hand if an unpaired flush card comes at the river. And it only costs you one bet on the turn.

Tom: Still I have a minor disagreement. When you bet into four or five players with one card to come, you are not a favorite to make the hand. If quite a few bets are in the pot, I suppose that you could make a case for betting, but what you don't want to do is get check-raised when all you have is a draw with just one card to come.

TJ: But remember that all of your opponents have already checked to you, they are showing weakness.

Tom: Yet, but it's tough to get them all to leave.

TJ: I don't necessarily need them to leave. Of course, I'd like for them to fold and let me win the pot right there, but obviously it isn't a very big pot yet or they wouldn't be checking, would they? If everyone checks to you, they're all showing a lack of strength. Probably the best thing you're up against is an underpair or possibly top pair-no kicker or some other type of draw (possibly even a lesser flush draw than yours). Here you have two overcards and either the nut flush (or nut straight draw), so why not build the pot? Would you rather make your hand and not win anything? You want some money in there when you make a big hand.

Sure, they've all put in the initial bet on the flop or they wouldn't be there to see fourth street. But if they are checking to you now, they aren't checking to set up a check-raise. If someone has a big hand and four or five players are in the pot, he's going to bet the pot because he *wants* to get raised. (Of course if someone bets and it's call-call-call, I'm not going to raise, I'm going to flat-call.)

Tom: Say that you have two big suited cards and raise before the flop. Several players call your raise. The flop comes eight-high with two in your suit. Aggressive players often automatically assume that you will make a play at the pot. Therefore they're liable to check-raise you with virtually nothing on fourth street because they think that you're trying to steal and take the pot away from them.

TJ: That's possible, but what does a check-raise cost you? Two bets to win a ton. Are you going to lay it down?

Tom: No, but a lot of times you're going to get paid off anyway when you make the hand because your opponents are not going to believe you when you bet on the end.

TJ: Okay, so you're going to get paid off when you make this hand. But how much more money are you going to make with three or four players in the pot who all check to you on the turn — and you make a bet? The chances are that they're all weak, so the most that they're going to do is just call. If one of them raises, it only costs you two bets instead of one. And when you make your hand at the river, these players are going to call you because there's so much money in the pot that they don't want to turn loose of any possible winning combination.

I understand that you're an underdog to make the hand with one card to come, but pot odds are what you go by in limit poker. And with 15 outs and four or five players in the hand, the pot is laying you pretty good odds, isn't it?

Tom: I agree that you're an overlay to the pot. We simply have two different points of view here: Mine the more conservative one, yours the more aggressive. I've been check-raised so many times betting a draw that I almost don't even *think* about trying to bluff these people because I know that they will call me with second pair, third pair, ace-high, virtually anything.

TJ: I don't consider it a bluff. If I'm in the proper situation where I know that I can win the pot with either one of my overcards or another flush card, I don't think of the bet as a bluff — I'm making an action bet. I'm betting to build the pot.

And when I'm in a later position, their passing to me is simply a small added feature. The times that they're all going to pass after I bet are minuscule — somebody's usually going to call. You aren't trying to win it right there by betting, but it's an added bonus if you do. And when you get called, you know that you're drawing at the nuts.

Summary. Tom: To summarize, our viewpoints on this play are different. One is the more aggressive approach in which, if the pot odds are favorable, even if you miss the hand you're getting enough action that if you continue making this type of play, you probably will win money to it over the long run. The more conservative play that I am in the habit of making is taking the free card when I can — and when I make the hand, I get it paid off a fair number of times anyway. Both types of play can be successful. Against opponents who are observant, you may want to play a flush draw aggressively some of the time and conservatively some of the time in order to create confusion in their minds. In other words, mix up your play to keep them guessing.

When You Make Your Hand but A Better Hand is Possible

Tom: You can't play too chicken. In limit hold'em, you play aggressively — your opponents will let you know if they have a better hand. However, if you make the idiot end of a straight you have a problem. Suppose that you were playing an 8-7 and the board is showing Q-J-10-9. Someone fires at it. Any king has you beat, so you're in trouble. The only time that I might bet the idiot end of a straight is when I'm up against a very conservative player who isn't very tricky. If I'm last to act and he checks to me, I might bet if I think that he probably has only two pair.

TJ: Another time that you might bet the idiot end is when, for example, an A-3-4-5 is on the board and you have a deuce in your hand. Although a 6-2 or a 7-6 makes a higher straight, you might lead at the pot because it is unlikely that a bigger straight is out.

But when big cards are on the board and you're drawing to the idiot end of the straight, you're always taking the worst of it. When you're drawing to the top end of the straight, you might pair one of your big cards and still win the pot. But if you're drawing to the low end of it and one of your cards pairs, someone probably already has a card that pairs one of the top cards so you're beat to begin with. Or the card that pairs you might make a straight for them.

Suppose there is a Q♣ J♦ 10♥ on board and you have a 10-9. If a nine hits on the turn, you double-pair but anyone who has a king or eight in his hand makes a straight. And of course, you may already be up against someone who has an A-K, so your two pair isn't looking so good, is it?

Tom: Of course, you can't always be afraid that the nuts are out against you. I've seen people slow down with the middle set because they're afraid that someone has the top set. Or it might come runner-runner straight or flush and they suddenly shut down because they're afraid that their opponent may have backed into a better hand.

TJ: If you're a good enough player to know what type of opponent you have, you have to lead at these hands to get a call. If you get raised, you can always throw it away. If you check and he bets, you're going to call anyway so why not take a chance to make money on the hand? You're betting because you want to get called. If he raises and you're a disciplined enough player to throw away your hand, so what? You would've called one bet anyway if you had checked it. By betting it, there's a chance that he will call you with the second-best hand and you'll make more money . We're talking about three-straights and three-flushes here as well as sets.

Tom: Especially on the turn card. Most players aren't going to throw away their draws, so forget about that. But you want to make them pay to draw out and they aren't a favorite with one card to come. So when you have a hand such as top two pair or a set and the turn card brings possible trouble, you usually still want to bet. You can always reevaluate if you get popped, but you at least want to make them pay to draw at you, particularly if you think that an opponent is drawing to a flush and a nonthreatening card hits on the turn.

TJ: It seems like you get drawn out on all the time, but remember one thing: If you *win* 50 percent of the time when you're leading with the best hand against only *one* player, you're going to break even to the hand. And even if you *lose* 50 percent of the time when *multiple* players are in the pot, you will be a winner to the hand because you have made more money on the hands that have held up than you lost on the ones that didn't hold up. Actually, the best hand should hold up a lot more than 50 percent of the time, but if that's all it did you would still make money to it.

When To Continue with the Draw

Tom: As long as you're drawing to the nuts or close to it, you're usually getting a good enough price to continue with the draw, even with only one card to come — unless you're playing against only one opponent. If you're drawing to the nut flush and there has been substantial action on the flop — and now the board pairs on the turn, especially one of the top two cards — bells should start ringing. This is not a good time to continue with the draw.

TJ: But suppose the board doesn't pair and you're in a multiway pot with the nut draw. You're in like Flynn.

Tom: You're going for it even if the pot is raised because there's usually enough money out there to justify calling a raise — as long as you're drawing to the nuts.

TJ: Here's an example of when not to continue, although it's something that you see players do quite often, especially in loose games. The pot was raised before the flop and a player called the raise with two fives or two sixes in his hand. The board comes something like A-Q-9. It's bet and he calls to try to hit the set.

You even see players who will call again on fourth street. When they make it, they think they're the greatest players in the world. But if they've been doing this on a regular basis, how much money do you think they've lost over a year making those kinds of calls? Certainly a lot more money than they've won for the year.

Tom: Any limit-hold'em player who violates percentages by taking longshot draws inevitably will lose his money. Sometimes they may take you down the drain with them in a session or two, but eventually they will sink their own ships. They win just often enough to enforce their mind set that they are doing the right thing.

TJ: Remember, too, that a lot of limit players are playing limit poker strictly because it doesn't cost them as much to make these kinds of plays. Or they think it doesn't cost them much — in the long run, it costs them a lot of money.

Tom: There's another factor that I think is also true. Some players get their kicks precisely by putting a beat on somebody. If you're a famous player, it's even more likely to find somebody gunning for you because there are so many players who want to go home with bragging rights. Or you may not be a world famous player, you might simply be the best player in your cardroom and the lesser souls will come gunning for you to try to pick you off.

TJ: Sure, they want to knock off the king of the hill. In the long run, of course, the king will benefit from these paupers. You see, there's always a reason why he's the best player in the game.

When You Had the Nuts on the Flop But Get Demoted on the Turn

Tom: This is in the same category as when you make your hand but a better one is possible. For example, suppose the flop comes J♦ 10♣ 9♦ and you made the nut straight with the K♠ Q♠. Now the 6♦ hits on the turn. Whether I would decide to continue with the hand depends on how many players are in the pot. If there has been substantial action on the flop with three or four people contesting the pot, someone usually has a flush draw. If I think that is true, I will pass the hand. If I'm up against only one or two players, I will lead into them if I am first to act. Or if it's checked to me, I will bet. If I get check-raised, I will reevaluate the nature of my opponent as to whether I think that he would have check-raised with a worse hand than my flopped nut hand.

TJ: Now let's look at another scenario. Suppose the board comes J-10-8 and you have a Q-9 in your hand. What do you do if a nine hits the board on the turn? You had the nuts on the flop, but someone with a K-Q might have flopped an open-end straight draw on the high end, right? On the turn you no longer have the boss hand, do you? A lot of times, this scenario will come up — one card in the straight sequence can change the whole outlook on a hand.

So how do you play it? First of all, you're not supposed to be in a pot with a two-holer such as Q-9 (or a three-holer like Q-8 either). Of course, maybe you were in the big blind in an unraised pot, but remember that you can lose a lot of money in the big blind with hands that you get funny flops to (bottom two pair, for example) and then become involved in the pot. You have to become very leery of these kinds of hands and know what types of players you're playing with. Is your opponent(s) the type of guy who will call you with a single pair? Two pair? A set or a big draw?

In our example, when the nine hits on the turn the board is J-10-8-9. The nine is a really bad card for you because there is a good possibility that your opponent(s) was drawing to the open-end straight on the flop and now has the top straight on the turn. You can't be aggressive with your Q-9, you have to shut down with it. You might still lead at it against only one opponent, but you have to slow down if you're in a multiway pot. You're just hoping to win the pot in a showdown at the end, or find out where you are on fourth street and if you think that you still have the best hand, bet it on fifth street if nothing else comes.

Now let's look at another scenario where you flopped the best hand but the turn card made a better hand possible. Suppose you were betting the boss pair on the flop and an overcard comes on the turn — you have Q-J, you flop a jack, and either an ace or a king comes on the turn. Now what? Obviously your top pair probably has been demoted. Remember that the most feared thing in limit hold'em is having a big pair against a lone ace. You're always thinking, "Please don't let an ace hit the board!" I'm always uttering that silent prayer to the poker gods. (The other time that you start praying is when you have two kings in no-limit hold'em and you have all your money in the pot. You're thinking, "Boy, I hope they flushed all the aces down the toilet!") The hold'em player's prayer is "Please don't let an ace come." That's the most sincere prayer I've ever heard — and I've even heard people utter it out loud.

A Tip from the Top
When an overcard to your pair hits, you have to shut down.

Tom: Back to the point: When an overcard to your top pair hits, you instantly have to shut down in a multiway pot. If it's an ace, you usually will have to muck your hand because it's too dangerous to continue. However, against only one opponent you might bet it anyway and if he raises, you can decide whether you want to continue playing the hand. If I am last to act and my single opponent, an action player, fires into me I usually will call him down. If it isn't Mr. Action firing the bet, it's Mr. Conservative, I'm probably going to fold.

TJ: If you've been watching your opponents, you know which ones have the tendency to call with second pair. So if an overcard hits the board you don't have to shut down against that type of player because he often is calling you with second pair to begin with. If he's this type of opponent, you can just keep going because you want him to call you, you don't want to lose those bets.

When the Board Pairs

Tom: If the board pairs on the turn, it is an "either-or" situation — either it has helped or it has not helped. It depends upon which card pairs. Obviously if no one has a card of that rank, the board's pairing helps the best hand the most. But any time the pot is multiway and a board card pairs, it can be fatal to your hand unless you have the paired card. Remember that in a raised multiway pot, especially in rammin'-jammin' games, a player will flop third pair, take a card off at the single-bet level, and may catch that card or double-pair his other card on the turn.

TJ: This happens at almost all levels of play, although it doesn't happen nearly as often at the bigger limits. Top players usually aren't in the pot with smaller cards to start with.

Tom: In the smaller hold'em games, even $20-$40, a lot of multiway pots are played and any card that pairs on fourth street can ruin you. This doesn't mean that you should routinely throw your hand away, it means that you should play with caution. If I have been betting the nut-flush draw, for example, and I think that my opponent has been calling with bottom pair, I won't necessarily throw away my draw — it depends on what hand I have put him on. If he has just been meekly calling the flop after everyone has checked to me and then fires out when the bottom card pairs, I may figure that it hit him but there usually is enough money in the pot that many times I will continue with my draw. But I have to be absolutely sure that I am not drawing dead — if there is any doubt in my mind that I am not drawing live, I will fold.

TJ: You can tell which players will call with third pair on the flop. A player may not have filled when the board pairs on the turn, but he might have made trips. If you think that he has a tendency to call with third pair and the board pairs the lowest card, you have to shut down. We're not talking about when you have a draw, we're talking about when you have top pair.

Tom: Suppose you have an overpair to the board, which is the same as having top pair, and you bet it on the flop and got called. The bottom card pairs on the turn and you bet again. If someone raises you and you're certain that he has tripped up, you don't have a play, you must throw your hand away. At the most, you may have only two outs.

TJ: Plus, a lot of times in limit hold'em, there might be three players in the pot who all check to you on the flop. You are last to act with second pair and so you bet it. Nobody had top pair on the flop, so your second pair is good. You figure that they don't have top pair since they didn't bet the flop, so what *do* they have? Now the bottom card pairs on the turn and bingo-bango, they bet. You're probably in trouble.

Tom: But if you bet the second pair on the flop and it pairs on the turn, it's hallelujah time.

TJ: If you have the top pair in this situation, you run into a big red stop sign when that second-best flop card pairs. Now you're moving into the shutdown mode with your top pair. When you have top pair and the second pair pairs, it matters who is doing the betting and how many people are in the pot. If the bettor has already check-called on the flop, he may have top pair with a weaker kicker than you have. Then when the board pairs the second-best card on the turn, he bets out.

A Tip from the Top
Don't compound your losses.

How you respond to his bet depends on what type of player he is. If he's the kind who usually calls with second pair and that card pairs on fourth street, check on fourth street. If he bets, throw the hand away. This is limit hold'em, so how much have you lost by folding? Not much. Why compound your loss?

When a Third or Fourth Flush Card Comes on the Turn

Tom: How you play your hand when the third or fourth flush card comes on the turn depends upon how many people are in the pot. Maybe you flopped top pair, top two pair or a set. Then a third flush card comes on the turn and you don't have any cards in that suit. Now you have to shut down.

If I have flopped a set, I usually call if someone bets. If the bettor is a super-aggressive player who I think might not have the flush, I occasionally will raise him. If he reraises I will call him down on fourth and fifth street if I have a decent hand, in which case I have to *really* know him. And it's very dangerous to make the call — I don't think you lose much by just passing in these situations if you don't have a really big hand or a draw to a bigger hand.

TJ: I have seen five callers on the flop when two of a suit are on the board — and not a one of them is drawing at the flush, but the odds usually are that someone is drawing to it. Now what about a flop that has two suited cards plus a straight draw? In limit hold'em a lot of players will draw to a straight when a flush draw also is available. And sometimes they win when a flush card hits that also happens to complete their straight. But it isn't a very good play.

Tom: It's always dangerous to be drawing to a straight when three suited cards are on board, although it isn't quite as dangerous when you're heads-up. In a multiway pot you usually are drawing dead. If you have an open-end straight draw and two flush cards are on board, you no longer have eight outs, you have six. You have to decide whether it's worth drawing to the hand. Is the pot big enough? Are you going to get jammed in the middle? You want to avoid that.

TJ: Plus, if you make a straight with the third flush card, you can't improve your hand, you're dead to it. You might decide to pay it off, but you could be drawing dead on fourth street. There's always the chance that someone has a single big card to the three-flush on fourth street and will snag the fourth flush card at the river.

Tom: Now suppose that the flop contained three flush cards and a fourth flush card comes on fourth street. Everybody checks and then at the river someone suddenly comes out betting. Sometimes a player will be slowplaying a big hand, but a lot of times a player will try to steal it on the end. If you bet on fourth street and they don't have the flush, they usually will pitch their hand. But if you don't bet, they're probably going to try to take the pot away from you at the river. So you have to know who these players are — and if I know them well, I often will call them down.

TJ: Plus, is it worth your while to call because you think that they might be bluffing? Suppose there was a bet before the flop and maybe a bet on the flop, or maybe it was checked all the way to the end after the flop. Now the fourth flush card comes at the river and someone bets. Does what you have invested in the pot warrant your calling the double bet? If you're playing $15-$30, you have only $15 in the pot and it will cost you $30 to call on the end. And the only reason that you're calling is that you think your opponent is bluffing. Is it worth it?

Tom: The size of the pot affects your strategy. Also, if three of a suit hit the flop and a fourth flush card hits on the turn, you need at least a set to continue playing if you believe that someone has made a flush. You have to call not only the turn bet but, often, the river bet as well.

TJ: Here's another thing to remember: A lot of players, especially in heads-up situations, will draw to a flush and make it on the turn — and check it. At the end will come an unsuited card that doesn't pair the board. Now they bet on the end and you might think they're bluffing. They checked it on the turn because they knew that you wouldn't call, and on fifth street they bet it to make you think that they're bluffing. Or they might check it and if you bet, they will check-raise you. This is one example of the delayed bet play.

Tom: This is the type of thing that you should be doing. If you've made the flush and you don't think that you can get any action on it on fourth street, many times your only play is to check on the turn and bet at the river hoping that your opponent(s) will think that you're trying to steal.

When a Four-Straight Is on Board

Tom: We have touched on this previously, saying that if you have the idiot end of the straight you have to shut down. Or if one of your straight cards pairs potentially giving someone a bigger straight, you have to play with caution.

TJ: The example we talked about earlier involved playing a two-holer (Q-9) or a three-holer (Q-8). You'll see a lot of players in action games playing these types of cards, especially if they are suited. But I suggest that you never play them, suited or unsuited. Why? Because you can never have the nuts with a three-holer, except for the A-10 when the K-Q-J are on board. And if you're playing an A-10, you aren't playing it for its straight possibility, you've playing it for its high-card value.

Tom: I occasionally will play a three-gapper suited on the button in a big multiway pot, but I'm not playing it for its straight or flush value. I'm playing it to make two pair or a set. Unless the ace or king in my suit is showing on the board, I am not playing a hand such as Q-8 suited for its flush value. These types of hands aren't just "trouble" hands, they are very troublesome hands.

Part of our suggested strategy in this book is to encourage you to avoid troublesome situations. The way to avoid them is to not get into them in the first place. One way you can do that is to stay away from hands such as suited two-gappers or three-gappers so that you won't have to make a lot of tricky decisions with marginal hands.

TJ: It costs you a bet to see the flop with a trouble hand, right? But in two minutes, you're going to get two more cards to play. So why play a hand that can get you in trouble and cost you all your chips? "I played it on a hunch," you'll hear players say. Well, all those hunch players can get in line over at the Salvation Army's soup kitchen.

When You Have an Overpair to the Board

Tom: If it was capped before the flop and you have jacks or queens, for example, you may be in trouble if someone else has pocket aces or kings. But say that you have been the aggressor with your big pocket pair and you flopped an overpair to the board. If you have no reason to believe that a bigger pair is out against you, you're in good shape so you take an aggressive posture until you have reason to slow down.

This is the type of hand that I will play fast. Remember that any one-pair hand plays best against fewer opponents, so my main concern is to (1) Win the pot; (2) Increase my chances of winning the pot by knocking out as many players as I can. My strategy will be directed toward eliminating as many opponents as possible.

TJ: If an opponent leads at the pot, I suggest that you *always* raise him. You must thin the field.

Tom: Many times I will bet into an aggressive player in the hope that he will raise so that everyone who is sitting behind him will have to call two bets cold to continue in the hand. Other times if I am in the middle with people yet to act behind me, I am hoping that someone in front of me will bet so that I can raise to thin out the field.

But what if the scenario is a little different? I'm up against solid players and I'm either in first position or middle position and it has been checked to me. Now all I can do is lead at the pot. If you think that someone in the blind is chaffing at the bit to check-raise, you might bet in the hope that he will raise to drive out the players between him and you. With five or six people in the pot, any big pair is very vulnerable so if all you can do is simply lead at it, that's what you do.

However, I may do something else a little trickier. If five or six people are in the pot and I know that a bet won't frighten them off, I may check — especially if I have a couple of people to act in front of me who are aggressive. In this case I may delay betting until fourth street and then put in the double bet. That usually is too much pressure, based on the size of the pot, for any sensible player to handle unless he has improved dramatically on the turn card.

Usually, however, I won't make this play, reserving it for very special situations. It is a play that I am more likely to use against either a novice aggressive player or a very sophisticated player who may think that his top pair is good on the turn. So it's a play that you can use against either a very poor player or a very good one.

Another way that you might handle an overpair is to try for the check-raise. For example, if you are in a multiway pot with an overpair, you might check in the hope that someone will bet behind you so that you can check-raise. Your check-raise may eliminate a lot of players between you and the bettor who may have been willing to call a single bet but probably will not call a double bet. This is a strategy that you can occasionally use with success in multiway pots.

When You Have Two Pair —
Top & Bottom or Bottom Two

Tom: Bottom two pair is a hand that is very vulnerable so you must protect it. This means that you have to be aggressive with it as long as you think that it's the best hand. If you have reason to doubt that it's the best hand, put on the brakes.

Top and bottom pair is a little bit stronger hand. A typical top/bottom hand might be something like A♦ 3♦ and the flop comes A♠ 7♣ 3♥. You can play this hand fairly strong. If there was any substantial preflop action, you might be concerned that a king or queen might hit on the turn or river and give someone else a better two-pair. But if a middle card hits the board, you can feel comfortable that you have the best hand. This is especially true if someone else is leading at the pot. Suppose you were in the big blind with the A♦ 3♦, a couple of people limped in before the flop, someone in late position raised, and you decided to call the single raise to see the flop. When you flop your two pair, you have two ways to go. One way is to lead at it and the other way is to check, knowing that if the preflop raiser has a big ace he will bet. Then you can put him precisely on where he's at and raise.

TJ: Suppose you flop the top two pair. The pot was raised before the flop and a few other players called the raise. You're on the button with J-10 suited. You know that you're getting good pot odds, so you call. The flop comes J-10-9. Everyone checks to you. Do you bet it?

Tom: I like to bet it in that situation.

TJ: Sure, everyone *likes* to bet it, but the hand is in such bad shape — somebody could have a set, somebody else could have K-Q and check it to you to put in a check-raise. These are hands that people play in raised pots. Even worse, suppose the flop comes Q-J-10 and you have either a Q-J, a Q-10 or a J-10. Now what do you do? I know what you do in no-limit — you shut down. But in limit hold'em, you're supposed to bet it.

Tom: If it's checked to you, you automatically bet.

TJ: Yes, but remember that there's a very good chance that you're going to get raised on fourth street. These guys will check a big hand so that they can get you for a double bet later. They check to you on the flop, let you bet, and flat-call to let you think that you have the best hand. Then on fourth street they check to you again.

Most players see no Indians behind the bushes and no red lights flash in their minds — all they know is that they have top two-pair — and here they come again and here comes the raise! And even though they get raised, they still think that they have a *hand* when all they really have is the *hope* that they fill up. And sometimes they don't even have those four outs, sometimes they're up against top set.

A Tip from the Top
Most players see no Indians behind the bushes.

Tom: Obviously if you're up against solid aggressive players who have made early position raises, you have to proceed with caution if you decide to call at all with your two suited connectors. This is particularly true if you bet and several people call but nobody raises. Somebody probably is laying in the bushes setting up an ambush on fourth street.

TJ: Remember that most hold'em players have heard the time-worm expression, "You can't make a straight without a ten or a five." So they see that J-10 in their hands and think, "Boy oh boy, I've got a couple of straight possibilities here.

This is a big-big hand." But with certain flops, you can be in worse shape than you ever imagined with that J-10.

Tom: There's no doubt that J-10 is a highly overrated hand that is misplayed by a lot of players. Certainly it is a hand that I like to play, but I don't want to take any heat with it. What I really want to do is hit the straight with an A-K-Q on the board and take out all the A-K and A-Q hands. Or hit the 9-8-7, of course. But flopping top pair or top two pair to it can get you into trouble.

TJ: It's similar to playing the J♣ 9♣, which everybody knows as "T. J." because I like the hand and have won a lot of money with it. But in my entire poker career, I cannot remember a single time when I have stood a raise with it in no-limit hold'em. I may have *raised* with it, but I've never *stood* a raise with it.

Tom: Back to two pair on the turn. Say that you were in the blind with the A♦ 3♦ that we mentioned earlier. An aggressive player whom you think might have a big pair or maybe an ace-big made a preflop raise. Several people called the raise and you decided to also call because you were getting a decent price. The flop came A-9-7. It was checked around to the raiser and he bet. Many times, whether the raiser has an ace in his hand or not, he will bet — that's just the nature of the beast. So you decide to take a card off. On the turn you hit your kicker, making two pair. The board is A-9-7-3.

At this point you can be pretty sure that you have the best hand. (Your major worry is that someone has a set.) You think that the raiser has ace-big, so you have two ways to go. If you think that he has ace-big, you know that he's going to bet so if your other opponents are still in the pot, you may want to go for the check-raise to blast them out just in case they're on a draw. Or if you don't believe that they are on a draw, or if one of them has dropped out, you might lead at the pot in the hope that the aggressor will raise so that you can reraise him. I probably would not lead at it unless I am pretty sure that he will play back at me. I know that I'm going to get two bets on a check-raise.

Also, if there is some doubt in my mind that the raiser has an ace in his hand, I would be better off to lead at it. If he only has a pocket pair he's going to shut down, so there is no upside to giving him a free card. There's only a downside against his two-outer to draw out on you and make the set whereas if you had bet, he might not have called. So you have to be reasonably sure that he's going to bet if you check — usually, he will if he is an aggressive player.

Bottom Two Pair. Tom: Suppose I am in the big blind with a dinky little hand like 7♣ 6♣. The flop comes with the 10♣ 8♦ 7♠. I have bottom pair, a three-flush, and four to the inside straight. Against any action I will fold the hand, so the only way that I will ever see fourth street is when it is checked all the way around. Now suppose that a six comes on the turn, so the board now reads 10-8-7-6 giving me bottom two pair.

TJ: With so many other players in the pot with you, there's a very good chance that someone has a nine and didn't bet it on the flop because all he had was an open-end straight draw. He also could have a 5-4 to make the low straight. This is the type of hand where you don't want to be very aggressive. You're in it for nothing and you're going to try to play a small pot with the hand. With a one-card straight on the board, if there is any action on the turn you're probably beat so why bet it? I would check with the bottom two pair and just hope that everyone else also checks.

When a four-straight or four-flush is on the board and you have bottom two pair, you're playing to check the hand to the river and win the pot with two pair in a showdown at the end. This is not a scenario when you bet-bet-bet and take the chance of losing money on a hand that you wouldn't have played if it had been raised before the flop.

In sum, when you have bottom two pair on fourth street in limit hold'em, you usually can be very aggressive with it —

but *not* when the board is showing four cards to a straight or flush. Of course, the only way that you will ever get there is when it has been passed all the way around on the flop — we've already told you not to play third pair

Now suppose you have 8-5 in the blind and nobody raises before the flop. The flop comes 7-6-5. You have bottom pair and an open-end straight draw on the high side. Here's a hand that you're going to play to see the turn card. But on fourth street comes an eight: 7-6-5-8. Now what do you do?

Now you have top and bottom pair, but you're in the same situation as before — you could be up against a one-card nine, a 10-9, even a four. The only time I might be aggressive with this hand is when I am playing against a single opponent. I might lead with a bet and hope that he will call so that I can win a bet with the hand. Of course, if you get called in this spot, your opponent usually has a lot of outs against you. The only way that you can make a straight is if the board makes a straight. You have top and bottom pair (which isn't that bad), but usually the only way that you will get action on the hand is when your opponent has an overpair. Then what happens if the seven or six pairs at the river? Now his two pair are better than your two pair. In a nutshell, you have to play this type of hand very carefully.

Tom: Let's look at a different scenario: Suppose you have 7-6 in the big blind. The flop comes Q-J-7. It gets checked all the way around so you're still in the hand. The turn card is a six, so the board now reads Q-J-7-6. Someone suddenly bets. What do you do?

It is unlikely that someone has a Q-J, Q-6 or Q-7 or they would have bet it on the flop. It also is unlikely that anyone has a J-7 or J-6 as those are hands that few people will voluntarily play. If someone bets on the turn, I will raise to try to drive everybody out because I think that I have the best hand.

The only time that you might check-raise in this spot is when you know that your opponent is someone who simply cannot stand it when someone checks to him twice. For example, suppose you're playing against a super aggressive maniac who might have bet second pair on fourth street because the hand was checked around on the flop. If you know that your opponent is this type of player, you can check to him and then raise.

TJ: Other than that, you're supposed to lead with the hand and try to win that double bet on the turn. Why give your opponents the option of getting a free card and end up losing that fourth-street bet? If you lead at it and have the best hand, you're going to win an extra bet if your opponent calls. If you check it to check-raise, you've lost money if he doesn't bet. You can't lose bets — you have to get everything you can out of each pot when you think that you have the best hand.

Just remember that the reason you're in the pot with the 7-6 usually is because it's an unraised pot. This means that all of those strange hands also are possibilities — the J-7 or J-6 suited, for example. You still have to lead at this hand if you are first to act, but you have to be careful. You don't want to play it for an enormous amount of money. If you get raised or reraised, you have to play it very cautiously.

Now suppose the flop came A-J-6. In loose-aggressive games it is possible that somebody has A-6 because a lot of players like to play ace-anything, especially if it's suited. The weak ace may not bet on the flop and if someone has a jack he may not bet either because he only has second pair, so it gets checked all the way around. Now the turn card is the six — A-J-7-6. You have bottom two pair, but the A-6 has top and bottom pair. Of course there are a lot of scenarios where you can get hurt, but this is limit hold'em so you can't get hurt too bad if you know how to play the game at all.

Tom: As long as you think there's a reasonable chance that you have the best hand, play aggressively until you have reason to believe that you are beat. You can't play timid poker. It is better to play too aggressively than too timidly.

It all gets back to knowledge of your opponent and what he's likely to do, especially on the turn, depending on what the action was preflop and on the flop. I once met a seven-card stud player who tried playing hold'em but found that he didn't like the game. "There isn't as much information available to you in hold'em as there is in stud," he said. Trying to tell him how wrong he is was like talking to a stone wall.

TJ: People are always giving you information if you're sharp enough to pick it up — and a lot of it has nothing to do with the actual playing of the hand.

Tom: The information that my stud-player friend was talking about is the knowledge that he receives from the board cards that have been exposed. In hold'em you don't have to rely on remembering all the exposed cards like you do in stud, but you have to remember other types of things.

Players misread their opponents a lot of times in hold'em. A card comes off and they say, "Well, he might have two pair, he could have a K-6 or a Q-7 and beat me," and they become timid in betting their hands. Theoretically it is possible that your opponent could have *any* two unrelated cards, but how likely is it?

Say that you are in the big blind with A-2 suited in your hand, the pot is raised, one person calls the raise, and you also call it for one extra bet. The flop comes 5-4-3 giving you a wheel. Is it possible that one of your two opponents has a 7-6 in his hand? Yes. Is it likely? Not very. So even though you don't have the nuts, you can play the hand as though it is the nuts. You can precisely put people on certain hands or take them off certain hands depending on what you know about them and how they play. ♠

6

Things to Think about ...
AT THE RIVER

T. J. Cloutier & Tom McEvoy

It's showdown time, folks, another of those either-or situations: You either enjoy the ecstacy of victory or suffer the agony of defeat. Either your superior play takes you to the cashier's cage or your lack of judgment (or some maniac who has caught runner-runner) sends you back to your pocket. This is the moment that all limit games are built around, the showdown at the river. Here are some questions that we answer in this chapter:

• **How can you get the most money into the pot when you make the nuts at the river?**

• **What do you do when a scare card comes?**

• **Is there a time when you can bet or call with the second-nut hand?**

• **Should you play to the showdown with only two overcards to the board?**

• **What about calling at the end with the lowest pair possible?**

• **When can you bluff?**

When You Have the Nuts

Tom: When you have the nuts at the river, your main concern is how to peddle the nuts whether you have just made it or whether you had it all along. If you think that your opponents were on a draw and missed it at the river, they probably cannot call a bet from you, especially if you have been leading all the way. So if you're up against only one or maybe two opponents whom you think cannot call a bet, you have no reason to bet if you are first to act. You're hoping that someone else will bet so that you will get some action on the hand.

If there isn't a logical draw on the board, or if you have more than one opponent and you think that one of them has been on a draw but not necessarily both of them but they're afraid of you so they might not bet if you check, then you have no reason to check. Your main concern is getting some money in the pot. So you use the strategy that will best maximize your profit.

TJ: The thing that dictates how you play in making the nuts on the end or if you had the nuts all the way through without raising is whether your opponents are being aggressive toward you, if they're doing the betting or if you're doing the betting. If you have one or two opponents, one who's betting and the other who's calling and you're just flat-calling all the way through with the nuts, let them do it again on the end — then put in a raise at the river. Of course, you bet if they both decide to check to you — you'll usually get a call.

Or suppose you make the nuts on the end. A lot of players will simply discount the draw at the end and will lead at the pot anyway. Let's look at a tricky situation that comes up. Four of you are in the pot. You're in second position to the man who's doing the betting and you have two players behind you. The first player bets. If you raise when you have a draw that hits, there's a good chance that the two players behind will drop out, you'll lose those guys. Is it better to try to get one extra bet out of the original bettor, or just flat-call him and allow the two players behind you to overcall? One more time: You have to know your opponents, how they're playing their cards.

If there has been action in the pot — it's been raised here and there through the hand so it's a good pot — there's a very good chance that they will overcall because of the size of the pot. But if you raise, they probably will dump their hands. And the original bettor might fold his hand too. Your big decision, then, is "I have the nuts, but do I want to raise?" Why not flat-call and hope that somebody else raises?

Tom: It's a thing of beauty when you flat-call, because then nobody thinks that you have the nuts. So one of them pops it behind you, you reraise when the action gets back to you, and they feel forced to call because of the size of the pot — and you wind up winning an enormous pot.

TJ: Now suppose that you've been drawing to the nut flush and one of your opponents sitting behind you has been drawing to a lower flush. When a flush card comes at the river, an opponent bets from up front. You flat-call with the nuts. Now the player who has been drawing to the lower flush thinks, "Ho, I've got 'em!" He raises. Now you have the first player's bet and the raiser's bet when you reraise him on the end. This scenario may not happen too often but when it does, it's sweet. You should recognize the situation when it's likely to come up to maximize your profit.

When You Have the Second-Nut Hand

Tom: If you're last to act and everyone has passed, it's an automatic bet. If someone check-raises you, you must reevaluate the situation.

Sometimes, of course, the second nuts is so powerful that you aren't worried about the stone nuts being out. If the flop comes Q-4-4 and you have pocket queens, you aren't too concerned that someone has pocket fours. In this case you simply decide the best way to get the most money in the pot. It is when I have the second-nut flush that I am more worried — for example, when I have a king-high flush and someone else might have the ace-high flush.

TJ: Or when an open pair is on board and you have top set with a king kicker when there might be an ace kicker out there. For example, the board reads Q-6-2-Q-9. You have a K-Q but an opponent might have you beat with an A-Q.

Tom: Another example is when you have the second-nut straight. Suppose you have a Q-9 suited, a hand that we do not recommend playing, but you played it either in the big blind or on the button in an unraised pot. Now the board reads J-10-4-5-K. You have the second-nut straight, but there's the possibility that someone drawing to the gutshot straight (with two overcards) has an A-Q. Now what do you do?

TJ: If everyone checks to you, of course you bet it. If somebody bets in front of you, you should flat-call with the second nuts against a tight player, and raise once against looser opponents. Suppose a bettor has been leading at the pot throughout the hand and the straight card comes at the end, giving you the second nuts. There's a pretty good chance that you have him beat — but suppose a new bettor comes out with a bet. Usually, the player who has been betting it all along has a hand other than a straight. But when the new bettor makes his bet, it probably is because he has made the middle-buster straight. You have a very tough call here — and you definitely should not raise.

When a Scare Card Comes

Tom: When a scare card comes at the river and I am first to act against only one opponent, I sometimes will represent that scare card as having helped me. If my opponent has enough of a hand to raise me, I can reevaluate whether he raised simply because he thinks I'm out of line or whether he really has a hand. Other times when a scare card comes and I'm against a single opponent, if I still have enough of a hand to play I may check with the intention of calling if he bets.

What I do depends on my knowledge of my opponents. Is this the type of opponent who will raise me trying to represent the scare card? If he is, it would be foolish to bet into him. You may want to call if he bets, but you don't lead at it. Sometimes you will have a bet that has a negative expectation — that is, you may not get raised but you can't get called unless you're beat, so you have no reason to bet. This especially is the case when a scare card comes and you are the last to act.

It is when there is more than one other player in the pot that you have to shut down. You have to evaluate whether your hand is still good — for example, whether your two pair will hold up when a straight or flush card comes. You ask yourself, "What hand are they in the pot with?" One of them probably has a drawing hand, and the scare card may or may not have helped him. Therefore I will shut down when I am the first to act against two or more opponents.

TJ: Remember this about limit hold'em: A lot of players call to the river with two overcards. They don't necessarily have to be ace-king, either, they can be *any* two overs to the flop. Suppose the flop comes 10-6-2 and a player has Q-J in his hand — some players are weak enough to play that Q-J to the end. So if an overcard comes at the river, you might be in jeopardy. Of course, if you've been watching the play throughout the session you should know whether your opponents are the types of players who will do that.

Tom: Other than a flush or straight card, or the board pairing a card other than one of yours, the most dangerous scare card is the ace because so many people will play any ace. Therefore when someone bets at the river, you should be inclined to be more leery of an ace that doesn't help you than some other types of cards. For instance, I am less worried if a king, queen or jack comes although that doesn't mean that the overcard didn't hit somebody — it is simply less likely than it would be if an ace hits on the end. You also have to be worried if the board pairs a card other than yours.

A Tip from the Top
The most frequent error that limit hold'em players make is continuing with only overcards in a raised pot.

One of the biggest flaws of many ring-game hold'em players, including those who play the higher limits, is continuing with only overcards in a raised pot. It seems like they think that they must take a card off, and they do just that. This can have two consequences: (1) You will suffer more drawouts, and (2) You will win a lot of extra bets that you ordinarily wouldn't win because your opponents were chasing with their overcards. When they get there, it's very frustrating.

It is almost as though things run in cycles, both positive and negative. The negative cycle occurs when your opponents are consistently taking off cards when they shouldn't, or going for draws with hands they shouldn't have played to start with — and drive you crazy because they keep getting there with them at the river.

TJ: You can sit down in a game and know that you're the best player, but that doesn't mean that you're going to hold the best cards and it doesn't mean that you're going to win in any one particular game you sit in. You're going to win over a year's time, yes, but not in every single session. Even a guy who's higher than a kite on alcohol or dope can pick up two aces when you have two kings, so you always have to give your opponents credit no matter how bad they play.

Tom: Theoretically the cards balance out in the long run, although in reality they don't always do that in the short run. But if the cards break even remotely even, you're going to wind up winning more bets in the long run when your opponents continually make these kinds of plays.

TJ: The difference between the pro and the bad player is this: Suppose a bad player has a weak hand like K-10 and he's been playing the hand straight through. A middle-buster straight card hits on the end or a flush card hits at the river. Against a *single* opponent, the pro will still bet the hand because he's good enough to know that he might get a call at the end by a hand that can't beat him (the same hand that's been calling all the way through), whereas a weak player will check at the end and miss that bet.

The pro will make the bet knowing that if he gets raised he can throw it away. He's going to call one bet anyway, so he figures that he might as well lead with it and take the chance that he might win the pot. The bottom-line difference is that good players will maximize what they get out of a hand while the weak ones won't — and that's your edge. Of course, if the same pro is against *multiple* players and a flush or straight card hits, he's supposed to check the hand. But heads-up, he has to bet it.

Tom: Yes, especially if the single opponent has just been calling along. If he has enough of a hand to pop you on the end, then you have to reevaluate as to whether he would have raised you on a bluff or a hand that you can still beat. You can always get away from your hand, but you're going to pick up an extra bet when your opponent called your last bet.

Therefore when a scare card comes at the river, you will have to make a quality judgment if someone bets into you. Your decision will be influenced by your knowledge of the player, the size of the pot, and the number of players in the pot. If it has quite a few bets in it and a loose-aggressive player who represents a lot of hands comes out betting, you're going to have to call him down almost 100 percent of the time.

TJ: But I never — and I emphasize *never* — call a bet on the end just because the pot may be big. A lot of players do, but I never make that long call at the river just because the pot may be big. I might make it when a scare card pops out and I think that the bettor is taking a run at the pot — if I believe that I have him beat. But I never let the size of the pot influence my last bet — that bet might be the one that you save four or five times a session and make you a winner for the day.

Tom: At the low limits, $4-$8 for example, the mentality often is that the final call will cost only $8 whereas if you're playing $30-$60, that's a lot more money to lose.

TJ: Sure, but the limit you're playing really doesn't make any difference. If you're a $4-$8 player you're only willing to put in a certain amount of money, and if you're a $30-$60 player you're only willing to put in a certain amount of money. The concept is the same. And it doesn't happen only at the lower limits — you also see players making those long calls all the time in the big games, too, even at the $50-$100 or $80-$160 limits.

Tom: Players get pot-bound in the big games just as easily as they do in the small games. After they put in a certain amount of bets, players simply will not give it up — they know they're beat, but they still call on the end. You know what another mentality is? Sometimes a player will call the end bet just to prove that he was correct about his read. This is truly dumb, but you'll find even high-limit players doing it just to confirm that they have read their opponent correctly.

Here's an example of that in action: You are first to act in the blind and you have top pair with a weak kicker. With five people yet to act behind you, you lead into the field to see where you're at. We've all done this, and occasionally you should do it depending on how the play has come down.

TJ: I'm not saying that there is anything wrong with betting that weak kicker in that spot. But if you're betting it to see if you have the best hand, to find out where you're at, that's ridiculous.

Tom: Sure it is. Then you get raised and you have to guess whether the guy is raising to get a free card. Or does he have a draw? Does he have second pair? Is he just playing position on you because you're in the blind?

You're putting yourself in a tricky situation, the type of thing that you want to avoid whenever you can. This is another reason why position is so important, why you want to avoid playing certain hands out of position — so that you won't be put to these tricky guesses.

A Tip from the Top
The less often you play hands
out of position,
the fewer tricky decisions
you will need to make.

When You Completely Miss Your Hand

Tom: Winning the pot with just a bet on the end is pretty hard to do in limit hold'em. In fact, more people lose more bets at the river by trying to make hopeless bluffs than they do at probably any other stage of the game.

TJ: The only possibility you have for pulling off a successful bluff is when you're heads-up. If there is more than one other player in the pot and you try to bluff on the end in limit hold'em, you might as well just donate your money to charity instead.

A Tip from the Top
Bluffing in limit hold'em in a multiway pot is an exercise in futility.

Tom: Bluffing in limit hold'em in a multiway pot is an exercise in futility. The big bluff is far more characteristic of no-limit play. Remember that in all forms of limit poker and particularly limit hold'em — whether it's ring play or tournament play — you're going to have to show down a hand most of the time. You possibly can bluff a little more often in limit hold'em *tournaments* because players cannot go back to their wallets, therefore they are a little more selective about which hands they get involved with.

TJ: Most of the pots that are won by bluffing in limit poker are won on the flop. Suppose you raised preflop with A-J and two players called your raise. The flop comes 8-6-2. They both check to you, you bet it, and they throw their hands away. You're bluffing at the pot, all you have is ace-high. You might have the best hand, don't get me wrong, but you're still bluffing with the best hand.

Tom: Or suppose the flop comes 9-9-4 rainbow. Unless someone called your raise with something like an A-4, nobody has anything and you can win it right there with a bet if it is checked to you. You're betting ace-high but it probably is still the best hand. Or suppose you raised it with K-Q in late position and a player called the raise with a rag ace. Even though he has a slightly better hand, he can't take a chance that you're bluffing when you bet the flop.

TJ: Now suppose that the flop comes ragged and a player bets his ace-high or two overcards. Then an opponent sitting behind him with top pair raises. I guarantee you that 95 percent of the time the person who bet with the A-J or A-K or two overcards calls that raise! Sometimes the turn card makes his hand, but still it is a marginal play.

You don't make the bet from up front with two overcards when the flop comes with that 9-9-2 we were talking about. You make it from late position. You get called, but not raised. Now what do you do? You had better shut down if you don't hit your hand. But a lot of players will bet a second time if they get checked to again. Suddenly they're thinking that the caller only has two overcards too!

Tom: If he checked to me on the flop and called my bet, and then he checked to me again on fourth street, I usually will also check. Suppose I have an A-J and I think that he may have called me with an ace with a weaker kicker. Then both fourth street and the river rag off. In this case, I may decide to call if he leads into me at the river. It depends on my knowledge of my opponent and how he has been playing that day.

TJ: Here is another mistake that a lot of players make at the river. Suppose "Joe" had position so he bets his two overcards on the flop when it gets to him. He gets called. Nothing comes on fourth street, his opponent checks and Joe also checks. On the end comes nothing again. The opponent checks again and now Joe bets. Bad play! He's supposed to show the hand down. If Joe bets at the river and gets called, he's a goner.

Tom: He's making a negative expectation bet. He will only get called by someone who can beat him. The only time that he *won't* get called is when his opponent was on a draw and missed it, or when the opponent knows that he cannot beat whatever hand Joe was bluffing with to start with. Some players think that they are being so clever when they make this play — they think that they have stolen the pot. But if they get called, they're beat and just wind up losing a bet. As a buddy of mine who reads his opponents superbly once told me, "Picking off bluffs is one of the great nonmonetary pleasures of poker."

TJ: If you just show the hand down and it's the best hand, you will win the pot without risking a bet. If you don't get called, you probably had the best hand anyway. In this scenario, you're simply putting up money just to see if you can get your money back — that's all you're doing. I know we've covered this point before, but this type of play comes up so often on fifth street that it's worth repeating.

Tom: When you miss your hand completely, your action partly depends on whether you were leading with a drawing hand and how much action you were getting. Suppose you have K-Q and the flop comes J-10-3. Or maybe you have A-K and the flop gives you either a flush or straight possibility plus you have two overcards. So you decide to fire at the pot. Any time I have more than one opponent in this type of situation, I like to shut down quickly if I get played with at all.

TJ: And I shut down on the end against anybody if I don't make anything. The players are good enough today that they can read the flop well — they know that there's a flush or straight possibility out there, plus the overcards — just like you do. If you miss your hand on the end and still try to win the pot, that's just doesn't make sense.

Tom: The bad players who are in there with weak hand values might have been calling you with third pair. But if you can't even beat third pair, who's playing worse? Weak players for calling with third pair, or you for trying to run someone off third pair who won't fold? I guarantee that you're making a worse play than they are.

TJ: Or how about the guy who's playing two sixes when two overcards and a straight draw is out there — and he keeps coming! He's called you all the way through and he's going to call you on the end even though you could've paired any card on the board and have him beat.

Tom: So you don't bluff these people, not once, not ever.

TJ: Some players make a living out of tournament poker by putting people on the correct hand, calling them right through, and then taking down the pot at the river. That's their strength, which is based on their ability to read opponents. Believe me, they know which players are betting their draws with nothing at the end and which ones aren't doing it.

Tom: I have read *exactly* what certain top players would do in advance in a tournament hand — and it hasn't done me the slightest bit of good! For example, I once raised with two eights in late position when I had a short to medium stack. I knew that a particular top player was going to take any two cards and try to shove them down my throat. Sure enough, he had an A-10 and practically jumped the fence coming over the top to put me all in — this in a spot where I was going to call 100 percent of the time. Of course, he paired both of his cards, won the pot, and knocked me out.

TJ: Erik Seidel is the all-time World Series of Poker money winner at limit hold'em. In fact, he's a great card player at all games. Who else do you know who has had a big bankroll put up for him to go to Las Vegas and play poker? But instead of just concentrating on hold'em, Erik realized that he needed to know how to play other games too. He didn't know the split games and seven-card games very well so he worked on them by playing at the $10-$20 level until he became proficient enough to move up. He had a huge bankroll to play in the big-big games, but he worked hard playing in those little games to improve himself as an all-around poker player.

Tom: Know anybody who wants to stake me?

TJ: Skip it, Tom. Let's get back to the major points we're making in this session: Always remember that a bet saved on the end is a bet earned. And if you do it five or ten times a night that money might add up to what you've earned for the entire day.

A Tip from the Top
A bet saved on the end
is the same as a bet earned.

Bluffing at the End

Tom: Remember that bluffing is far too overrated in limit hold'em. Players bluff way too often. Most of the time, you're going to have to show down a hand at the river. Thinking that you're going to run over players simply isn't going to work in limit poker. Even the weakest players, the loose-passives, are going to call you if they have any part of the flop. And if you can't beat even the weaklings, it is suicide to keep trying to force the action.

TJ: Also remember that raising with hands such as 7-5 or 9-8 suited before the flop is bluffing — that is *bluffing*. Say that the flop comes with an ace — the guys who continually raise preflop with connected small or middle cards will take off bluffing at it *again* if they don't think that anybody has an ace. All they're doing is burning up money.

A Tip from the Top
Bluff bets are chip burners in limit hold'em.

Tom: Bluff bets are chip burners in limit hold'em. It's OK to *occasionally* raise with one of these types of offbeat hands for advertising purposes. But people do it far too often — they get away with it once in a while and think that they can continue to get away with it, whereas if they never did it at all they would be better off in the long run.

One of the most difficult plays at the river is deciding whether to value-bet with a marginal hand. Good players sometimes are afraid that if they don't bet they will miss winning an extra bet on the end with the best hand. However if you simply check, an opponent may see your check as a license to steal and will bet a hand that is worse than yours.

The other advantage of checking a marginal hand rather than betting it is avoiding a decision if you are raised. Once again this gets us back to trying to avoid having to make tricky decisions whenever you can.

TJ: The ideal play in limit (and even no-limit) hold'em is to run a bluff and then show it at the river after you've won the pot. You make the bluff, win the pot, show the bluff hand — and then take it out of your repertoire for the rest of the day. Of course, Tom and I both have taken it to another level once or twice. "This guy knows that I wouldn't be bluffing at him again," I'm thinking, "so I'll just run one more past him." But I don't recommend this ploy to most players.

Tom: You have to get inside your opponent's head and know that he knows that you wouldn't do it again. You must understand his mind set.

TJ: Of course, you're never going to try it against one of those loose-passive weak players or a maniac because you'll never even win the first pot against them! They're going to call you from here to Dooms Day. ♠

Tom McEvoy accepts the trophy in Limit Hold'em
at the 1997 Seniors World Championship of Poker.

7

LIMIT HOLD'EM TOURNAMENT STRATEGIES

Tom McEvoy & T. J. Cloutier

Tournaments have changed since I wrote my first book *How to Win at Poker Tournaments* in 1985. As public gambling has become legal in more and more places across the nation, poker and poker tournaments have mushroomed during the last ten years. In this section we discuss the latest changes in tournaments and how they affect strategy.

You can do some things in a ring game that you cannot do in a tournament — but everything you can do in a tournament, you *also* can do in a ring game. In fact, by using these tournament strategies in your next cash-game play, you might just save yourself from having to go to your pocket.

I strongly believe that everything I advised readers to do in the limit hold'em tournament chapter of *Tournament Poker* is very useful for limit hold'em cash games as well. I encourage you to read that section as an adjunct to this chapter on tournament play.

Although T. J. and I base our discussions on solid theory, we write from a practical point of view rather than a theoretical one. The advice that we give you has helped us become successful players in ring games and tournaments alike. We try to use common-sense terms in a conversational style of writing that is easy to read so that Joe Blow from Idaho can understand it — and so can Ginny Genius from MIT.

In this chapter, look for answers to these questions and many others:

- **How do the size of the blinds, the amount of the buy-in, the number of chips you start with, and the number of entries affect tournament strategy?**

- **Why should you seldom play small pairs and drawing hands?**

- **Should you always rebuy in rebuy tournaments?**

- **How can you outlast the maniacs?**

- **Why are some tournament structures better for players than others?**

- **What adjustments should you make in your ring-game play for tournaments?**

- **Should you change the way you play in very small buy-in events?**

- **What about playing satellites?**

Tom: Management has found that sponsoring tournaments is a money maker for the poker room as well as the casino. Casinos have a threefold purpose in holding tournaments: (1) Tournaments bring players into the cardroom. The casino makes a little juice on them, but you're actually playing for the money that the players put up, not the house's money. In addition the casino will sometimes post a guarantee, which they usually meet without having to cover any deficit. (2) When players bust out of the tournament, the cardroom counts on their playing side games from which it takes the drop. The drop is where the house makes its real money. (3) In casinos where other forms of gambling are permitted, the house drop rises substantially. Tournament players, their spouses, friends and relatives often gamble at other games such as blackjack, video poker, craps and sports wagering. Wise casino executives realize this and factor it into their projected profits.

Tournament fields today are much larger than they were a decade ago (and even five years ago). No matter how talented a player you are, the more people you have to play against the more difficult it is to make it to the money. However, don't be concerned about the number of entries, just remember that no matter how many hundreds of players there may be in the tournament, the only ones you have to worry about at the moment are the eight or nine opponents who are sitting at your table. Take it one table at a time — you have no control over what's going on anywhere else, but you have a fair amount of control over the action at your table.

You have to change your mind set to play in a modern, big-field tournament, otherwise you will become overwhelmed. T. J. just finished second in a tournament with a field of 490 players and I'm certain that he was not intimidated by the huge field, but I know that there were a lot of players saying to themselves, "Oh my god, we've been playing for several hours and look at how many players are still left — there must be 200 of us!" But instead of thinking about how many opponents they still have to go through to get to the money, they should be concentrating only on what's going on at their table.

TJ: Just remember one thing: In a tournament with 250 players, which was a large field in days past, if each player knocks off one other player that takes it down to 125 players left. If you use the same formula in tournaments with 600 players, there are that many more people knocking other players out before *you* have to knock anybody out. Do you know how many players I want to knock out in a tournament? One!

So, the size of the field should never bother you and it should never change your strategy one iota. All it should do is make you feel better knowing that the purse at the end will be that much bigger.

Tom: I once came in second in a WSOP stud event in which I didn't personally eliminate one single player in the entire field. I had the opportunity to knock out my one final opponent, Men Nguyen, but unfortunately luck was not on my side that day and he drew out on me with a gutshot straight draw against my aces and nines.

TJ: I agree that there are some monster fields in tournaments today. The opening limit hold'em event at the 1999 WSOP attracted 609 players at $1,500 a shot. The first $120 limit hold'em event at the Orleans Open drew 1,085 entries.

The fields are bigger, yes, but I still stress the point that the size of the field should never intimidate you and it should not change your play. Think of it this way: Everybody starts with the same amount of chips. At the end of the third level, one-fourth of the field usually has been eliminated, no matter if the tournament started with 1,000 players or 200 players. On a ratio basis, you're still going to lose the same number of players at the same rate, it's just that there will be more of them going out in the bigger events, so the math shouldn't change at all. Bigger fields simply make bigger prizes — and you have to be prepared to play longer.

When I won the opening limit hold'em event at the inaugural Carnivale of Poker, there were 480 players. We began about 1:30 in the afternoon and played until 8:30 the next morning, which made it a long tournament. The limits rose at a slow pace every hour. Today the final table at Carnivale events are played the next day. But personally, I prefer playing a tournament straight through to its end. I've always thought that it takes two or three hours to really get into the feel of things in a tournament, so if you have to come back the next day to finish, it's just like starting all over again. Even though there is only the final table left to play, it's still a full table and that's all you were ever playing against at any one time anyway — but you have to get your mind set back again. Of course, the World Series of Poker championship event is different. You know before you start that it's a four-day tournament and you pace yourself accordingly.

Tom: Whatever level of tournament play you like, there is a veritable plethora of events available to you. If you are in Las Vegas or Southern California, you can play a tournament every day of the week, twice a day. These tournaments have buy-ins from $12 to $120, and most of them are rebuy events. A lot of the players who enter the big-field, small buy-in tournaments in Las Vegas are recreational players on vacation who are longshots to win.

TJ: There also is a regular group of tournament players who travel around from casino to casino playing all of the low buy-in events. They don't mind putting up $100 and shooting for $10,000, but they don't want to put up $500 and shoot for winning $50,000.

If you travel the tournament circuit in Southern California, you'll run into the same group of $100-$200 tournament players almost anywhere you go: The Bike, Commerce, Hollywood Park, Lake Elsinore, Oceanside, Normandie, Crystal Park. Then there's another echelon of players who won't play any event that has less than a $300 to $500 buy-in. There also is a group who won't play any tournament with less than a $1,000 buy-in, and a select few won't play anything except the championship event in $1,000-and-up tournaments.

General Tournament Concepts

Although limit hold'em tournament play is closer to the ring-game style of play than it is in any other form of poker, there are significant adjustments in strategy that you must make. Here are some of them:

• Mathematics can go out the door in tournament play

Some mathematically oriented authors (who do not regularly play tournaments) use the same math theory for ring games as they do for tournaments, but in doing this they leave out the most important factor in tournaments: You can't go back to your pocket for more money. Maybe you make a call saying to yourself, "Well, the pot's laying me 4-to-1 odds." But if that's all the money that you have left and if you will get knocked out of the tournament if you lose the hand, you're better off folding the hand. If you're out, you're out, and that's all there is to it whereas in a ring game, you can go back to your pocket and continue playing.

Am I saying that math isn't important in poker? No. It's just that the math, the statistics, are more useful to you in ring games where you can put more money on the table when you get broke than they are in tournaments. A lot of people don't factor these things into their tournament play. They forget how important it is in tournaments to play situations and to play your opponents.

• The size of the blinds affects your play

The smaller the blinds in relation to the number of chips you have, the less reason you have to get involved with anything other than premium hands. The bigger the blinds in relation to your chips, the more likely you're going to have to go after the blinds with less than premium starting hands. You'll have to make more positional plays and gamble a little bit more with hands that you might have folded earlier.

Many tournaments have a very small blind structure in the opening round — for example, a $5 small blind with a $15 big blind. In this structure you virtually should never defend the small blind unless the value of your hand warrants it.

• Avoid drawing hands as often as possible

A draw that might make sense in a side game where you can put more money on the table if you miss can be fatal to your chip stack in a tournament. If you don't successfully make the draw it can deplete your chips so drastically that it may not be worth playing the hand.

Any draw that you try for should be a double draw in which you have, for example, a straight draw and the nut flush draw. Or you might have the nut flush draw and two overcards that could win for you if they pair. In other words, you need to make more outs than just a simple draw.

TJ: You need to have as many outs as I recently had in a no-limit tournament. I had the A♠ K♦ and the flop came with the J♠ 10♠ 6♠. I had two overcards, the nut-flush draw, and a middle-buster straight for all the money against a player who had a pocket pair of nines. I went broke to the hand.

Tom: An unfortunate outcome indeed, but the point is that you want to have other outs than just the single draw. If you can only win by making a flush or straight draw in which you might be a 4-to-1 dog depending upon whether there are two cards or one card to come, a lot of times you're better off abandoning ship rather than risking your precious chips that you cannot replace.

TJ: Remember that in any multiway pot where you are not drawing to the nut flush, you might make your hand and lose the pot anyway. This is a particularly dangerous draw in a tournament because you can lose all your chips that way.

Tom: Always ask yourself, "Do I really need to get involved with this hand?" For example, I once played a 9-8 suited on the button in a tournament, made the flush and lost to a better flush. I didn't need to get involved with that hand in the first place and I paid a dear price for my mistake.

TJ: You should ask yourself that question *before* the flop. If you get involved with it, invariably you flop two to your suit just so you can get broke to the hand. It seems like you always either make it and lose or miss it and lose.

• You must be able to make proper laydowns in tournaments

A hand that might be playable in a ring game often is far too dangerous to play in a tournament. The hand requirements that players usually come in with in tournaments are higher than they are in ring games. Suppose you have A-J. It's raised in early position and called before it gets to you. Should you call with this hand in a tournament? No.

TJ: Here's an example from a tournament that I played at the Four Queens a few years ago. It was raised in the first seat and reraised in the second seat by a solid player. I was sitting in the big blind with A-K — I threw it away. And if I threw it away every time under those circumstances, I would be a big winner to it.

Say that you have A♠ 10♠. It's raise, call, call and then it comes to you. If you call you're hoping that the flop comes A-A-10, two tens, K-Q-J, or three spades. You don't want an ace to come because you don't have a quality kicker. You have to ask yourself how often those flops come *before* you get involved with the hand. The fact that you can *win* with any two cards doesn't mean that you should *play* any two cards, even cards presumably as good as A-10 suited.

Making the correct laydowns in the right situations separates the winners from the losers, the men from the boys. Winners realize that it is critical in tournaments to get away from hands that they may very well continue playing in ring games. This requires discipline.

Tom: As in any form of poker, you must exercise strict discipline, especially in tournament poker. If you have no discipline in tournaments, you may as well just save your buy-in because you have to play good poker for hours to make it to the money in a tournament.

I have seen big-big laydowns twice in major tournaments and both times, the player who folded pocket kings won the tournament. When seven players were left during the 1992 World Series of Poker, Hamid Dastmalchi, who had the tournament lead, folded in a key hand against Mike Alsaldi. Seven players were left, six of them to play the final table under the lights the next day. Mike had made it clear that he was determined to play the last day, no matter what. Hamid made a fairly substantial raise with pocket kings. Mike came over the top of him for all his chips, everything. It seemed clear that he had pocket aces. After Hamid folded, Mike indeed showed him the aces. Actually, Hamid didn't ponder the fold for very long — he just showed his kings and whisked them into the muck. Hamid won the title and Mike came in fourth.

A Tip from the Top
Making quality laydowns separates
the players from the pretenders

At the inaugural 1999 Tournament of Champions, winner David Chiu folded kings against an all-in raise by second-place finisher Louis Asmo, who showed his aces after Chiu had folded. The gallery hung on in suspenseful silence as Chiu took a long time to make the decision to fold. The ability to make quality laydowns in tournaments separates the players from the pretenders.

• You can raise with some hands that you cannot call a raise with

There are hands that you can raise with from a *late* position that you cannot call a raise with from *any* position. Remember that in tournaments as well as ring games, it takes a much better hand to call with than to raise with. This is especially true in tournaments where players usually are playing more solid hand values. For example, if you have A-J or A-10 suited or unsuited on the button or in the blinds (with no action in front of you), you might raise with this hand. But if somebody raises in front of you, you probably should throw it away. You simply have to duck these types of hands because you can get into so much trouble with them, even when you flop to them. That's the biggest danger — it isn't so much calling the first bet, it is all the subsequent bets that you lose when you flop something to a marginal hand and the hand is no good.

TJ: Suppose you have $600 in chips at the $100-$200 level. You have A♠ 10♠ on the button. The first man raises and the second man calls. Now it's going to cost you $200 to call. Then an ace and two rags come on the flop and the raiser bets into you. Now you're gonna call him again. Another rag comes on the turn and he bets $200. Again you call. Now $500 of your $600 is in the pot. Then no matter what comes at the river, you're going to call again for the rest of your chips — with a hand that you shouldn't have played at all.

Tom: The point is that you should be very careful about the hands that you commit with in tournaments. There are many hands that you might commit with in ring games that you cannot play in tournaments. You need more strength in tournament events because your chips are so much more precious, leaving you with only a narrow margin for error.

TJ: Here's a situation for you to think about: You have a pair of tens on the button. It has been raised and called. What do you do with the hand? When you're short or medium-stacked, you probably should throw it away. If you have only a few chips left, you may decide to gamble and go all in because you might not get a better hand before the blinds eat you up. When you have a lot of chips, you might call to see the flop hoping to flop a third ten and take somebody out.

• Staying out of tricky situations after the flop is very important in tournaments

Tom: Staying out of tricky situations after the flop is even more important in tournaments than it is in ring games. Here is another example using a pair of tens: I was playing the $2,000 opening limit hold'em event at the World Series of Poker. We were at four tables with very high limits and three tables were being paid, so I was getting close to the money. A man with a lot of chips raised under the gun and I called with those two tens. To my surprise, the small blind also called.

The flop came with three baby cards, making it hard to determine what to do with my tens. The weak player in the small blind, who could have had any two cards, led at the pot on both the flop and turn, and the original raiser just called. Being totally lost as to what to do in this hand, I also just called. With an all-baby-card flop, the small blind could have flopped two pair, a straight draw, or a small pair and a straight draw (which is what he had), but in any case it was a hand that he should not have defended the blind with. At the river an ace came. The small blind checked, the raiser fired out a bet, and I threw away the tens.

This example illustrates the point we are making about trying not to play hands with which you will have to make close decisions. Under the playing conditions I have described, the two tens required very tricky decisions and they wound up costing me dearly. If I had saved those chips I would have made the money whereas I finished just a few spots out of it.

With a raise and a caller, the two tens are not a favorite to be an overpair to the flop. Even if they are, they may not be the best hand. Remember also that the chances of flopping a set are 7.5-to-1 against and many times, that is what you'll have to hit to play the hand. And if one overcard comes, what are you going to do with the hand?

TJ: There are two scenarios with this hand: Either you call the raise to start with and the flop comes with an overcard or two (A-K-X or K-Q-X or Q-J-X). Or it comes with a baby flop such 8-4-2 and you really get taken out. Somebody has a pair of jacks or queens and you get toasted just like you're supposed to get toasted.

Tom: A lot of people say, "Well, if you don't play two tens, what *do* you play?! You don't get a pair that high very often." Just remember that you're playing the *circumstances.* If you have solid players betting and raising in front of you, you can't play this hand with any degree of confidence.

TJ: It doesn't even have to be solid players doing the raising, it can be weak players — anybody can be dealt a pair. Of course, you can raise with the hand in the right situation.

Tom: Sure, it's a whole different ball game if you can be the aggressor with the hand. If you're the first one in the pot, or if one guy has limped in and you figure that you have a better hand than he has, you can attack to try to isolate with superior position against one player. But coming in cold for two bets puts you on the defense right from the start.

• Seldom play small pairs

We have stated that many players are playing medium and small pairs aggressively in the new brand of hold'em ring games. You can follow our ring-game advice for playing these pairs in tournaments, remembering that you should duck them most of the time. Even if you suspect that your opponent is in the hand with a slightly weaker pair or just overcards, if he's super-aggressive and is willing to keep firing you can't play your pair with any degree of confidence unless you flop a set — and you're never a favorite to flop the set.

Remember also that you can play a medium or small pair for a single raise from the small or big blind in a tournament *if* there is multiway action. If four or five players already are in the pot after calling an early position raise and you're in the small blind, the only player who can reraise you is the big blind. If you're in the big blind no one can raise you.

In this case you can call the double bet and try to flop a set in a multiway pot. Just remember that it's "no set, no bet" after the flop. You're getting a big price to the hand and you can get away from it quickly and easily.

We don't want to confuse you by implying that it's okay to play a pair of eights or fours but it's not okay to play a pair of tens. It all depends on the circumstances, how the play comes up. In tournaments you always have to be aware of special situations — and the same thing applies to side games.

The players who win so many hold'em tournaments make the plays we've been talking about and they don't make the plays we're warning against. It isn't an accident that certain players are consistent winners at tournament poker.

• You must have an acute sense of timing and a feel for situations in tournaments

In particular, you have to know when to duck the traps and when to take advantage of favorable situations. The great tournament players are the ones who adapt to existing and changing circumstances. Players with the best overall results are the ones who have the best ability to do whatever they have to do to adapt.

Tom: Top players know how to adjust their play based on their chip count and what's going on with their opponents. Sometimes their opponents will go from a big stack to a little stack or vice-versa, and that immediately changes their play. The top players recognize the change and adjust to it instantly. This is why T. J. is so successful at tournament play — he is adept at making adjustments very rapidly and getting inside his opponents' heads.

TJ: You're good at that yourself, buddy. Now let me tell you about a play that came up during a no-limit tournament at Lake Elsinore Casino that also applies to limit hold'em. I raised the pot $200 with Q♣ Q♦. The little blind reraised me another $200 and I flat called. The flop came J♠ 10♠ 8♠. He led at the flop and I threw the queens away even though I had an overpair to the board. Of course, I didn't have the spades and I wasn't going to try to catch a queen to make a set (which also would have put a four-straight on the board). And if the spade queen came, a four-flush would be out there and he could have won with any spade. He showed me pocket tens.

• Determine whether your opponents usually play ring games or tournaments

The great majority of players you run into in limit hold'em tournaments are ring-game players who play tournaments exactly the same way that they play in cash games. The top players don't — they switch gears to play tournament hold'em. When you're playing a tournament, you need to know which players will pull in their horns and which ones will play their usual sidegame strategy. If you play regularly in a cardroom, you usually will know who plays regular cash-game strategy and who shifts gears for tournaments.

The ring-game players get A-6 offsuit and here they come. If you raise the pot with two kings, one of them is liable to call you with A-2 offsuit just as he would in a loose ring game. You have to be prepared to take the beats from these types of players and not let them influence your play whatsoever — you just have to go on to the next hand.

TJ: And I've had plenty of experience in doing just that! In a limit hold'em tournament, I held A♠ K♠. An opponent raised and I reraised before the flop. He called. The flop came J♠ 10♠ 4♦. He had the Q♥ 9♥ and bet on the flop. I called. On fourth street he checked and I bet. He called with the open-ended straight draw. At the river came a nine. He checked and I checked. He won the pot with a pair of nines. He had raised and called a reraise with that Q-9 before the flop! I had flopped a royal flush draw with two overcards and lost the pot, but that's the way it sometimes goes in limit hold'em.

Tom: I agree that his play was loose, but you can't play ultra tight in tournaments either. Tight players don't win tournaments. They just never catch enough cards (by their standards) to be able to win. And when they do catch cards, they don't get maximum value for them if they're up against any real players.

TJ: I get a big kick out of the fact that a lot of "nonplayers" think that I'm a tight player. (Nonplayer is a term that we use on the circuit to describe other tournament players who aren't considered to be real *players*.) That's beautiful for me. They think that everything that I've ever accomplished is because I just play solid-O. And I've got more moves than a mongoose!

Tom: Sure, but a lot of the moves that you make are in the middle to later stages when you've read the situations and players right. Tournament players should not be making a lot of moves *early* when the blinds are small — they should make their moves later when those plays are more significant.

TJ: Correct. Tight's right when you first start out.

A Tip from the Top
Tight is right early in the tournament.

Tom: I have told the players that I teach the same thing. You start out playing not ultra tight, but certainly very solid. The blinds and antes are very small at the start of tournaments, so you have less incentive to try stealing them.

TJ: Another thing that I hope you're teaching them is this: Play right in every situation. And then add: Adapt these strategies to your own play, your own style. You should play solid and use your own kinds of moves when the situation is right for you. You and I both have been very successful at poker but believe me, we don't play the same style.

Tom: Right. There is more than one way to be successful in ring games and there is more than one successful tournament style. And when you really get into it, you adjust your style to the table that you're playing.

• You Sometimes Must Steal a Few Blinds to Stay in Action

Tom: T. J. played a tournament a while back when he stole just enough blinds and antes with no hands to stay alive. He never held a pair or an ace for two hours, but he didn't lose his discipline and play recklessly. This is what separates the true tournament players from the wannabes. The class player is able to wait, to pick his situations and survive the drought until some cards come his way.

TJ: Let me tell you how I stole them. This happened to occur in a no-limit tournament, but it could just as easily have been a limit hold'em event. I had $875 left at the $50-$100 blinds level. Never did I ever put my whole stack in the pot. I was making $275 or $300 raises, but never put in the whole enchilada. I always gave myself an out in the hand. Then at the $100-$200 level I moved in with the 6♦ 2♦ against a top lady player who happened to have an A-Q behind me in the big blind and called my all-in raise. Fortunately I snagged a deuce at the river to win the hand. She took it like a champ.

Tom: Sure, you got lucky at the end but you weren't *calling* with the 6-2, you were making a play at the pot. But back to a point we made earlier: Stealing is an important ploy at certain stages of a tournament.

The Stages of Tournaments

Tom: Generally speaking, tournaments progress through four stages of play — slow-fast-slow-fast. You will find discussions of these stages and tips on how to play them in *Poker Tournament Tips from the Pros* and *Poker Tournament Tactics for Winners* (which is out of print), as well as *Tournament Poker*. D. R. Sherer's explanation of these stages is about as good as you will find: "If the tournament has started with adequate chips (50 to 100 times the size of the big blind), the opening round is slow and you should be able to steal with smaller cards. However, if a fast-playing maniac is at your table, you must identify him quickly and play only big cards if there is any chance that he will be playing the pot with you.

"After a few limit rises the first fast period begins. Players start getting eliminated, there are many short stacks in action, and some desperate play is going on. This fast stage lasts through a few more limit rises until all the chips are concentrated in fewer players.

"The second slow period begins when (for example) about six tables remain from a starting field of twenty tables. At this time, a lot of big stacks are in play. Most of the maniacs have been eliminated or are so impressed with their big chip piles that they cease playing wildly and begin to preserve their stacks. Now it is the foxes against the rocks, making for a great time to try to steal a few pots.

"Then comes the final table. When it gets to about six-handed, the on-marching rise in limits again forces some fast action. The fact that three or four players have been eliminated at the final table is itself an indication that the raisers are holding sway and fast is back."

Understanding these tournament stages can help you to judge your style of play, depending on the type of opponents at your table. Just remember that in the opening stages, tight is right, as T. J. puts it. Your goal is to build a stack through solid play that you can take with you to the next level.

Adjusting Your Play from Ring Game to Tournament Strategy

Tom: Other than playing somewhat more conservatively, you don't have to make huge adjustments from regular ring-game strategy to tournament play during the first level of play in a no-rebuy event (or one with only one rebuy). However if I am playing a multiple rebuy tournament in which the rebuys are not very expensive, I usually will play a little faster because I always plan to take the rebuys. But in a no-rebuy tournament I am not going to play very differently from my usual ring-game strategy — I am just going to play very solid hold'em and be aware that most of my opponents are playing a little more conservatively than they normally do in ring games.

Once the second level hits and the chips start to get redistributed, that changes a lot of things. If you're shortstacked, you have to tighten up a little bit and wait for that one hand when you can push it for all it's worth. If you have a bigger stack you can start bullying the smaller stacks a little bit. Just remember that in limit poker, it is more difficult to push people around so you have to know your opponents.

TJ: Most of the bigger hold'em events on the regular tournament circuit are no-rebuy events. In fact until a few years ago when the Commerce Casino started giving big guarantees, you never saw a limit hold'em tournament with rebuys. The main thing that you must remember is that the biggest difference between cash games and tournaments is that you cannot go back to your pocket. You must always be cognizant of this fact.

Tom: Which is why a lot of players must play more conservatively in tournaments.

TJ: A lot of ring-game players who play for hours on end will get a 6-5 suited with two or three players in the pot, it gets raised in a couple of spots in front of them, and they call because they want to take off three or four players if they hit a perfect flop. If they lose they can go back to their pocket and get all the chips they need to continue. But if you play this way four or five times in a tournament, suddenly you don't have any chips left. This is why the selection of hands that you're willing to play is so important to you in tournaments.

Say that you have $1,000 in chips and you decide to call a $300 raise with a very marginal hand such as J-10 or J-8 or even A-Q, and you had to fold the hand after the flop. If you hadn't called the raise, you could double the $1,000 on the next hand and have $2,000 to play with. But that $300 call has left you with only $700 in chips. If you double that $700 on the next hand, you only have $1,400 left, which is just $400 more than you had to start with.

By making these kinds of marginal calls, you have lost not only the power of your chips but your earning power as well. The whole idea of tournament poker is to win all the chips, so you have to be very careful when you're throwing them off. If you keep this factor in the back of your mind, after a while you won't have to think about it when the situation comes up. Keep thinking, "What is this call going to do to my chip stack?" Pretty soon, it becomes automatic.

Tom: Back to the second round of play: If I have a lot of chips and my opponents already are in their survival mode, I will make more positional plays trying to take advantage of their conservatism. That is, provided that I am pretty sure that they will surrender. If there is no chance that they will surrender, they're just going to gamble no matter what, I have to play strictly according to hand values.

TJ: Every time you make a positional play, you're either bluffing or semibluffing to try to steal some money from your opponents. Always ask yourself, "Is the money I'm trying to steal worth what it's going to cost me to steal it?"

Suppose you started with $10-$15 blinds and $15-$30 limits. Now you're at $15-$30 blinds and $30-$60 limits. With a marginal hand, is it worth the $60 that you have to put in to raise to try to win the $45 that you can steal from the blinds? If you get called by a better hand, you could end up losing more than it was worth to you to try for the steal.

The only time that it is worth trying to steal the blinds is when they become huge at the higher levels. This is why I prefer waiting until the later rounds to try these positional plays. And believe me, you will be playing against better players in the later rounds so that your positional plays will work better. The loose goose that was still in there in round two will call you whereas the better player will not.

Tom: Naturally you should not be making a positional play with a piece of cheese. You might raise it with a couple of face cards, a K-J for example, which is more of a semibluff. And if you're attacking the blinds, you want to be sure that you're the first one in the pot and there's a reasonable chance that the blinds will lay down their hands against a raise. If someone has already limped in the pot or you're up against loose blind defenders, the positional play will not work.

TJ: In the Practice Hands chapter, Tom and I discuss playing a hand such as K♦ 5♦. Suppose you have this hand at the $100-$200 limits ($50-$100 blinds) on the button and everybody passes to you. To make a positional play in this spot means that it will cost you $200 to raise. This means that if both blinds pass, you will win $150. If you get called and lose, the minimum that you will lose is $200. Is it worth it? No, I don't think it is. It's a lot tougher to steal in limit hold'em than it is to steal in no-limit.

Some players will defend with *any* two cards in limit hold'em tournaments. At the earlier levels (and sometimes even at the later levels) a greater percentage of players protect their blinds that you would ever think was possible. I never think about protecting my blind — I figure that my blind money is already lost the minute I put it up. If I happen to pick up a hand, that's great, but I never plan to protect my blind. After you've played a couple of rounds you will know who is likely to defend and who won't. If the pot is raised and the blind is calling a lot, sometimes he will even show his hand when he throws away after an ace hits the flop. They will defend with hands like 8-5 or Q-7, junk like that.

Tom: You'll also see fast players such as Dan Heimiller playing back with their blind hands. They will have something like K-10 offsuit and come over the top of the raiser. Be aware of this type of player.

TJ: I get a little tired of that stuff, so one time I showed Dan a little trick in a no-limit tournament. The antes were $25 and the blinds were $100-$200. It was passed to me on the button and he was in the big blind. I raised it up to steal the blinds. Here comes Dan with a reraise. But he made a big mistake: He didn't raise all his chips, just a nominal amount. Well, I came right back over the top of him with all my chips. He chucked that hand so fast it would make your head spin. But in limit hold'em, he is totally bluff-proof. "Well, you caught me bluffing," he said and showed me a piece of junk. "Who was bluffing who?" I answered and showed him my hand. Of course I didn't make that play at him again during the tournament. In another no-limit tournament I bet on the end against a player and he raised me. I repopped it and he laid down kings-up. Then I showed him a stone bluff.

If you raise from a late position, this type of player automatically assumes that you have no hand and you're stealing. We mention this play as an example so that you will be aware that they are out there. You need to know whether the two players on your left are aggressive blind defenders.

A Tip From the Top
At some point in most tournaments,
an A-K will be the deciding hand for you.

In tournaments you have to be successful in 11.5-to-10 situations. Even in limit hold'em tournaments where you raise with an A-K, if you get played with by two queens or jacks (or any other pocket pair), you have to win with the A-K. You also have to win with the other side of the coin, when you're up against A-K with a pair. At some point in most tournaments, Big Slick will be the deciding hand for you.

Rebuy Tournament Strategy

TJ: In *no-limit* hold'em events, I suggest not rebuying or adding on until you have to, whereas in *limit* hold'em events you should make your rebuy as soon as you are eligible for it. I take this approach because limit hold'em tournaments have structured betting limits and you may find yourself playing better poker with a lot of chips in front of you, not being tempted to make marginal calls because you're short on chips. "Well, I've only got $200," you say, "and I'm gonna rebuy the next hand anyway, so I'll just make this call." But suppose you get $500 for the rebuy, which is only $300 more than the $200 you already have. If you had enough chips in front of you, you might not be making that long call.

Tom: I always want to be prepared to make a rebuy and an add-on. Suppose that I start with $500 in chips at $15-$30 limits and the second round rises to $30-$60, after which the rebuy period is over. Now suppose that I've been fortunate enough to double up to $1,000 in chips when the add-on comes up, which will give me $500 in additional chips. Any time that I can add 50 percent to my stack, I almost always will take the add-on, and I might even add on if it amounts to a little less than 50 percent.

If I have $1,300 in chips, for example, there's a good chance that I still will take the add-on because it gives me at least one or maybe one and a half extra hands that I can play — and that makes a difference, especially at the very next level. But if I have been on a hot streak and have $2,500 in chips, then I would save the add-on expense. It is when I am in the in-between range of $1,000-$1,500 that I think that I can never go wrong in taking the add-on.

TJ: I have a standard policy for add-ons. If I have less than $2,500 in chips and I have not rebought, I will always take the add-on. When I enter a $120 tournament, I always figure that it's a $220 tournament because I plan to take the add-on with anything less than $2,500 in chips.

I do that for this reason: In every tournament there comes a time for almost every player when he has a lull, a time when he might go five or six rounds when he doesn't have a hand to play. When the rebuys are over, the limits usually are up to $25-$50 blinds, $75 a round if you don't play a hand. If you go five or six or seven times around the table, that extra $500 that you added on will give you a cushion for when you can't find a hand to play, and that happens lots of times. So adding-on is something that I suggest doing but it's something that you yourself have to feel good about doing.

Tom: T. J. is somewhat more liberal in this respect than I am. If it's a $100 tournament, I am far more likely to add on when I have $2,500 in chips, but if it's a $300 or $500 tournament I am less likely to put in the extra money. In this respect, the size of the buy-in affects my action.

TJ: In reverse, say that you have $200 in chips in a $500 tournament. It's time for the add-on and you know that the new limits will be $50-$100. You will only get three rounds at the table ($450) for that extra $500 in add-in chips. In this case, I suggest just going with your $200 and not adding on.

Let the ante size dictate whether it is correct to add on. If the add-on will do you some good, fine. But if it won't help you enough to justify the added expense, you might just as well play with the short stack you have in front of you. You're going to have to win the first hand that you play, anyway, so why not just gamble with what you have and reduce your investment? But say that you're playing $50-$100 limits with $25-$50 blinds and you're sitting on $500, the amount of your original stack. Then it makes sense to take the add-on.

• Incremental Rebuy Events

Tom: There's a fairly new type of rebuy tournament setup that offers incremental rebuys. For example, you get $500 in chips for your initial $120 buy-in and then you get $800 in chips if you make the $100 rebuy plus $800-to-$1,000 in chips for $100 if you add on. Basically, this type of event is telling you that although it only costs $120 to buy in, you should not play it if you aren't willing to invest $320 because you'll be taking so much the worst of it if you don't rebuy and add on. Other tournaments of this ilk have a single rebuy with incentive chips added, and in those you also should take the rebuy.

TJ: Remember that the main reason you're playing the tournament is to get a big return on a small investment. If you play in one of these incremental rebuy tournaments in which you get $500 to start with, $800 for the rebuy, and $1,000 for the add-on, you should consider it to be a $320 tournament, not a $120 tournament. Situations will come up where you never have to do anything, you just hold the deck and never have to add on. But those are rare, so be prepared to invest the maximum amount in incremental rebuy events.

This example is not from limit hold'em, but it still addresses rebuys. Anyone who plays in a pot-limit Omaha tournament who decides in advance not to take any rebuys is taking much the worst of it. In pot-limit Omaha you can lose your whole buy-in on one hand, even on the first hand dealt, because the pots get so big and there are such fluctuations in the game. Therefore, pot-limit players plan in advance for rebuys and the add-on. You should do the same in incremental rebuy events.

Suppose that limit hold'em is *your* game but you also want to play a few other events during the tournament. If you have to forfeit playing one of the other events to take a rebuy in the limit hold'em tournament because you don't have enough money to play the others *and* make a rebuy in the hold'em event, do it. Always play the game at which you are more proficient, the one where you think you have the best chance of winning.

• When Should You Rebuy?

Tom: I've been asked if it is always correct to rebuy when you go broke. My answer is no. The later you are in the rebuy period, the less reason you have to rebuy. The rebuy has less value to you at this stage because the limits are much higher.

In the Los Angeles area, the casinos hold a lot of $300 rebuy limit hold'em tournaments in which you're allowed to rebuy for three levels. You start with $500 in chips and get $500 for each rebuy you make. Suppose you get to the third level of play, you're in for just your original $300 buy-in, only 15 minutes are left at that level, and you go broke. If you take the rebuy, then you're probably going to have to take another rebuy and possibly the add-on, increasing your original investment from $300 to $1,200 real fast in order to have a chance to win. To me it makes a lot more sense to surrender at this point rather than to quadruple your original investment unless, of course, the prize money is so huge that you think it's worth it, which occasionally happens.

TJ: Any time the tournament will pay you 40-to-1 on your original investment, it's worth it to rebuy and/or add on. Say that first place gets $70,000, second place gets $35,000 and third place gets $17,500 and it goes on down the line from there so that 18th through 27th will get in the money. A lot of players will just be trying to finish in the money.

In no-limit hold'em rebuy tournaments there used to be a formula that we used for rebuys. The rebuy period lasted for three levels and you played for one hour at each level. The formula was that the rebuys would work out to just about 1.5-to-1 the original buy-in for $500 tournaments on up. Of course, this increases the prize pool by 1.5 times the original buy-ins. By this we mean that if the original field of 100 players equaled $50,000 the rebuys would equal 150 X $500 or $75,000. To show you how things have changed, there were 490 players at the Orleans Open $100 no-limit hold'em event and there were 931 rebuys, which works out to about 2-to-1. This means that the average cost for the field was almost $290 per player (not counting the $20 juice).

Guaranteed Tournaments

TJ: A lot of players make it a point to enter small tournaments that have guarantees. When a small out-of-the-way card room such as the Lake Elsinore Casino sponsors a tournament with a $30,000 or $40,000 guaranteed prize pool, it's often worth it to players to travel there because they only have to invest a couple $100 to win a big prize. In their minds, the tournament gives them an overlay.

Even if you don't play a lot of tournaments, the guaranteed prize pool may make it worth your while to enter one of these events sponsored by small cardrooms, so long as you can drive to it. Don't fly from the East coast to the West coast to play in a $100 tournament, guarantee or not. But I think that if you're within 150 miles so that you can easily drive there, it's to your advantage to play these small guaranteed tournaments because they are good values.

If the guarantee is $30,000 and first place pays 40 percent, the winner gets $12,000. I know that's a very good payout for a $100 or $200 investment, but you still have to beat all of them before you get that money.

Most guaranteed tournaments are rebuy events because the house wants to make the guarantee. With a $30,000 guarantee the card room is expecting 300 players if no rebuys are allowed, or around 200 players if they allow one rebuy. Some of these tournaments might have one rebuy only, or one rebuy with an add-on, or even multiple rebuys with an add-on. Before you enter any rebuy event, you should set your mind straight on how much you're willing to invest in the tournament and stick with the plan.

Playing Against the Maniacs

TJ: Just remember that being able to rebuy should not change the way that you play — you should not make a call that you wouldn't make in a freeze-out tournament just because you can rebuy. But being able to rebuy *will* change the play of the weaker players in the event. They will call with open-ended straight draws, middle-busters, second pair (even third pair), ace-anything and any two suited cards. Although the percentages are against drawing out with these hands, they will play them because they know that they can rebuy.

Tom: In small buy-in tournaments that attract big fields, you will be playing against the maniacs, the weak players, the rocks and the "pros" (expert players). In the opening stages, the maniacs and the weak players dominate the action.

TJ: That's right — they always seem to get a hold of chips early. If they get lucky, their play can knock out the rocks and the foxes early on. You should always remember that maniacs and weak players rule in the early stages.

Let me give you an example of this phenomenon: Tom and I were playing in a $1,000 buy-in, no-limit hold'em tournament where we started with $10,000 in chips. The chip leader had $50,000 in chips after the first hour, which was incredible — it meant that he had had to break four players when the blinds were still small. But he did *not* make it through the second hour!

Tom: You have to realize that you're up against these types of players in the early stages, and they're the ones who can take you out. Remember that the maniacs are going to take somebody down almost every time. In fact, maniacs sometimes win tournaments when they get a hold of so many chips early because they just keep bulldozing their way through other players, catching enough cards to make it to the end. If you're up against a known maniac, you're forced to give him more action than you would a more solid, conservative player. Even a maniac can wake up with two aces, you know.

TJ: I was playing a tournament at the table with a guy who won a ton of chips during the first two levels. He didn't happen to get my chips, but he could've if the situation had come up just right. He fired at every pot and hit everything he needed — I think he started with the best hand one out of ten times, but he happened to win all ten pots. I leaned over to a friend sitting next to me and said, "I'd like to lay you 20-to-1 that this guy doesn't make the final table." Well, I could've laid 1,000-to-1 that he wouldn't have made it to the last four tables because it just couldn't happen. If you laid that bet against the same man every time, you'd win it 100 percent of the time.

In another case, a man was transferred to my table at the Orleans Open with $30,000 in chips with six tables to go. He would limp in, somebody would call and somebody else would reraise, and he would call every single time. Less than an hour later, he was broke. After he got broke he came up to me during the break and asked, "Where did I go wrong, T. J.?"

"Well, I think you might've called a few too many raises," I answered. But you get what I'm saying, right? The way these players get their chips is by doing those types of things or sucking out, getting lucky, and when that luck goes away they don't know how to play.

They acquire chips early by playing loose, gambling with a lot of marginal hands, but they forget to shut down when their luck runs out and move on to some other type of play. For example, suppose this type of player is in the $50 big blind with $2,000 in front of him in a no-limit tournament. Another guy moves all-in for $1,000 and the big blind thinks, "Well, lookie here, I've got an A-4 offsuit. I'm calling!" and shoves in the $1,000. He's up against A-K but he snags a four and wins the pot. Do you think that he can do that for the rest of the tournament? No way. But he remembers that hand and he thinks that he can make a repeat performance.

Tight's right early. The reason why some people are a lot more successful than others is that they know when to open up and when to shut down, who to make plays against and who not to make plays against.

Some Tips on Playing Satellites

TJ: Say that you start with $200 in chips in a supersatellite. Every 20 minutes the limits rise. You start at $5-$10, then $10-$20, then $15-$30. By the time you get to $15-$30, which means that after four rounds at the table you will be broke just from posting the blinds. If you go broke and rebuy at that level, it might not be worth your while. Remember that right after the break, the blinds will be $25-$50. You almost would have to go for the single and double add-on, or even the triple add-on, and suddenly you're in for $800 instead of $200 with no more than $600 in chips in front of you. With the blinds at $25-$50, that isn't a lot of chips to play with.

I don't think that any supersatellite that costs $120 is worth more than $420 total (a buy-in with three rebuys, or two rebuys and one add-on). This is for a $5,000 seat in the main tournament.

It is *when* you make the rebuys that counts. A lot of times, we wait until the end of the rebuy period before we even enter the supersatellite. At that time, some seats usually are open and you can come in for the $420 and get $800 worth of chips. You'll have almost as many chips as anybody else at the table instead of getting $200 at a time. Some people do the same thing at the supersatellites for the $10,000 seats at the WSOP. They come in late for $800. You put your name on the list to come in as an alternate. You're not starting with $200 in chips, with which you can't blow anybody out of a pot. The first hour in supersatellites is racehorse poker — they're pushing it all in on anything. If you raise with two aces, they'll call you with 4-3! With any type of pair, they'll go right to the center with all their chips.

Professional satellite players sometimes will get caught up in the heat of the action, lose their perspective, and make excessive rebuys. I once saw a player make seventeen (17!) in a $220 supersatellite for a $5,000 seat. He was in $3,620 to win a $5,000 seat! There weren't even enough players to award multiple seats, so they were only giving away one seat — and he didn't win it.

You can get into a one-table satellite for $1,000 ($200 more than you're likely to spend on a $200 supersatellite with two rebuys and an add-on) and only have to play against nine other players. For this reason, they probably are a better value than the supers.

Tom: In a nutshell, one-table strategy is a sort of hybrid between what works in regular tournaments and what works in shorthanded play. Because the betting rounds in one-table satellites are only 15 or 20 minutes long, you must play faster than you would in either a ring game or a regular tournament. (In Chapter 15 of *Tournament Poker* I give a more detailed explanation of one-table satellite strategy.)

Steady but controlled aggression, plus a lot of good judgement, is necessary to win. Because the luck factor is higher, I am willing to gamble in multiway pots with speculative hands. Chips are power and I want to win as many as I can as early as I can. I don't advocate playing a lot of trash hands, particularly in raised pots, but it only takes one winning hand in a raised multiway pot to gain a commanding chip position.

Some of the hands that you are looking for to gamble with in multiway pots include suited connectors and small pairs. You might even play them somewhat out of position if it looks as though there will be four or five-way action. If I win one of these big pots and double by stack, I will immediately put on the brakes because I have enough chips to wait for a premium opportunity. This doesn't mean that I won't play decent hands or take a few more calculated risks, just that I won't be gambling quite as much once my goal of doubling up has been achieved.

If you lose the multiway hand, look for either another multiway pot or a heads-up situation. If you can't find either, simply tighten up and wait for one good solid hand to push in all your chips. If this also fails, you're in bad-bad shape, but still never give up. It only takes a chip and a chair to win.

The Tournament Structure

Tom: The more chips you start with, the smaller the limits, and the longer the rounds the more important skill is to your tournament success. The fewer the chips, the larger the limits, and the shorter the rounds the more important is the luck factor. Under this second set of conditions, you have to play at a much faster pace — and this is where maniacs are truly in their element.

The top tournament players raved about the tournament structure at the inaugural Tournament of Champions. They liked it so much because they started with a lot of chips and the limits rose rather slowly. They were unanimous in predicting that no maniac, no weak player, was going to win the tournament — a world-class player would win it. David Chiu proved them to be correct.

The point is that the slower the limits rise and the more chips you have to start with, the more it favors quality players because they have more time to outmaneuver their opponents. This is why the WSOP championship event is considered to be the ultimate test of skill.

TJ: Some tournament directors are scheduling 40-minute rounds for the first three to five levels and then going to one-hour time frames for the later rounds, which I think is also a very good structure. You have enough time at the lower levels and when the chips really mean something later in the tournament, you have a full hour to work with.

Tom: There is a tendency for tournament directors, including myself, to give players more chips to start with in lower-limit tournaments and give them a premium on their rebuys. Or give a 2-for-1 add-on (as happens at the Orleans daily tournaments) in which players get double the starting amount of chips for the same cost as a rebuy. In this format, it is virtually never wrong to take the add-on.

TJ: I thought that the 2-5-10 buy-in at the Super Bowl of Poker was the best tournament structure that I've ever played. The original buy-in was $200 for which you received $500 in chips. The first rebuy cost $500 for which you got $500 in chips. Any subsequent rebuy cost $1,000 for which you received $1,000 in chips. Except for your original buy-in, you paid an amount of money equal to the number of chips you received and, of course, all that rebuy money built up the prize pool. Let me contrast that setup to a modern, incremental rebuy $300 tournament format in which you pay the $300 entry fee and get $500 in chips, pay $300 for a rebuy and get $800, and then pay $300 again and get $1,000 for the add-on. You get more chips in this structure, but the additional chips do not reflect on the size of the prize pool as they did at the Super Bowl where the dollar amount of the rebuys increased the payouts proportionately.

Phil Hellmuth once laid everybody 8-to-5 on a last-longer bet at the Super Bowl and wound up putting $8,800 into the tournament just to stay in it because he had all those bets going. That was a lot of additional money in the prize pool — and he didn't win the tournament either.

A tournament structure that I don't understand is the one used at the Orleans Open, where there is a no-rebuy tournament that starts at noon each day and a $100 second-chance one-rebuy tournament that starts at 7:00 pm that night. Why not also give the main tournament players the opportunity to make one rebuy? That way, the prize pool would build and everybody would be happier (and richer). If I was the director of a $100 tournament I would always allow at least one rebuy.

Tom: A common structure in daily casino $20 rebuy tournaments is to start players with $100 in chips, $5-$5 blinds, and 30-minute rounds. The second round also is 30 minutes long but beginning at the third level, the rounds are 20 minutes long. Players can make $20 rebuys for which they get an additional $100 in chips. After the third round, players can make an add-on in which they get $200 in chips for $20. After a 10-minute break, play resumes with 20-minute rounds. In other words, the casino is running the tournament in reverse with longer rounds earlier and shorter rounds later in the event. Although we advocate that you start your tournament career by playing in low-limit tournaments, we want you to be aware that some of them have a weak structure.

Tournament directors should print tournament structure sheets in advance so that players will have full knowledge of how the tournament will be run before they decide whether to play. Structure sheets usually are passed out at the sign-up table and include the amount of chips you start with, the limits at each level, the length of the rounds, and how many places will be paid proportionate to the number of entries.

Knowing in advance exactly how the tournament will be structured is important in making a yes-no decision to play it. For example, if you know that the rounds will be comparatively short in proportion to the number of starting chips, and the beginning blinds will be higher than warranted, you may decide against putting up $200 to enter an event. But if you are satisfied with the number of chips you start with, the opening levels of the blinds, and the length of the rounds, you probably will go ahead and enter the event knowing that it favors skill rather than luck.

TJ: Some tournament directors say that they want to spread out the prize money pool to pay more places. The reason that they want to do this is so that more players will come into the casino, play the tournament, and then play ring games in which they will be paying time after the event is over.

The players themselves at the first Tournament of Champions voted to spread the prize money to pay more places. This will happen in any tournament where a vote is taken. Why? Because there are so many players who figure that they have no chance of winning the tournament, but would love to see their names in *Card Player* magazine as a money finisher. If you read over the lists, you'll find that somebody new is always winning a limit hold'em tournament.

As far as I'm concerned, that is the worst attitude you can have when you play a poker tournament. From the first time I ever played a tournament, I wasn't sure that I was good enough to win it but I sure as hell was going to *try* to win it. I certainly wasn't going to settle for just getting my money back. When I win a tournament, I want to *win* something.

I believe that if the tournament starts with nine tables, nine places should be paid. If there are three tables, three places should be paid. In other words, for every table of entrants, one place should be paid.

So many people enter the WSOP these days that the percentage for first place has gone way down. It's still $1 million, but that's only 26 percent of the prize pool. Eventually, the Series will have to increase the first-place money. In 1985 when I placed second, first place was $700,000 and second place was $285,000. Bill Smith and I saved $50,000 so I received $335,00 for second. Today second place is more than $700,000. The fields now are huge, which is why a lot of players like having more spots paid. With fields of 500-600 they like the idea of getting their $10,000 buy-ins back plus maybe just a small profit, so there is a case to be made for the spread payout.

But have you ever entered a tournament in your life, Tom, where you thought to yourself, "I'm gonna make it to 27th place, get my money back, and I will have had a good time?"

Tom: No, that's not my attitude but it is the attitude of a fair number of recreational players who just like to say that they have competed with famous world-class players and would be delighted just to get their money back. I think that one of the reasons why tournament poker has increased so much in popularity is because the payouts have been expanded to pay more places. In the not so distant past, only three to five spots were paid in many tournaments. Then they began paying nine places. When the fields reached 150 or more, they decided to pay a second table as well, and so on. As directors decided to start paying more and more places, more people started playing tournaments. Most tournaments now pay at least two tables, and that has increased attendance.

Adjusting Your Play According to the Buy-In

TJ: People have asked me if they should adjust their play when they're playing in big buy-in events as opposed to when they're playing the smaller tournaments. I am a proponent of playing the same way no matter what the size of the buy-in is for the tournament. Because if you change your play and loosen up in a little tournament, it's going to hurt your play when you enter a bigger buy-in tournament. You might think that you can continually change your play back and forth, but you can't do it. You can't say, "Well, I'm going to play X-style for this size tournament and Y-style for that size tournament, and I'm *really* gonna play good for this big one." Why not play your best in any tournament you enter?

So it's just a $20 tournament — ask yourself, "Am I entering this tournament to win it or am I here to just have fun?" If I enter a tournament I'm trying to win it, no matter what the buy-in is. I think that if you enter a tournament, you ought to take it seriously and play good. And learn something. I've never seen a poker player with any intelligence at all who didn't learn something every single time they played.

If you don't learn something all the time, your ability to learn, your I. Q., must be pretty low. Even if it's just a little quirk in somebody's play that you notice, you've learned something. Nobody is good enough that he can't learn, I don't care if it's Doyle or Chip or anybody.

There are two types of tournaments: The ones designed for the house and the ones designed for players. Any tournament that starts with short rounds is a house event. The casino wants to bring you in, eliminate you quickly, and get you to move into a side game so it can get the drop.

A tournament designed for the players usually has the same length of time periods throughout the event, or it starts with 30-minute rounds and then goes to 45-minute rounds, or begins with 40-minute rounds and moves to 60-minute rounds.

If you're accustomed to playing those short 30-minute or 20-minute rounds and then move into a tournament where you have twice as long to play, what can you do to help yourself adjust to the longer rounds in the higher buy-in tournaments? Say that you're playing a $20 rebuy tournament with $10 rebuys any time you have less than $100 in chips. You can rebuy through the first three limits and then make a $10 add-on. The first two rounds are 30 minutes each and the third round is 20 minutes long. All the rounds after that also last 20 minutes. (This is the typical daily tournament structure at the Orleans in Las Vegas.) You start with $100 in chips and the blinds are $5-$5 with the betting at $5-$10. In this structure, I suggest that you take the $10 rebuy right away. Then you have enough chips that you don't have to rush your play because the blinds aren't going to eat you up.

Even if you don't rebuy at the $5-$5 level, you don't have to rush your play. During the first 30-minute round you're going to get about 15 hands. That's only about twice around the table. Even if you don't play a single hand, it's only going to cost you $20 total and you still have $80 to play with. So why would you have to rush into a hand?

But Tom and I both advocate that as soon as you put that first blind in the pot, you should rebuy if you lose your blind bet. With those added chips in front of you, you can avoid the tendency to play fast. If you're accustomed to rushing your play in these fast tournaments, this is one way that you can help yourself to adjust when you start moving up to bigger tournaments with longer time frames.

TJ: People also ask if the competition gets stiffer as you move up. Sure, but a lot of the people who play the $20 daily tournaments also will play $100 tournaments under the right conditions. These players are not tournament players *per se* so a $100 tournament might look a lot bigger to them than it does to a regular tournament player. To a regular tournament player the $100 tournament is not a big event, it is a very small one. The competition is stiffer in the $100, $200 and up events than it is in the $20 buy-in tournaments.

Tom: There is quite a difference in attendance between the $100 and $200 tournaments. For example, the $100 opening event at the Orleans Open attracts multitudes of players, but when the buy-ins start hitting the $200 and $300 levels the fields decrease dramatically. This is because most players are willing to put up $100 but no more than that.

TJ: When the buy-in is $500 it matters which tournament it is. At some tournaments, $500 is the starting low buy-in like it used to be at the World Series, so you're going to see a lot of dead money in these lower buy-in events. But at a Lake Elsinore tournament or at the Hollywood Park tournament that Tom hosts, the $500 tournament is the championship event, so you'll see a lot of top players coming in to play it. In the tournaments where $500 is the top buy-in, there will be less dead money playing in it. So if the lowest event in a tournament costs $100, the live ones will be playing in that event. And if $500 is the lowest level at another tournament, that will be the event that has the most dead money in it.

The Carnivale of Poker was a good example. When I won the inaugural $500 buy-in limit hold'em event there in 1998, it was so overbooked that players were selling their seats at a premium. One player actually paid $1,100 for a guy's seat and gave him a 10 percent freeroll on his action — in a $500 buy-in tournament! If any idiot paid me $1,100 for my seat, I wouldn't even want the freeroll — this man is so ridiculous he can't have a chance to win!

A player once approached both Lyle Berman and me asking for a $10,000 loan to play a couple of events in a big tournament. He promised to pay the money back, plus give us a one-third freeroll. We both turned him down. "Why would a man want to guarantee money that he borrows from you and then give up one-third of it on a freeroll?" Lyle asked. "If he's that desperate, how's he going to win?"

So, the caliber of players might be different depending on whether $500 is the lowest buy-in event or the biggest one in a tournament. If a player is moving up from $20 tournaments, he might have played enough of them to get a feel for tournament poker and advance directly to a big tournament. Or he might be better off going from $20 to $60 to $100 buy-ins and so on. It all depends on how much he has learned at the smaller tournaments. I don't see that much difference in the caliber of play between a $20, $60, and $100 tournament. There might be a significant difference in the quality of play between a $20 event and a $200 event, but the caliber of play in between those two buy-ins isn't that different.

One other comment: If a tournament is marketed correctly it can attract 600 players who will pay $10,000 each to play it. We had more than 600 players at the 2001 World Series of Poker. One reason for that is because satellites for the World Series are held all over the world these days.

Tom: Satellites not only increase the size of the field but also weaken the overall caliber of players who enter tournaments. There is more dead money in the first limit hold'em tournament at the WSOP and in the championship event than you can imagine. Players who have virtually no chance of winning or even placing in the money are playing the big tournaments because they have won a seat in a satellite. Anybody can win a satellite but not everybody can move from there to win a tournament.

TJ: A lot of people are trying to catch lightning in a jug. And with that $1 million guarantee at the WSOP as temptation, they're willing to gamble that they can catch it. Hal Fowler did it in 1979. You hate not winning it yourself, but it's good for poker that a carpet manufacturer from Ireland (Noel Furlong) can win the World Series. Everybody reads these stories and they want to give it a try themselves.

When the Betting Changes from Limit to No-Limit at the Final Table

Tom: In some of the daily tournaments such as those held at the Orleans in Las Vegas, the betting format at the final table changes from limit to no-limit hold'em. In the bigger buy-in tournaments, changing from limit to no-limit at the final table virtually never happens but in the small buy-in daily tournaments with 20-minute intervals, the cardroom sometimes designs the final-table play with a no-limit structure in order to conclude the tournament in a timely manner and move players into the side action.

A lot of limit players panic at the thought of having to play no-limit because the word *no-limit* is intimating to them. In reality, if the limits at the last table are so high that you have only enough chips to play one hand, you already are playing no-limit hold'em (a concept that I discuss in *Tournament Poker*). For that reason switching from limit to no-limit is not as big a change as you might think, although you have to be just as selective (if not more so) about which hands you decide to play. Although playing no-limit does change your strategy somewhat, it doesn't change your play so drastically that you should play erratically or irrationally.

In fast-action daily tournaments there usually are a lot of chips in play, but the limits are so high that the size of the limits compensates for the huge number of chips on the table. And because the time frames are so short, the chances are that you'll have to put them all in on one hand anyway either by just shoving it all in before the flop or by putting one-half of your chips in before the flop and shoving in the other half on the flop.

If you have put in one-half your chips before the flop, you still have a chance to back off the hand by putting on the brakes if you don't catch a good flop. For example, suppose you raise one-half of your chips before the flop with pocket nines and get called. The flop comes with an ace and a king. You can save the remainder of your chips by folding on the flop in the hope of catching another good hand that you can go all in with. Other times you will put it all in before the flop with your pocket nines. One advantage of shoving it all in preflop is that someone who has a random ace (an ace with a small kicker) may not feel comfortable calling your all-in bet.

A lot of players who are unaccustomed to playing the no-limit structure continue to play limit hold'em at the final table. For example, if the blinds are $1,000-$2,000, they will bring it in for a raise to $4,000 rather than betting more (such as $6,000 or $9,000). In other words, they will only raise double the amount of the big blind, the way they are accustomed to doing in limit play. You need to be more aggressive than that — if you're going to play a hand, you may as well put as much heat as possible on the pot in order to discourage calls. Even if you have a big pair, you're usually happy just to win the pot uncontested.

This is the time when you definitely want to pick up some blinds and if you use a few no-limit strategies, you should be able to do that. The blinds are so big that just winning them can substantially increase your chances of winning the tournament. Of course if you're never called when you have put all your chips in the middle, you're never in jeopardy of being drawn out on. Therefore the purpose of the raise before the flop always is to win the pot immediately — to play it uncontested or possibly against the big blind only.

Second Chance Tournaments

TJ: I think that one of the best things that Tom has done as a tournament coordinator and host is to design and set up second-chance tournaments. This was a terrific innovation. These are the smaller buy-in events that are run in the evenings during a major tournament. Anybody who gets knocked out of the main event can get a second chance at winning something by entering the $100 evening tournament. When he first started them at the Queens Classic a few years ago, a ton of players entered the night tournaments. In fact, the fields were bigger than the day tournaments.

Tom: Sometimes the prize money in the $100 night events (with one rebuy) was very close to the $500 day events. I actually designed them originally to draw more players to the Queens Classic and the idea has caught on in several tournaments since then. Today these smaller evening events are very popular — you'll find them at the Orleans Open, the Peppermill tournaments and the Reno Hilton's Pot of Gold events.

Second-chance events are good opportunities for small buy-in tournament players who want some experience at a higher level. They also will give you an opportunity to play against some of the top tournament specialists who have busted out of the main event and are taking advantage of a second chance to win.

Tournament Rules

TJ: There is no uniform set of rules for tournament play. Floorpeople make different rules from one casino to the other. For example, in a hand that came down in a recent tournament, the floorman made this ruling: The dealer wanted to move the button over one place, but the player in the big blind objected saying that the button was supposed to stay where it was, so the dealer dealt the cards. At that point the big blind realized that he was wrong, that indeed he already had taken the blind. But the man in first position already had brought it in for a raise. In a standard ring game, the hand would be allowed to be played since action had already commenced when the mistake was discovered. However, when a mistake like this happens in a tournament, the hand cannot be played. In fact, all the way through the "push" (when the dealer pushes the pot to a player), the hand has to be reconstructed and the money given back to each player — because nobody should have to be required to put in the big and/or little blinds twice in a row in a tournament.

The floorman, however, made an incorrect decision in this instance. He ruled that the hand played. (To his credit, he came back to the table a little later and apologized to the table.) Unfortunately, things like this happen all the time in tournaments. My one big squawk at the Orleans Open is that the floorpeople who have to manage the huge fields that turn out for the tournament do not make consistent decisions on particular issues. Why should a decision be made *this* way one time and the *opposite* way another time?

When you enter a tournament, you should find out what the policies are for that particular event. Always be aware of the house's rules, because they may be different from where you have played before. What will the house's decision be in certain situations? Although tournament rules should be standard, they indeed are not.

One of the crying needs in the world of poker is a uniform set of rules for tournament play. The Trump Taj Mahal has such a manual for its ring games so that if a ruling is questioned the floorman can refer to the policies manual and make a standard ruling. But they do not have one for their tournaments. Back in the '80s Bob Ciaffone worked with the Las Vegas Hilton to write its rules book, a policies manual that still is considered the standard for ring games. What we need today is that type of policies manual for tournaments.

Tournament Etiquette

Tom and I recently played a series of tournament events at Crystal Park Casino in Southern California. On the bulletin board in the tournament area we noticed a list of rules titled "Tournament Etiquette," the first time either of us had seen such a thing posted for a tournament. In fact, it was a xeroxed copy of a page from *Poker Tournament Tips from the Pros*, which our publisher Dana (Shane) Smith wrote in 1992 for novice tournament players. Here is the list:

- **Don't show your hand to other players.**
- **Don't talk to railbirds.**
- **Don't throw cards when you lose a hand.**
- **Don't announce another player's hand before he shows it down.**
- **Don't distract other players during a hand.**
- **Don't play table captain — that is the floorman's job.**
- **Don't make derogatory comments to either the dealer or your opponents.**

- **Don't talk to another player while he's in a hand.**
- **Don't do anything that delays the action.**
- **Don't be an inconsiderate smoker.**

I'm sure that this list could be expanded ad infinitum, but you get the point. In the chapter titled "Tales from T. J.," I talk about two other breaches of poker etiquette that I think are horrible in both side games and tournaments. One is slow rolling the winning hand (see "The Ultimate Slow-Roll") and the other is asking the losing player to show his hand on the end. The best way that I can think of to describe these two practices can be summed up in one word — rotten.

In her book Dana adds, "Of course, I know a player who likes to break these etiquette rules. He thinks that it creates an obnoxious table image that gives him an edge over his opponents. Whether he's right about getting the edge with rudeness is debatable, but I certainly agree with him on one thing — he definitely is obnoxious. Myself, I prefer calm and quiet at the tournament table. I am not there to make enemies, nor am I there to make new friends. I am there to make money."

Amen. When the day comes that tournament players adhere to the common courtesies of etiquette, that will be the day that we come closer to corporate sponsorship.

Tournament Ethics

Tom: In "Tournament Talk," my regular column for *Card Player* magazine, I often am asked about ethics issues that pertain to tournaments. Here is a reprint of a 1999 column titled, "Tournament Ethics — Improving or Slipping Away?"

In my last column, I discussed a hand in which a player involved in a very large pot was up against a weak player who had inadvertently been exposing her cards to him. Knowing that she was drawing to an inside straight in a very large pot, he briefly considered showing his trips to the lady in hopes that she would fold. I expressed a strong view that intentionally exposing his hand would have been a breach of proper ethics and mentioned that there are penalties for such violations in most tournaments. (Although I know of no penalties for such actions in ring games, I believe that some penalty should be enforced in them, as well.)

I strongly believe that we need a code of ethics to govern our actions in tournaments. Tournament poker has expanded remarkably in the past few years and because of that expansion, poker itself has become more popular, enjoying greater visibility than ever. Some of the stars on the tournament circuit are indeed the celebrities of the entire poker world because tournament winners are written about and talked about more than any other players. When tournament stars, who should set good examples for other players, behave in a fashion that is contrary to what high ethics and good behavior dictate, they are setting a poor example for poker. Any corporate sponsor who sees a major player misbehaving in a big tournament (which unfortunately happens far more often than it should, although not as frequently as it used to) would have to give serious thought as to why his company should be represented by people whose behavior is improper.

Unethical conduct takes a variety of forms. One example is softplaying. A California player recently e-mailed me a story about playing a local tournament in which he and a friend were "playing hard at each other like we always do," but two of his opponents at the table were softplaying each other — not betting when they had good hands and allowing their friends to survive in the tournament by not playing the way that they normally would play against opponents who were not their friends. He brought the situation to the attention of the floorperson, who promised to take action against it in the club's next tournament. However, the same scenario repeated itself the next week and the floorperson did nothing. As a result of management's lack of action in the matter, the reader decided not to play there anymore.

A situation of this type recently occurred in a large California tournament that I was hosting when it was down to two tables (both of which were in the money) with the final nine players advancing to the final table. One of the players was contending for the best all-around player award and called a preflop raise with pocket eights. The raiser held A-J. The flop came Q-10 and both players checked. The turn showed a rag. A king came at the river with no flush possibility, giving the A-J the nut straight. The first player checked and — with last action heads-up — his opponent also checked the nut straight. The other players at the table immediately complained that the player with the A-J had intentionally softplayed his opponent.

When I was called over to the table, I was faced with the dilemma of what action to take. I strongly believe that soft playing is a violation of proper conduct, but sometimes it is very difficult to do anything about it because you can't always prove it, and you cannot force someone to play his hand. This is what I chose to do: I immediately relocated the player with the A-J to the other table and put him in the blind. Then I high-carded a player from the second table and put him at the first table, announcing, "These two players will not play at the same table together unless they both make it to the final table." Giving him the benefit of the doubt that perhaps he wasn't aware that he had the nuts, I didn't penalize the player with the A-J, but I gave him a strong verbal warning that if anything remotely similar ever occurred again, he would forfeit his rights in the tournament by being blinded off.

I wanted to make sure that there wouldn't be even the appearance of collusion. At the break I asked the points-leader contender, "Do you have any idea how bad this situation looks to others?" He answered by claiming that he had never even seen the other player before (and neither had I).

One prominent tournament player has been accused of having people not just softplaying him, but deliberately dumping off chips to him. These players reputedly are people that he himself has placed in the tournament by putting up their entry fees. If the rumor is true, this practice violates every standard of good ethics. In fact, I believe that it is outright cheating. Other types of behavior that tarnish the image of would-be role models are drinking at the table and exhibiting loud or rude behavior. Of course, cursing, throwing cards, and abusing dealers, floor people, and other players also are inadmissable infractions of common etiquette.

Almost all tournament rules state that the floorman's decision is always final and I sometimes joke, "no matter how misguided." The floormen and the tournament manager are the referees and the umpire of the game. Just like umpires in any sport, they are only human and may occasionally make a borderline decision. But to keep the game flowing at a smooth pace, once the decision has been made, that should be the end of the discussion even if people disagree. Later on, players can express their disagreement and reasons for it to the tournament official in private.

Soft playing, exposing hands, and proper player conduct are three of the major issues that tournament rules are designed to address in order to maintain a high standard of ethics in poker. Tournament managers need to put an early stop to misbehavior, particularly by notable players who should be role models instead of part of the problem. And highly visible tournament stars need to accept the responsibility that comes with fame. Of course, many of our tournament stars do set fine examples for the rest of us — I think of them as the "John Waynes" of poker. I only wish there were more of them. ♠

"McEvoy is a proven, durable winner." — Howard Schwartz, Gamblers Book Club. In this vintage photo, Tom is shown shortly before his victory in the Pot-Limit Hold'em championship event at the Superstars of Poker. In 1983 he won the World Series championship in both No-Limit Hold'em and Limit Hold'em.

8

TOURNAMENT PRACTICE HANDS

T. J. Cloutier & Tom Mc Evoy

In this chapter we give you our opinions about the best way to play various types of hands in limit hold'em tournaments. Although we have written this with tournament play in mind, if you apply this tournament strategy to your cash-game play it can do nothing but help you. You see, you can successfully play tournament strategy in a ring game but the reverse isn't necessarily a good idea. In fact, you may find that a lot of the things that you're doing wrong in ring games will suddenly go away if you apply tournament strategy to your cash-game action.

Tom has played a lot of limit hold'em, but I'll guarantee you that he's a better ring-game hold'em player today after years of playing hold'em tournaments than he ever was before he started playing tournaments. This is one reason why he has been able to make his living at poker for so many years.

We have pictured most of the practice hands unsuited. We have done this because we want you to understand that the ranks of the cards that you select to play are more important than their being suited. Some players use being suited as the reason to play certain hands when they should be looking more at a hand's high-card value than its suitedness.

Before you read our suggestions on how to play various tournament hands, think about how you would answer the following questions:

- **When is the worst time to check?**

- **What is the real strength of J-10?**

- **Which hand is the Holy City to most limit hold'em tournament players?**

- **What is the worst play that you can make from the blind in tournaments?**

- **What is the cardinal sin of poker?**

- **Should you ever slowplay pocket aces?**

- **From what position do a lot of players lose huge amounts of tournament chips?**

- **Why is it okay to sometimes fold a winner?**

- **What determines the value of pocket jacks?**

- **When should you try to trap in a tournament?**

- **What is the cardinal rule of hold'em?**

- **When does it seem as though there are 50 aces in the deck?**

Hand One

TJ: Suppose you're under the gun in a tournament and you look down at the boss hand, two aces. It doesn't matter what stage of the tournament you're playing or what your stack size is, you will bring the pot in for a raise. In limit hold'em you never limp in with two aces *unless* there is a maniac sitting behind you who raises every pot. In that case, since you know that he's going to raise the pot anyway, you could limp in and then put in the third bet after he raises. However if he's that loose and aggressive, he probably will reraise you anyway, so the main thing to do is to always raise with two aces. If you're in first position, middle position or last position, raise with this hand. Don't give any free flops.

Aces in a Front Position. A lot of people think that they can get funny with aces and slowplay them. But suppose you have aces in first position, just limp in, and get five callers (which can happen at any time in limit hold'em). Now the board comes 7-6-2. There's a pretty fair chance that someone might have either sevens and sixes, an open end straight draw, or even a set. But if you had raised with your aces, you probably would have narrowed the field enough that you would only have to beat one or two players so that if the flop came 7-6-2, there would be a pretty good chance that you had the best hand.

The idea is to limit the field. You don't mind playing aces against one or two players, but you don't want to have to play everybody. You have the best hand that you can start with in limit hold'em and you might as well try to win a pot with it without giving your opponents every reason to beat you. If the opponents who called your bet or raise before the flop are just regular players, lead at it on the flop *unless* big connected cards or a pair flops.

Dangerous Flops. A dangerous flop to your pair of aces is any pair or any three big connected cards. Say that you raised and were reraised before the flop. The flop comes:

Or it might come K-Q-J, K-J-10 or Q-J-10. If you have put in a third bet before the flop, you had better shut down. Don't lead at it because there is the possibility that a set, two pair, or a straight is out against you. You're playing in a tournament, so why should you risk losing a ton of irreplaceable chips with your aces? If somebody comes out betting at you, make up your mind right then whether you should play any further with your aces or throw them away.

But suppose the flop comes Q-J-9. In this case, you probably would want to lead with your aces. Although a K-10 or 10-8 would give somebody a straight, players usually won't raise or call a raise with those types of hands. Of course, somebody could have flopped two pair such as queens and jacks, but you can't be fearful of that.

Other Types of Flops. Suppose the flop comes J-7-2. You can't give your opponent(s) credit for flopping a set, there aren't that many sets flopped in poker. You have to become very aggressive with the aces, so lead at it.

Now suppose the board comes with three of a suit and you have the ace in that suit. This is another time when you should lead with your aces. Even if somebody has flopped a flush, you have a redraw to the nut flush. See how it gets played out — if you lead and it gets raised and reraised, you know that somebody already has a flush. In limit hold'em, you probably would continue with the hand to see at least one more card.

Of course, your ideal flop has an ace in it. If that happens, you just keep leading at it. Why would you miss a bet? If a guy has called you on the flop and then an ace comes on the turn, bet again. Don't try to set a trap by checking to him. If you check, he usually will check. Then when you bet on the end, he throws his hand away and you've lost one or two bets.

The only time that you should ever trap in a tournament is when you have the nuts, when you cannot be outdrawn. Say that you have A-K and the flop comes Q-J-10. Your opponent bets and you just flat-call because you've decided to trap him. Then the board pairs on the turn. He bets again. Now you have to make up your mind how you want to play it. Are you going to raise him here? I say yes, give him one shot. But if he comes back over the top of you, at best all you have is a crying call (if you know that the guy can play at all).

In summary, forget about limping with aces in the first seat. I've seen lots of players lose big pots because they limped with big pairs from up front and let somebody get into the pot with a 9-8 or 6-5. Their opponent flops two pair and those aces are dog meat. Don't give free cards.

Aces in Late Position. Now suppose you have a pair of aces in a later position. The people at your table are playing pretty decent poker, and somebody brings it in for a raise and another guy reraises it. Don't just flat-call, put in the third bet. Don't be thinking about trying to trap by just flat-calling because sometimes when you try to trap, you don't get the full value out of the hand that you should have gotten. (Remember that before the flop, there's no such thing as the nuts.) So put in the third bet and hope that you get called by both of them. You want to have the strength position. If you get unlucky and lose the pot, so be it.

Suppose the flop comes:

One of your opponents leads at you. You *hope* he leads at you with his (probable) A-K. When he leads, raise him so that any of the little straggling hands that might have come into the pot will get out. You want to get it heads-up if you can. If he bets at you again on fourth street, just call. If he checks, bet. If the board rags off or pairs a little card on fifth street, raise if he bets into you (as long as no straight or flush card comes).

Tom: There are even occasional tournament situations in which two aces shouldn't be played. For example, suppose multiple seats are being awarded in a supersatellite and two or three people go to war before the flop. When you will win a seat in the big tournament if one or more of them is eliminated, you should pass even pocket aces.

Hand Two

TJ: The way that you play two kings in limit hold'em is pretty cut and dried. You treat kings the same way you treat aces, but you have to understand one thing about this hand — if an ace hits the board on the flop, you have to shut down.

Suppose it's been raised by someone in an early position and another player has called the raise. You must reraise with your two kings before the flop. You'd hate for one of them to have an A-4 and then see an ace hit the board. They will have to pay you first to get a chance at catching that kind of flop with their weak ace. Of course, there are some weak limit hold'em players who wouldn't lay down an ace-anything before the flop for all the tea in China. But even though you might lose to them now and then, these are the kinds of players you want to play against.

You have to play it by feel. You must raise with kings and if someone raises in front of you, it's a reraising hand. You want to get it heads-up. If you put in bet number two and your opponent puts in bet number three, you still have to call him. There's a chance that you might be up against aces, but not necessarily in limit hold'em. Again, it gets down to watching your opponents, how aggressively they play two jacks or small pairs. Do they put in a third bet with two queens? Always be alert.

In summary, play two kings very aggressively before the flop and hope that an ace doesn't hit the board. Remember that when you're playing against only one or two players, a big pair has a good chance of holding up, but if you're playing against a big field of players in the hand, all you have is one pair and you can't be nearly as aggressive with it. This is why you always raise with your kings to try to get it heads-up.

When an Ace Hits on the Flop. Are there players at your table who will bet an underpair if an ace hits the board? If you check, will they bet with two jacks or two tens? Although this sometimes happens, they usually will have the ace if the pot has been raised before the flop. Know the people you're playing against, watch how they have been playing.

Suppose the flop comes:

The first person to act comes out betting and the next player just calls. It's up to you with one player left to act behind you. Now what do you do? Your kings aren't looking quite as good as they did before the flop, are they? In fact, they're looking a whole lot like a piece of toilet paper! So you throw them in the muck.

Before the flop you're supposed to raise and reraise with kings, but after the flop you have to play them as the board dictates. You face the same types of danger flops with pocket kings that you face with pocket aces, only more so because of the danger of an ace flopping. You're starting with the second-best hand that you can be dealt, but when you have kings it seems like all the other 50 cards in the deck are aces!

Never be afraid to throw away two kings if an ace hits the board. What do you have? After the flop, you have two outs

twice, two more kings to hit on fourth street and fifth street —
that's it. When you're up against an ace after the flop, you're a big
dog to the hand, so you have to get away from it.

When You Flop a Flush Draw. Suppose you have the
K♠ K♥ and three spades come out on the flop:

Are you going to continue with the flush draw? Yes. You
have second pair to the aces and your kings beat the board's
second pair (tens). You also could make the nut flush or three
kings. Play this hand through unless the board pairs. Then you
have to make a decision as to whether your draw is still alive.
In a big action pot, the board's pairing can mean that a full
house is out against you.

Hand Three

TJ: Two queens is a raising hand before the flop from any position in limit hold'em. Is it a *reraising* hand? Sometimes, but not always. Remember that there are two overcards to the queen that people play all the time in limit hold'em. Suppose a solid player in seat one raises before the flop and another solid player calls the raise before it gets to you. One or the other of them might have two aces, two kings, or A-K. So you call with the queens, but you don't reraise.

Now suppose that a player in the first seat has been raised and a solid player in the second seat has reraised. You're in the third seat with a bunch of players to act behind you. What do you do now? Unless you're playing against maniacs, you throw them away. Sure, you've picked up a pretty nice hand but you don't have any money involved in the pot and it's been raised and reraised before you even had a chance to act. It's so easy to just throw them away in this spot. So what if the guy in the first seat only has two tens — the player next to him might have two aces or two kings or A-K or even A-Q.

Let's say that you have the pocket queens in the big blind. The pot has been raised and reraised and now it's up to you. You're already part of the way into the pot, so you call. But if an ace or king comes on the flop, you're through with this hand. Of course if a queen comes, you're in Fat City.

Now suppose once again that you are in the big blind with pocket queens and a player in late position raises with either two, one or no limpers already in the pot. In this case, reraising with your queens definitely is in order to try to narrow the field and get it heads-up if possible.

What if a queen flops along with an ace or king? For example, K-Q-6. Play it strong. Set over set doesn't happen all that often, you know. Against this type of flop, your opponents might put you on a king when you bet. If one of them has an A-K, he's probably going to raise you. In that case you do not reraise, you smooth-call the raise and then play for a check-raise on the turn.

Now suppose you have raised the pot before the flop with pocket queens. If you don't flop a queen, a great flop for your hand is J-10-9. If you're up against K-Q, too bad. Of course it would be much better for you if the flop came J-8-2. In that case you hope that your opponent has something like an A-J so that you can make a play with the queens.

People talk about having two queens beat all the time, but remember that it's still a very good hand. It's just that as you descend the ladder on the ranks of the pairs, you have to be more and more careful with them because the lower you go the more overcards there are. Aces have no overcards, kings have the ace as an overcard, queens have aces and kings. And in a raised pot, people usually have some of those cards.

If the pot has been raised and reraised, there's a pretty good chance that even though you might have the best starting hand, somebody has two overcards to your queens. People also raise with middle pairs from sevens on up in a lot of limit hold'em tournaments (and cash games as well). Say that an opponent raises with A-K, you call with two queens, and a player with two sevens also calls. He has two sevens that he can catch and the other player has an ace and a king that he can catch to beat you. You are less of a mathematical favorite versus two opponents, but you are more of a money favorite.

Remember that if you're playing in a ring game you can be a lot more aggressive with two queens than you can be in a tournament. Sometimes you simply have to get away from a hand. "How do you win so many tournaments?" people ask. Well, the good players get away from the bad situations — they're not afraid to throw a hand away. Sometimes you even throw away a winner — but if you can't throw away a winner once in a while, you can't win at poker because then you're just a calling station. I've never felt bad about throwing away a winner when I wasn't heavily involved in a pot. When I throw a hand away it is because I believe that the percentages are in *their* favor, not mine. The hand hasn't cost me that much — why should I give it a chance to cost me a ton and find myself suddenly down to no chips?

Now suppose the flop comes 10♣ 7♣ 2♣ and you have the Q♣. From there onward, it's draw poker. You don't necessarily want to make the flush if someone is betting at you because he might have the A♣ or K♣, but there's a pretty good chance that you still have the best hand.

Let's look at another flop: Q-J-10. You have top set but there's also a straight possibility out there. What do you do? You still lead with your queens. If you get raised, you call the raise but you're finished with leading at the pot unless the board pairs. If a player bets in front of you, you raise him on the flop. If you get reraised, just call and hope the board pairs. If the reraiser has A-K, more power to him but you still have redraws to the hand.

I don't ever suggest not betting the hand or not raising with it — why give them a free card? If somebody has a king, a nine or an eight in his hand, he can catch a middle-buster and beat you if you're just checking along and giving him a free card. For example if a nine comes on the turn, there's a one-card straight out there and suddenly your set doesn't look too good with only one card to come. So you have to lead with this hand — you can't just let everybody get into the deck against you without having to pay for the privilege.

Hand Four

TJ: I will raise with jacks from any position when I am the first player in the pot. If I get reraised I will just call, see the flop, and then decide whether to continue. Now suppose you're in late position and a couple of players have limped in front of you — you're still going to raise the pot. Why? To eliminate the blinds and everyone still to act behind you, if possible, and to build the pot.

If you're next to the button or on the button, you should always raise with the jacks if the pot hasn't been raised yet. If you get unlucky and an ace, king or queen flops, you can always get rid of the hand. By raising you also might knock out the people between you and the first bettor. If you get reraised, you just smooth-call.

Obviously if the flop comes jack-high or with any jack in it, that's a big-big flop. But any time that it comes with overcards and you have two or more opponents there's a pretty good chance that you're already beat. Then you're down to four outs, two outs twice. Look at the scenario where the flop comes 10-9-8. You have an overpair and an open-end straight. This is not a bad flop to the hand but it isn't one that I would go to the bank with either.

Remember once again that limit hold'em is a big-card game — people call raises with Q-J in this game. And if someone is in there with a Q-J, you're trying to catch a queen for a tie. As you get lower on the totem pole with your pair, other hands seem to be bigger holdings in limit play (A-K, A-Q, even K-Q is only an 11.5-to-10 dog against two jacks). Two jacks just don't cut the mustard that well — you like to play against only one opponent and hope that you get a small flop or a jack.

A broken board is a fabulous flop to the jacks, something like 9-5-3. Certainly an opponent could have a pocket pair to the flop, but that could happen with any hand and in that case, the play will dictate what you do with the jacks. Against that 9-5-3 flop you're sure as heck going to bet it if it's checked to you, and if somebody bets you might even give them one raise.

Raising on the flop is a lot better than waiting until fourth street to put in the raise because, in many cases, you can limit the field. If the flop comes 9-5-3 and a ten comes on the turn, giving no straight or flush possibilities on the board, that's fine but somebody might have made two pair, tens and nines, especially if you didn't raise on the flop. Somebody also could have picked up a straight draw, but you like that. You like your opponents to pick up a draw with one to come — if they get there, so be it, but you're a big favorite in the hand.

Late in a tournament the jacks are no better or worse than they are early in a tournament if you're playing at a full table. The limits are higher but the hand values remain the same at any time that the table is full. A pair of jacks is a lot better hand *shorthanded* than in a full ring — you can be aggressive with them before the flop shorthanded. For example, if you're at the final table with five players left, you can play the jacks a lot stronger than you could when the final table first starts with nine or ten players. Just remember that if an ace, king or queen hits the flop, your hand usually is nothing.

The thing that determines the value of the jacks is the number of people playing in your game. Heads-up, two jacks is a big-big hand. The more players in the pot, even if an overcard does not flop, the more vulnerable you are.

"If there is one player that all of us fear the most at the final table, it is T. J. Cloutier." — Berry Johnston. T. J. is shown here accepting the winner's plaque in Limit Hold'em at the 1996 Queens Classic.

Hand Five

TJ: Big Slick — that's what everybody in the rest of the world calls A-K, but in Texas we call it Walking Back to Houston. Why? Because if you go to Dallas and play A-K enough times in no-limit hold'em and get broke to it, you'll be walking all the way back home to Houston.

To be successful in tournaments, you have to win *with* an A-K and you have to win when you're *against* an A-K. In other words, you have to win the 11.5-to-10 situations. I recently lost both ends of the spectrum and finished seventh whereas if I had won both hands, I probably would have won the tournament. In the first hand, I didn't win with an A-K against a pair, and in the other hand I didn't win with a pocket pair against an A-K.

In limit hold'em A-K is a big hand, a reraising hand, whether it's suited or unsuited. Being suited just gives it a little extra value, that's all. There's an old story about two guys who both held an A-K. The first one says, "Well, I have A♣ K♣ and you have A♥ K♠. I only need three cards in my suit to make a flush."

"Well, hell!" the second man answers. "I only need four cards in two suits — I have *two* flush draws against your one!"

Ace-king is a hand that you raise with from any position in limit hold'em. And if you've been watching your opponents, you might even *reraise* with it against most of them. But I do not suggest that you ever reraise with this hand from the little blind or the big blind because you will have to act first from the flop on, which puts you out of position.

A-K is a *positional* hand. Suppose several people are in the pot and the flop comes something like 9-5-3. You don't have any pairs, so you should check it. A lot of people like to lead into the field with the A-K against this type of flop. Then they get played with and almost invariably they call the raise. Here's a typical scenario: Joe Blow bets it, somebody raises him, and he calls the raise because he has two big overcards — you see it all the time. Now it rags on fourth street and Joe still doesn't have anything. He can't lead at it again but he calls when somebody else puts in a fourth-street bet — he's trying to catch that ace or king on fifth street because he's so accustomed to sucking out at the river. But the percentages are way against him.

In any position other than the small or big blind, you reraise with A-K. You can raise from the blinds but generally, do not reraise. If you're around back and somebody has raised in front of you, you reraise with an A-K because you have them on the defensive (they will have to act first after the flop). If you're in the first three position, you bring it in for a raise. If you're in four, five, six or seventh position, you will reraise with A-K. If you're in the one or two position (the small and big blind), the most you should do is raise with the hand, you should not reraise with it.

Most of today's limit hold'em players play A-K, or ace-anything in fact, like it's the Holy City. They raise it with A-Q, A-J, A-10 — even with A-9 on down — because a lot of players love playing any suited ace, and they like to raise with it too. Over these types of hands, you're a big favorite with an A-K and that's why you always reraise with it *in position* (when you don't have to act first). Of course you also lose a lot of those pots when your opponents spike their only outs, but in the long run you're going to win a lot more of these pots than you lose because you started with the best hand.

I was playing a limit hold'em tournament with the limits at $2,000-$4,000 when the first player raised and the man in the number three position reraised. The player in fifth position called. I had A-K in the big blind. What do you think I did with the hand? I threw it away. At least 80 percent of the time, you would be correct in folding an A-K in this type of situation. All you have in the pot is your blind. It's going to cost you a double raise to see the flop when you might already be up against aces and/or kings or even a suited A-K (which also would be a favorite over your hand). And you're out of position on the hand.

As it turns out, I would have won the pot because I was up against a pair of jacks and an A-Q, and the flop came with an ace. I didn't tell anybody that I threw the hand away, I did it without comment (which is what I suggest you also do when you muck the winning hand before the flop). But if the play came up again tomorrow, I still would throw away the hand because in the long run, especially in tournament play, it will save a lot of money.

Dangerous Flops. If you don't hit a pair to your A-K, any flop is a dangerous flop. Suppose the board comes Q-J-4. What do you do with the hand? Are you going to play to catch a 10, ace or king? A lot of players do that, but not me. If you catch an ace or king, it could make a straight for somebody else. Other than catching a 10, what else will make you the nuts? Nothing. Sure you might be up against a Q-7 because people play some strange hands, and if you catch an ace or king it would make you the boss. But for every time that you catch it, you'll probably miss it seven or eight times. Do you think that you could ever make enough money in the one pot where you catch to make up for the amount of money that you lose in all the other pots?

Hand Six

TJ: I raise with A-Q in limit hold'em from any position, just as I do with A-K. I don't want to reraise with it, but I do raise. If the flop comes ace-high or queen-high, I have a pretty good hand. The reason that I raise with it before the flop is to limit the field.

An A-Q is a good hand in limit hold'em because so many people are playing small connectors and lesser holdings. When the flop comes queen high, you have top pair-top kicker; and when it comes ace-high you have top pair with second-best kicker. You also might be up against a K-Q or Q-J when the flop comes queen-high and then you're sitting in clover.

The only time that I would reraise is in a situation like this: Say that I'm sitting on the button and a guy raises the pot with only one more bet left to his name. I'm going to reraise it to put him all in and we'll see five cards each. That way, I'm not going to get blown out on the flop if it doesn't come with anything that helps me.

Other than this type of scenario, an A-Q is not a reraising hand. Say that you're up against an A-K and the flop comes A-9-4 — now you're trapped. Although it's a very good hand in limit hold'em, still you don't want to put yourself in a bind with an A-Q.

Say the flop comes J-10-9. Although a lot of people play K-Q, you don't automatically put someone on it, so you can continue with the hand. If a king comes, you have the stone nuts, and an eight gives you the second-best possible straight.

Hand Seven

Tom: This is a hand that a lot of people play from almost any position — but if they play it from early position, they're making a mistake. You must play an A-J under the right set of conditions. If you are the first player to act in a full ring with aggressive players in it, this hand is a loser. Remember that in tournaments, players usually play a little more solid than they do in ring games. This means that if anybody comes into the pot in front of you, or if it gets raised behind you, you probably are already beat. Also, you probably are beat if someone brings it in for a raise in front of you, especially if it is raised by a player sitting in the first two or three positions. Or suppose you come in first and decide to bring it in for a raise. Now someone raises behind you. You probably are up against a better starting hand that has position on you.

An A-J is a big trouble hand that is played somewhat similarly to a K-Q. Being suited makes it a little more attractive, of course, but too many players overrate the value of suited cards.

There are times, however, when I might play an A-J very strong. For example, if I am shortstacked I may decide to commit to the hand, particularly if an action player raises from late position and I know that he has been bullying the table with a big stack of chips. In that case, I may reraise with A-J and get the money in before the flop, with the intention of committing the rest of my stack after the flop. This is a situation in which I will take a stand with this hand.

I also will defend the big blind with it against a late position raiser. However if a solid player raises from very first position when I am in one of the blinds, I don't like this hand at all. What is he raising with? And what am I trying to make with this hand? The ideal flop for A-J is K-Q-10, but the chances of getting that particular flop are remote. If you flop an ace to the hand, you're in trouble with a mediocre kicker.

Or suppose your opponent is drawing to a big pair and you flop an ace to the hand. He probably cannot give you any further action with the ace on the board. If you lead into him from the big blind, he probably will give up the hand if he is playing a big pocket pair, so you can't win any extra bets with it. But if he has raised with A-K or A-Q, you're going to get all the action you want and more. The only problem is that you're down to a three-out hand to hit your kicker, so you're in bad shape. These are the kinds of situations that we urge you to avoid as often as possible. This often means passing the hand or at the least, playing it very selectively.

The time when I like to play A-J is when I am in middle to late position and I am the first to act. It also is a reasonably good hand to be aggressive with when you are nearing the payoff spots and your opponents have retreated to their shells. Late in the tournament the hand becomes more valuable to you, even in a full ring, because so many players are just trying to survive to make the payoff spots at that time. Obviously if there are a lot of big stacks at your table who are willing to mix it up, this is *not* the time you want to become aggressive with A-J. Of course if *you* are the one with the big stack against a lot of short stacks, A-J is a good gambling hand in the later stages of the tournament.

You have to use good judgment in playing this hand — you have to duck it when it might be a potential trap hand, and you have to play it aggressively with it when you think that you either can win the pot uncontested or when you believe that you have the best hand.

Hand Eight

TJ: The only times that you can raise before the flop with a K-Q is when you're sitting from middle position on. If only one player has limped in front of you, you can raise him. If nobody has limped in, you can raise the pot because there's the possibility that you have the best hand. If you raise before the flop and a player reraises, you would call the raise, particularly if the K-Q is suited. A lot of players reraise with jacks, tens and nines. If you have been observant and know that the raiser is a player who will raise with those types of hands, you're only an 11-to-10 underdog to catch one of your overcards, so you call the raise. If you don't flop to it, you can fold.

Now let's say that you limp in with K-Q and someone raises. You can call the single raise. Obviously, if an ace hits the board you're through with the hand. But suppose you're sitting in a late position and the pot is raised in front of you. Since you have nothing invested in the pot, why not just throw it away? No matter what comes on the flop, if you throw it away every time you'll be ahead of the game.

If you're in the big blind and the pot is raised in front of you, you can make the call for the single extra bet if you know that it cannot be reraised behind you.

Limit hold'em is a big-card game — K-Q is a hand with two big cards. A fair number of flops will come king-high or queen-high, and you will have the second-best kicker at all times. And if the pot hasn't been raised, you can be fairly sure that an A-K or A-Q isn't out against you, so the K-Q ought to be the boss hand. It might come with both of them or it might even come A-J-10 or J-10-9, which would be terrific.

As always, it matters who you're playing against once the action starts after the flop. Suppose the flop comes Q-6-2. In an unraised pot you can be pretty certain that you have the best hand. You have to lead with this hand. You want to prevent your opponents from catching an inside straight card such as a five, four or trey. And you don't want the board to pair either the six or the deuce on the turn, which can happen if you allow them to have a free card when they're sitting there with second or third pair. So you lead at it — if your opponents want to chase, let them do it. The idea is to get the most money you can get out of the hand, so you don't check these types of hands.

I believe that the worst time to check in poker is when you have a one-pair hand. You probably could've won the hand with a bet, but you check, your opponents check behind you, and they all get a free card. Then they hit their second pair on the turn and you're in trouble. Some players check top pair because they don't want their opponents to know where they're at in the hand. They think it's good to be deceptive so that they can get them for the double bet on the turn. Wrong!

King-queen definitely is a playable hand in limit hold'em, but you have to be very careful with it because of the ace factor. Any time you have raised before the flop with K-Q and one or more players have called the raise, you must be willing to release the hand if an ace hits on the flop. Suppose the flop comes A-K-Q. Obviously, you have to call with your two pair if someone bets into you — if it's an unraised pot. But if the pot has been raised before the flop, you must be very careful. Make your best decision before you make the first call. If someone leads at it, there's a lot to be said for throwing the hand away. Your two pair may not be any good, meaning that it's possible that you have only two outs in this hand. For example, if an opponent has A-K or A-Q you're playing to catch the opposite card, the only card that you have that is live. Or he might have J-10 for the straight. Actually, you have more outs drawing against the straight than you have drawing against A-K or A-Q. At least you have two kings and two queens to fill up.

If the flop comes K-Q-10 or K-Q-J and it's a raised pot, you also have to be very careful. You have two pair, but in a raised pot there's a very good chance that you're up against a straight or a set on the flop.

Or suppose the flop comes K-Q-6. You bet it and get a couple of callers. The turn card is an ace: K-Q-6-A. Anybody who has a J-10 would have called your flop bet with the open-end straight draw. Anybody who has an A-K will be there too. If the ace comes on fourth street in a raised pot, you have to be very careful with it. If the pot is unraised, you lead at the pot. Your opponents will let you know where you stand.

But you can't be fearful just because an ace hits on the turn. In loose games it isn't unusual for players to have hands like A-8 and call to see the turn card. Then when the ace hits, they become aggressive with it. This is one more reason why you have to know your opponents. In some cases when an ace hits the board on fourth street and an opponent raises you, you know that you're beat so you fold. But against opponents who like to play a lone ace, the raise is not as meaningful. When they hit that ace on fourth street, they think they have the best hand even though they have no kicker. If you understand which type of player you're against, you can make your best decision.

We can tell you a lot of things in these books, but you still have to develop and use insight about who is doing what and at what time they're doing it. You have to know what's going on at your table at all times.

Hand Nine

TJ: As we've said before, limit hold'em is a big-card game and Q-J obviously are big cards. But Q-J usually is a non-raising hand in most positions; it is a limping hand only. If the pot has been raised in front of you, throw the hand away. If players have entered the pot in front of you, just call or fold. If everyone has passed to you and you're either the first one in or next to the button, you can consider raising against players who often will fold their blind hands.

There are several scenarios in which you could flop a big hand to Q-J, but still it is not a raising hand. Think of it as two random cards, two random *big* cards, and play it that way. In an unraised pot, if you hit either the queen or the jack you have a decent kicker, though not a great kicker. If you bet it on the flop and get raised, you have to make a decision as to whether you want to go any further with the hand. Remember that in many low-limit hold'em tournaments, people forget about the importance of a kicker when they flop top pair.

Suppose you're playing in a multiway pot and the flop comes Q-J-6. You have top two pair and obviously you're going to play the hand. But anytime the board comes Q-J-10, K-Q-J, A-Q-J you're in trouble. Even if it comes Q-10-8, there is a potential straight on board since some players like to play hands such as J♣ 9♣. Any time the board has straight potential, you have to be careful about how you play Q-J. If the flop comes with a broken board — J-4-2, for example — then you can play it stronger.

Hand Ten

TJ: The real strength of J-10 is the ten. A straight cannot be made without a ten or a five, so the strength of J-10 is the multitude of straights that can be made with it. You can flop a lot of different made straights to this hand, and you can flop a lot of straight draws. If I have top pair and it is checked around to me, I will bet unless I suspect a trap.

The myth that J-10 is such a strong hand falters when the pot has been raised. In a raised pot, you're automatically gone (you fold) with a J-10. Although a lot of players believe that J-10 is a super hand, suited or unsuited, they forget that even a lowly Q-6 offsuit already has you beat. If you flop either a jack or a ten as top pair, you don't have much of a kicker, do you? The J-10 also can be a trap hand when you catch certain types of flops. For example, suppose you catch a 9-7 to it, which gives you two overcards and a middle-buster straight draw. A lot of players get themselves pot-stuck in this type of situation and wind up losing a lot of money to the hand.

The J-10 is a hand to be played, but it is one that you must play very carefully. You don't want to give it too much credit because it has definite liabilities. Obviously if you flop jacks and tens, you have a pretty good hand. But suppose you called a raise before the flop with J-10. What are you going to do if it comes A-K-4 or A-Q-5? Obviously you can take off a card to make the inside straight, but the chances of hitting those middle busters are pretty slim.

Although you seldom raise with J-10 before the flop, it still is a hand that is a part of the big-card family, as is any hand with two cards ten or higher. If someone raises in front of me, I don't cold-call the raise with J-10 although I know that a lot of players do. I won't call a raise because I know that I have the worst of it and who wants that?

The whole idea of poker is for you to have the best hand while your opponents are trying to draw out on you, not for you to have the worst hand trying to draw out on them. If you have your opponents in the bind of having to draw out to beat you, you always have the edge — you don't want to be the one who is going up against the edge. Remember this basic maxim of poker when you're playing hands such as J-10 and 10-9. If it's raised before you, you haven't lost a thing by not calling, and you will be getting two new cards the very next deal. So how hard is it to throw it away?!

In the early days of poker there was a lot of conversation about a J-10 suited being such a great hand — it was the original "computer" hand. We are picturing all of our big-card hands unsuited because we want to emphasize that you should put more value on the ranks of the cards in the hand than on their suitedness. If a pot has been raised and called before it gets to you and you have a suited J-10, you are a definite dog in the hand — suitedness does not increase its value that much. If the pot is raised and nobody else calls between you and the raiser, you still are a dog. Even if the raiser has only two deuces, you're only about even money with a J-10 offsuit. Not many people raise with pocket deuces, but the point is that against *any* underpair, you're only about fifty-fifty.

This is a hand to play when the pot has not been raised, and you prefer playing it in late position. If you limp in, you can call a single raise and take a flop to the hand. But here's the key to playing a J-10: If you don't flop to it, get rid of it immediately. You don't want to get involved in a situation where you flop a jack or a ten, an overcard is on the board, and you continue with the hand — this can cost you a whole lot of money.

If you flop good to it, that's another story. You may flop a straight to it, three jacks or three tens. Even the K-Q-4 flop might be OK, in which case you can take one card off. I don't suggest continuing with the draw if you don't hit it on fourth street — why pay a double bet for the draw? However, the pot odds come into play in this situation. Even though you don't usually like to play drawing hands in tournaments, you might continue if the pot odds are good enough.

Suppose you have the J♠ 10♠ and the flop comes with the K♦ Q♥ 4♠. Now you have an open-end straight draw and a three-flush to go with your J♠ 10♠. In this case you can draw to the hand. Let's say that you don't make the straight on fourth street but you pick up a flush draw to go with it — the board now reads K♦ Q♥ 4♠ 7♠. You can continue with the hand.

If you make a pair on fourth street against the K-Q-4 flop, you have a big decision to make. Say that the turn card is a jack and the board now reads K-Q-4-J. Obviously the jack might have made a straight for someone else. Now you have bottom pair and a four-straight. What do you do? Someone else could already have an A-10 or a 10-9. At the most you would be drawing for a tie against them.

Now suppose it is late in the event, maybe it' down to two shorthanded tables. At this stage of the tournament, hands like K-Q, Q-J and J-10 increase in value. The discussion so far applies to full ring action, but as the tables shorten these big-card hands increase in value. When you're playing nine-handed at a table, 18 cards have been dealt. When you're playing five-handed, only 10 cards have been dealt, moving your high cards upward in value.

Just remember that you want to flop something nice to the J-10. You don't want to put yourself in a position where you can get killed with it. In tournaments this is the type of hand that can cost you all of your money. You call a bet before the flop, you might even call a raise before the flop, you flop some possibilities so you call another bet on the flop, you don't make it on fourth street and now you have to decide whether to continue. Your thinking goes something like this: "Well, I've already lost two bets before the flop and a bet on the flop. Now it's going to cost me a double bet on the turn. Should I pay for it or not?" Then you rationalize, "Hey, I've got so much money in the pot already, I'm gonna continue." That's bad poker. Take your loss and move on to the next hand.

Now suppose the action is multiway and the pot is huge. You'll probably take the card and go on to fifth street with the hand because you have the possibility of winning a big-big pot. Now you have proper pot odds in multiway action. But if you're playing heads-up or against only two opponents, your pot odds are terrible. The odds are so far against your making the hand versus the amount of money in the pot that it isn't reasonable to continue in this circumstance.

Multiway pots tend to come up earlier in the tournament when you're gambling at a lower level. Very seldom do you see multiway pots late in a tournament. This is a factor to take into consideration with drawing hands — and J-10 is a drawing hand from the get-go. You don't have much to start with, you only have a jack-high hand — any overcard is a favorite over the J-10. Enough said?

Hand Eleven

TJ: If everybody has limped and you're in late position with a lot of chips, this hand might be worth taking a flop to because if you catch a good flop you may be able to take somebody off with it. But it isn't a raising hand, suited or unsuited. Ten-nine is a very tenuous hand, just two cards that you might draw to once in a while from late position.

Of course, you also can play it from the blinds in unraised pots. When it costs you only one half a bet extra or nothing extra, it can be a very nice hand because there are a lot of flops that will help it — but there are a lot of flops that can hurt it too. Say that someone raised the pot and you called the raise with 10-9 on the button. The flop comes 10-6-2. Aces, kings, queens and jacks could be out against you. And A-10, K-10, Q-10 and J-10 all have you beat. You have flopped top pair, sure, but you have no kicker.

Remember that a kicker is a big item in hold'em. When I first started playing poker, it took me all of a week to learn that kickers are important. I thought that when I had an ace, I really had a hand, but all I had was a piece of cheese.

Hand Twelve

Tom: The 8-7 suited is virtually unplayable in early to middle position. If you're in late position and a few limpers are in the pot, that's a different story — now you have position. You need to have at least two callers in front of you to play the hand, even when you're next to the button or on the button. This advice also applies to other suited connectors such as a 7-6 and 9-8. You don't want to have to take any heat with this type of hand.

If I am extremely short-stacked and have a chance at a multiway pot, I might call a raise with the 8♣ 7♣ and even put in the rest of my chips with it, but only because I'm in bad shape anyway. Also, it is unlikely that other people are playing these kinds of cards in a raised pot so I think that my hand is live. Therefore I might go for the value in winning a multiway pot and maybe get four or five times on my money. Therefore if I am extremely shortstacked, I am subject to gambling with this hand if I can get a good price to it.

TJ: I believe that if you have a lot of chips or a medium stack and your hand is only eight-high, it's a chip burner. Even if you're playing an 8-7 against a short stack, there's a pretty good chance that he can beat an eight-high hand, so you're taking the worst of it. Instead of breaking the man, you're giving him a chance to double up.

The only time that I might play this hand is when I am in the blind in an unraised pot or in the small blind where it will only cost me a half-bet extra to see the flop. Now if I get a good flop to the hand, obviously I can play it further. But you have to get a fantastic flop to a hand that's only eight-high, otherwise it's just a chip burner. Therefore it just isn't a hand that you want to play at all in a tournament.

Tom: I know some players who don't mind taking a shot at the blinds with this type of hand when they're in late position and are the first one in the pot, especially if the blinds are either exceptionally conservative players or are extremely shortstacked. What do you think about this play?

TJ: I don't like it. Some players rationalize playing this type of hand by thinking, "I've got some chips and I have a chance to break this guy." Suppose you're playing $300-$600 at that stage of the tournament — although it really doesn't matter what limits you're at because if you have $1,000 when the blinds are $10-$15 and you have $5,000 when the blinds are $200-$400, the relationship of your chips to the bets is still about the same. The point is that if you are making plays late in the tournament with hands like 8-7 suited, you're burning up your chips. And if you make it two of three times, you might find yourself suddenly down from $5,000 to $3,000 in chips. "I wonder where my chips went?" the player asks. "I haven't made any bad plays." But he has.

So you let the other guys make these kinds of plays, not you. It isn't your job to knock people out of the tournament. You only have to knock one player out, the last one. This reminds me of the guy who has J-2 in the big blind in a limit hold'em tournament. It's $1,000-$2,000 blinds and somebody who only has $4,000 in front of him puts in the full $4,000 on a raise. Everybody passes to the big blind and he says to himself, "It's only gonna cost me $2,000 more, so I'm gonna call and try to bust him" This is the worst play in tournament hold'em. It isn't your job to break him. It isn't your job is lose an extra $2,000 on a hand that you had no business playing in the first place, yet I see so many players doing it.

In a limit tournament that $2,000 might be worth $8,000 in a later hand when you have a good hand with three callers in the pot with you. But if you lose that $2,000, you don't have it to win their $6,000 with. When you think about it, that can be the difference when you get deep into the tournament.

Tom: I have to admit that I came in with the 9♥ 8♥ in a recent tournament in which a player had limped in from first position with the K♥ J♥. He led at it all the way and I just called with two hearts on the board. Unfortunately, we both made the flush on the end.

TJ: When you play those kinds of hands, you should always ask yourself, "Do I want to put my money in with the best hand, or do I want to have to draw out to win the hand?" Players ask me questions about tournaments all the time, and this is what I tell them to run through their minds.

Tom: Sure, but there are exceptions to every rule of poker. If I'm in the big blind with the 8♠ 7♠ and someone raises it, I'm going to call and see the flop *if* I have a lot of chips. And I'm going to see the flop for a half-bet in an unraised pot when I'm in the little blind.

TJ: Sure, but in virtually any other situation you're not supposed to play the hand.

Tom: You're right. There are very few conditions when you can play a hand like 8-7 suited in a tournament. These conditions include playing it in the small blind for an extra half-bet in an unraised pot; in the big blind for a single raise if you have a lot of chips and it's multiway action; or on the button for one bet when several limpers already are in the pot.

TJ: Just realize that you have to get a perfect flop to a hand like this. The hands that you really want to play in tournament poker are the ones that you *don't* have to get a perfect flop to. This is the big difference in tournament play and ring-game play. In a cash game I would say yes, call with the hand. In a tournament, no.

Hand Thirteen

Tom: Two nines is a very tricky hand to play up front. It's a little too good to throw away, but it's also very vulnerable in an early position. I put nines, tens and jacks in about the same category. A pair of jacks is about 50-50 to catch one or more overcards on the flop, so a pair of nines is weaker of course. In early position I would just limp in with the nines because I want to see the flop cheap. Now suppose you're on the button with this hand and one or two people have limped into the pot. Still I would just call because if I raise, the limpers are going to call the single raise. And the types of hands that they often limp with often are the connecting cards such as Q-J or J-10, overcards to your pair. It is possible that you might force out the blinds with a raise, but that's debatable.

TJ: Now here's the case for raising: Two nines is a hand that is past the "halfway point" (the halfway point is a pair of eights) and better than all lower pairs. You know that you're probably starting with the best hand and it only costs you one extra bet to raise. Nothing says that you have to play it past the flop if the flop comes with overcards, you know.

Tom: That's true. If the flop comes with overcards, the limpers often will check to the raiser and then you have a chance at a free card by also checking.

TJ: When you raise, you know that all the limpers are going to call you. All you're doing is building the pot and hoping to win a decent pot with the nines, knowing that you can get away from them if overcards hit the board. You must be a good enough player to get away from them, of course. The cardinal sin of poker is to bet after they've all checked to you when the flop comes with two or more overcards. Why not take the free card? If you're check-raised, you're in trouble. You have to give up the hand immediately and wind up losing a bet to it when it didn't have to cost you anything to see the turn card. With just one overcard on board, I would bet if it is checked to me.

Tom: I still would rather see the flop cheaply if three or four limpers are already in the pot. And raising out of the big blind with two or three limpers is something that I would not do.

TJ: Sure and there's nothing wrong with seeing the flop cheap. Like we said earlier, it matters how many players are at your table. Suppose there are five players or less at your table and you're in the big blind. If somebody has limped in before you, you automatically raise with those two nines because you probably have the best hand.

Here's another scenario: You're playing at a high level in the tournament and you're on the button with two nines. Two limpers have entered the pot in front of you. There's a good chance you might just throw the nines away. You're thinking, "We're playing at a high level and I don't want to risk $3,000 on this hand if overcards pop out on the flop. I just have a feeling about this hand." So you just chuck them in the muck. Any time you throw away a decent pair, the thing to think about is that although you didn't make money on the hand, it didn't cost you anything either.

Tom: When I have the nines in middle to late position and I am the first player in the pot, I like to bring it in for a raise unless I have a strong feeling that someone is ready to tromp on me with a reraise. This is when three or four people have passed and I am the first one in the pot. When I am on or next to the button with one weak limper in the pot, I want to raise to get it heads-up against the one opponent. And if the table is shorthanded, I might even raise it from first position.

Hand Fourteen

Tom: When you play a pair of sixes or lower, you virtually always see overcards on the flop. And when overcards don't flop, a straight possibility usually will be out there. Sometimes you even will have a straight draw yourself with the sixes. So unless the flop comes something like 4-4-2 you almost never will have an overpair to the flop.

As with medium or small connectors, if you play these small pairs (sixes, fives, fours) from early position, you obviously are very vulnerable. Of course the hand can be very deceptive if you happen to flop a set to it and if that happens, you often can win more money with it than you can win with connectors because the set is more disguised.

I like to play these small pairs from late position for the minimum bet when there are several callers in front of me, but these are not hands that I want to take any heat with. Or if I am on or next to the button and am the first one in, I might take a shot and raise with two sixes. I'm hoping to win it right there or at least get heads-up with the big blind when I have position on him with what probably is the best hand.

TJ: Just always remember the cardinal rule of limit hold'em: This is a big-card game. If you play sixes, fives, fours, treys or deuces from early position you're just asking to get beat and lose money. You absolutely have to hit a set or get some other fantastic flop to win with these little pairs. So the best formula for playing sixes on down in the first three or four seats is simply to play them as though they were a 3-2 — throw them away.

Tom: I finally have trained myself to just dump the small pairs. Even though I might put a guy on overcards only, I still pass these types of hands.

TJ: "The first rule to get in your mind," Lyle Berman taught me years ago, "is that you have to get rid of those small pairs out of position." I do agree with how to play them late when you're the first one in the pot. You can't weaken your hand by just limping with them. If you're on the button with two sixes and nobody else is in the pot, you either fold or raise with them. You don't just limp. You have the semblance of a hand against two players, the blinds, or at least against one of them (the big blind). So in that situation you raise with the sixes. But from up front, two sixes is toilet paper.

Yet you see people playing these kinds of hands all the time from an early position. If someone brings it in for a raise in front of them, they routinely call a raise with them. Their thinking is that the raiser probably has A-K whereas they already have a pair and can flop a set to it. They forget about all those pairs that are higher than theirs, or that their opponent might hit the ace or king.

Tom: Would you say that these players are just a touch optimistic?!

TJ: It's not even a question of optimism, it's a question of playing the game correctly. And playing the game right says that playing little pairs up front spells t-r-o-u-b-l-e. Now suppose you play the game correctly *after* you make your initial bet — you get raised and throw the small pair away. Well, you knew that you could get raised when you made the initial bet, so why did you make it? Any time you come into a pot from the first five seats in limit hold'em, you had better be able to stand a raise. Otherwise you have made a bad play.

Remember that people play a lot more hands in ring games because the pots are multiway more often than in a tournament, especially in California where it isn't unusual to see five people in a hand in ring games. But in a tournament it is seldom that you see five people in a hand. They're looking to hit a little set playing those small pairs in ring games, and there's nothing wrong with that I guess. Just don't do it in a tournament because small pairs do nothing but burn up your money.

Hand Fifteen

Tom: Any-ace suited is another hand that has "toilet paper" written all over it, but there are situations when it is playable. You should call from the small blind for half a bet in an unraised pot. From the big blind you might call a single raise from a late-position raiser who you know could be out of line. You may also call with this hand when you're on or next to the button in an unraised pot with several limpers in it already. In this case you figure that the ace might be good because if someone else had a big ace, he probably would have raised it. If everyone has passed to you on the button, it probably is correct to raise with this hand to attack the blinds.

TJ: But just remember that if several people have limped into the pot and you call on the button with A♦ 7♦, the flop that you're looking for is three diamonds or aces-up. You're not looking to win with a lone ace — if you happen to win with the ace by itself, that's just an auxiliary win. So when you put your money in the pot, you're looking for two sevens, an ace and a seven, or three diamonds on the flop.

Tom: But suppose I'm in there with a suited A-7 on the button when three or four players have limped in front of me, and the flop comes with an ace. If everyone checks around to me, there's a good chance that no one else has an ace or they would have bet it, so I will bet the hand and see what develops. If I get check-raised, I can reevaluate.

You have to avoid problem hands in tournament poker. The best way to avoid them is simply to *not* play them. Certainly avoid playing hands like A♦ 7♦ from the first three or four spots in front of the big blind. Get rid of it so that you can avoid having to make a lot of tricky decisions later in the hand.

Actually the A♦ 2♦ through A♦ 5♦ is a better hand than the A♦ 7♦ in a multiway pot because you can make straights as well as nut flushes with the wheel-type aces. Having a five along with the ace gives you a straight card for either the wheel or a low straight. If you're going to play an ace-wheel card suited, play it in the same situations that we have outlined above — calling a half-bet from the small blind, defending the big blind from a late-position raiser, and limping in late position.

However if that late-position raiser is the guy with a layer of dust on his chips, it isn't worthwhile trying "to keep him honest." You know that either you're a dog with your ace or you have only one overcard. Remember too that you're taking the worst of it trying to hit your suit to win.

TJ: In the loose ring games you'll see a whole lot of people playing any-ace, particularly if it's suited. Then when they come into the tournament they're playing with that same mentality. You'll see a lot of these players in the first three levels of the tournaments — but they aren't around later.

Tom: These people play excessively aggressive, always overbetting their hands and giving a lot of loose action. Don't forget that maniacs rule the early stages of the tournament.

Hand Sixteen

Tom: A king suited to any small card (not a connecting card) is a bad-news hand. What do you do if you flop a king? You have no kicker.

TJ: Do you know when you *can* play this hand? When you're in the big blind in an unraised pot. You might also play it in the small blind for a half-bet. Just remember the old adage that Tom and I have emphasized in our other books: If nobody has a hand in front of you, that one player behind you might have a hand. Remember this at all times.

Tom: If I am in the big blind and a player has raised all-in, I might call the raise with a king-small suited to try to beat him *if* no one else has called, but I virtually would never play it on the button.

TJ: Time and time again you'll see people play these big-small suited hands in tournaments. They play Q-7 suited, J-8 suited, all those hands. And you'll even see players occasionally win with them — but over a period of time these types of hands will burn up all their chips. So let *them* play them, but not *you.*

You know something else? I would rather play 7♣ 5♠ on the button than K♠ 5♠ on the button strictly because the 7-5 has a straight possibility and *no* flush cards are involved — I sure won't be in there drawing to a seven-high flush! When you play the A♦ 5♦ your premium hand is the nut flush. With that K♠ 5♠ you could make a flush and still lose to the ace-high flush,which would cost you a ton of chips. Of course the flush also might be your premium draw with the K♠ 5♠ since the chances that you're up against the ace-high flush are slight, but it *does* happen. And when it does, you lose several extra bets.

Tom: Another scenario in which I might consider playing the K♠ 5♠ type of hand is when I'm up against very conservative players, especially when they're trying to hang on for the money late in the tournament. In that case I might make a raise that is based more on position than on the strength of my hand — I'm just trying to muscle them.

TJ: Sure, but you can do that with any two cards. It doesn't necessarily have to be a king-suited, it can be a 3-2 offsuit, because all you're trying to do is pick up the blinds. The hand itself might have no value. If you hit something to it, fine, but you're not raising to hit it, you're just hoping to pick up the blinds. It's just a steal.

Tom: I once saw T. J. go broke with a king-high flush in the very first hand of a tournament.

TJ: That's right. The man who broke me was the only player at the table that I'd never played before. It was a three-way pot and I knew that the man to my right had a set. This was the first hand dealt in the $5,000 no-limit tournament at the Hall of Fame.

Tom: Your nemesis won the pot and became the chip leader. Then he was the second player broke at the table, so you can see what type of player he was.

TJ: When I made the call I even said to him, "If I had ever played with you before, I might not make this call." He had limped in first position with the A♦ J♦ and got a couple of calls. I was in the big blind with K♦ 9♦ and the flop came with three diamonds. The guy in the small blind flopped a set. There was a bet, a call, a raise and a reraise. The only way that I could've called a reraise in that spot was by my not knowing the player, otherwise I would have folded.

Even the guy with the trips called the reraise so I was getting big odds on my money. I could have trippled up on the first hand and become the chip leader, but one hand could beat me and it was out, that's all there was to it. Instead of trippling up, I got trippled out.

Hand Seventeen

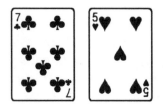

Now let's look at the 7♣ 5♥. Say that you're playing in a rebuy tournament at the $15-$30 level (the start of it), five limpers are in the hand for $15 each, and you're on the button. With all those limpers in the hand, now it's worth your while to put in the $15. If you don't flop to the hand, you can sure as heck get rid of it. But you also might get a big flop to it and make a lot of money on the hand. In any other scenario, the hand is nothing.

Hand Eighteen

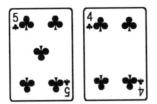

Tom: The small suited connectors, of course, are not as strong as the middle suited connectors because many times they make the weak end of the straight. If you have a 5-4 suited the only time that you have the nuts is when A-2-3, 2-3-6, or 3-6-7 comes. If it comes 8-7-6 you can be in a world of hurt with the idiot end of the straight because a lot of players like to play 10-9. Therefore the higher your connectors, the better off you are. It goes without saying (but I'll say it anyway) that if the hand is suited there is no guarantee that you'll make the best flush with it. A flush is *not* what you're hoping to make with a hand like this.

Suppose you flop a flush. Any player who has a single higher card in your suit can make a bigger flush on the turn or at the river if a fourth suited card hits the board. Most players who flop a four-flush with a suited overcard in their hand will take a card off to see fourth street at least. The fourth flush card comes a fair amount of the time, so you have to be very selective in playing the small suited connectors.

I like to play this type of hand when I am in the small blind and it costs me only one-half a bet more to see the flop. I also might defend the big blind with small connectors in a multiway pot. Or I may play it on the button or in very late position provided there are at least two other people already in the pot (the two-limper rule must be in effect), and if I don't think that someone will raise behind me. If I sense that there are too many people yet to act behind me, any one of whom is likely to raise the pot, I will pass the hand.

Occasionally (*very* occasionally) you can raise with this type of hand. Suppose it is the later stage of the tournament, you are in late position with a decent amount of chips, and you know that the other players at your table are just trying to hang on for a payout. In these situations, it doesn't matter so much what your cards are. With two suited connecting cards you at least can make a straight or a flush with the right flop and ambush the opposition.

This play is one type of semibluff. You have three ways to win: (1) Your opponents surrender without a contest; (2) You outflop them if they call the raise; (3) You could win with a bet on the flop and your opponent folds because he missed.

It's pretty sweet when you've raised the pot with 5-4 from a late position, get there with it, and trap someone with a better hand. T. J. tried this play in a hold'em tournament at Lake Elsinore Casino when he was the first one to enter the pot and raised on the button with 5-4. The big blind flat-called the raise with a pair of jacks. The flop came A-5-5. Needless to say, T. J. took the pot.

Hand Nineteen

TJ: Let me give you an important tip about playing these types of two-gap suited hands: You prefer playing them against a single opponent. If you do play this type of hand in a multiway pot, the hand's suitedness helps, but your flush possibilities could get you in trouble because of the possibility that someone else is holding a bigger flush draw.

With hands such as these in a multiway pot, you don't necessarily want to make a flush. You play a hand like Q♥ 9♥ more for its rank and connectedness than you do for its suitedness. Any time you play a suited hand that doesn't have the ace in it, you are playing it for its straight value or possibly to make two pair or trips with it. Making top pair with it usually isn't enough to take the pot.

The value in a hand like this is when somebody raises with A-Q, you're sitting in the big blind with Q-9 suited and decide to call the raise, and the board comes Q-9-rag. Now you've trapped the A-Q.

Tom: The times that you play these types of hands are: (1) When you're in the small blind for half a bet; (2) When you're in the big blind for a single extra bet; (3) When you're in late position in a multiway pot, preferably an unraised one.

TJ: Never initiate the action unless it's blind-against-blind. Or possibly, *possibly*, when it has been passed to you on the button and you can attack the two blinds. Other than these two situations, you don't initiate the action yourself with hands such as Q♥ 9♥.

Tom: This is not a hand that you can take a lot of heat with, but I've seen people fall in love with this kind of hand. Any suited two-gapper must be played under the right set of conditions using a lot of judgment and caution. Certainly these are not hands that you play in the first two or three positions in front of the big blind. The only suited two-gapper that can be played from early position is an A-J.

Hand Twenty

Tom: In this discussion we are primarily talking about playing a two-gap hand suited or unsuited from the small or big blind. Generally I will play this type of hand for half a bet in an unraised pot from the small blind. But if the pot has been raised, I will surrender this type of hand from both the big blind and the small blind.

TJ: I am always afraid of getting trapped with these hands. Invariably you flop either a ten or a seven as top pair and you're a gone goose. You catch a little tiny piece of the flop and you die with it. You have to be leery of "free" hands.

Tom: In tournament poker players lose a huge amount of chips when they defend their blinds with hands that they would not have played if they had not been in the blind. Too often they call with a substandard hand, catch a piece of the flop out of position, and wind up losing a lot of extra bets with a hand that they shouldn't have played to start with. All of these types of hands are big-big trap hands. Even on the button I would much rather have a one-gap hand of lower connectors than a two-gap hand such as 10-7 suited.

TJ: Suppose a player goes all in with his $2,000 in chips. You're in the big blind and have $10,000 in chips. For some reason, people think that it is obligatory for you to call. It is not. Calling the raise in situations like this is one of the worst moves you can make in tournament poker. The idea is to break your opponent, sure, but you don't want to lose a lot of chips to try it. Why would you want to double up an opponent by playing a bad hand?

The reverse to this situation goes something like this: Suppose he has $2,000 and you have $30,000. Now it's worth taking a chance to break him out of the tournament.

Tom: In this situation you can take a shot at trying to break the guy because the worst that can happen is that he will have $4,000 and you will still have $28,000. But when you have only $10,000 and he has $2,000, he doubles up to $4,000 if he wins the hand and you're down to $8,000. Now how do you like it? You have allowed him to get up off the carpet. I can't tell you how many times I've seen someone play a sub-par hand because he thought that it was mandatory to call, double up his opponent, and then see that same opponent came back to haunt him later in the tournament. ♠

9

A LITTLE MORE

Hold'em High-Low Split
Fort Worth Hold'em
Widow Poker

This chapter is just a little added feature about games that aren't played very often in big casinos but are popular in home games and some of the smaller cardrooms.

Hold'em High-Low

TJ: My first exposure to hold'em high-low split was at Len Miller's former Oceanside Card Club a few years ago when I went there to play some sidegame action. Len had scheduled a little weekend hold'em high-low tournament for the day after I arrived, but the night before the tournament they started up a $10-$20 hold'em high-low cash game. Although it's fairly popular in a lot of smaller California card rooms, I'd never even played high-low before, so as soon as I sat down I began watching to learn the hand values and see how the game was played.

I won a little bit of money in the side game and the next day I won the tournament. Ron Stanley came in second and he had never played the game either — we beat all the locals at their game and won the tournament too, which is just one more example that shows that no matter what the game is, you have a good chance at winning if you just play the basic tournament strategy.

Ace-Rag. In hold'em high-low split, the strength of ace-rag is fantastic. Obviously, two aces is still the best hand but to my preference, two kings is no longer the second-best hand. The ace with any wheel card probably is a better hand than two kings. A deuce, trey, four or five with an ace, particularly if it is suited, probably is preferable to a pair of kings because everybody who plays a hand usually is trying to scoop the pot high and low.

Anybody who is dealt an ace probably is going to play it. Even hands such as A-10 go way up in value because any time an ace hits the board you have a strong hand. In fact, I am more likely to play any-ace than I am to play big pairs. Since it's a two-way game, the object is to scoop the pot and I might be better able to do that with ace-rag than a big pair.

However the big pairs such as kings, queens and jacks are preferable to any of the little hands such as 3-2, 4-3, 6-5 or any combination of these. Even playing with an eight qualifier for low, there still will be more high scoops than there will be scoops with straights or flushes or the little cards. You're going to play the high hands even if you don't have an ace (although it's a key card) because an ace doesn't hit the board any more often than any other card does (although it might seem like it does when you have kings).

You might occasionally win the low end with rags such as 6-2, but you shouldn't purposely come into a pot with those kinds of hands because your earn value usually is minus. It is only when you have an ace-rag that you are aiming to win the low end of the hand. You're always trying to win both ends of it and that is why the ace-rag is so important. You might win the high with the ace and the low with the deuce and rake in a nice pot for yourself. This is why hands such as A-10 also go up in value: If the ace hits the board against the big pairs, you've got 'em. And people do play the pairs.

A perfect betting situation is when two aces are against ace-rag because a lot of times the aces obviously will hold up and the ace-rag won't get there. A pair of aces is still the best hand, period. I know that a pair of kings is a great hand because an ace doesn't always hit the board, but let me repeat that I would rather have A-2, A-3, A-4, A-5 or A-6 (preferably suited) than the kings.

The whole idea of playing hold'em high-low is to win both ends of the pot. One player might have A-K while another one has A-2, in which case the A-2 could scoop the pot or at least take a half of it. And how far can you go with A-K in this game? If a guy is rammin' and jammin', he could have a set or a low draw, particularly if three low cards are on the board, so you prefer having a two-way ace.

Now let's look at an unusual high-low hand that Dana played in a $5-$10 game in her hometown cardroom in California. The pot was raised from middle position by Dennis, who had pocket queens. On the button Dana looked down at the 3♦ 2♦ and decided to call the raise in a probable five-way pot. The flop came Q♠ 4♦ 8♦. A player bet, Dennis raised, and Dana called. The two blinds dropped out. The turn card was the K♣. The first man checked, Dennis bet, Dana called.

What was the perfect card she could dream of catching? It came at the river — the A♦. The first player checked, Dennis bet and Dana raised. "OK, I'll pay you off," Dennis shrugged and called the raise in the hope that she only had the best low. That dinky little 3♦ 2♦ won the whole pot. Later she apologized to her good friend, saying "The devil made me do it!" But she didn't need to make excuses for playing the hand, since she took a chance on the button with a low hand, flopped good to it, and got a payoff at the river.

Fort Worth Hold'em

A popular home-game version of hold'em is Fort Worth or Greek hold'em, which is hold'em's form of Omaha. The big difference between this game and regular hold'em is that you must play *both* of your hole cards — you cannot play only one card from your hand *and* you cannot play the board. You must play precisely two cards from your hand and three cards from the board.

Say that a set is showing on the board — A-8-8-5-8, for example. A lot of players make a mistake because they forget that both of their hole cards must play with the three cards on the board. If a player has an A-K, he might think that he has a full house when all he really has is 8-8-8-A-K. So somebody with a lowly hand like pocket threes will take off the A-K because he has a full house — 8-8-8-3-3.

This is a very good game to play against bad hold'em players because they get confused on these types of hands. Now let's say that the board is showing J-10-9-7-6. The poor player with the bad memory has an A-8 in his hand so he thinks that he has a straight. Wrong! All he has is ace-high.

Forth Worth hold'em is a tighter version of hold'em if the players really know the game. The structure itself tells you that it's a tighter game than traditional hold'em because you can't make those one-card straights, flushes and full houses. I would venture to estimate that about 25 percent of the straights and flushes that are made in traditional hold'em are made by using only one card from your hand. If you must use two cards out of your hand and an ace hits the board, you still have aces with the best kicker, but those straights and flushes that you're accustomed to using one card to make are no longer possible.

Therefore the hand values change. Two aces is still the best hand but *all* pairs go up in value, big or small. Suited connectors also pick up value in this game. If you catch three or even four suited cards on the board, you need two suited cards in your hand to make the flush. And if you catch three or even four straight cards, the same thing goes — you still have to use two cards from your hand to make the straight.

We used to play this game occasionally back in Tyler, Texas and it was a great game. Tighter, yes, but still an enjoyable and profitable game for the best players.

Widow Poker

I'll bet that most of you have never heard of widow poker, right? I was in Boston a few years back and I found out where a card game was going on. It turned out that I was playing with five cops and two firemen. Widow poker is draw poker that is played seven-handed. An eighth hand is dealt facedown in the middle of the board. Every time someone bets, the bet doubles so if the first player bets $5, the second man has to make it $10. If you're in first position and you don't like your cards, you can pay $5 and exchange your hand for the widow hand sight unseen. Every deal has only one widow hand and it's only available to the first player. Nobody else can buy it. From there onward, it's draw poker.

A lot of players would never buy the widow hand. They play so tight that even if they have a bad hand, they would never think of paying $5 to buy the widow hand sight unseen. They know that if their $5 bet gets called, they're going to have to call $10 because the bets double every time somebody comes into the pot. So if a second man plays the hand, he has to bet $10, and if a third player comes in he has to bet $20. It's a fabulous game, an interesting form of draw poker that's fun to play in home games. ♠

10

TALES FROM T. J.

T. J. Cloutier

Nominal Affection

Red Ashey, Jess Stuart and Dave the Bookmaker, the four of us leave Shreveport together to drive to Lexington, Kentucky, to bet this one horse called Nominal Affection. Keeneland has two meets a year, a 15-day meet and a 17-day meet, separated from each other. They get all the class horses at these meets and they have the Keeneland Sales there too. Right at the backdoor of the racetrack sits Calumet Farms and those other big, famous race horse breeding farms.

So we get there and we all love this horse, Nominal Affection. He's coming down the stretch and he's neck and neck with a gray horse called Native something, and I mean they're battling all the way. Nominal Affection just nosed out Native so we won our bets. We thought for sure that he was going to go off at 4-to-1 but he went off at 6-to-5, otherwise we never would have driven that far.

About six months later I'm in California with my dad at Bay Meadows racetrack. A race comes up and here's this Native-something horse, the one that just lost by a nose in that classy field at Keeneland, running in a claiming race in California. He'd only run one race in between the two and had lost it. This was the first race he had ever run in California and was 10-to-1 on the board. My dad, who's a $2 bettor, had already made his bet.

"Dad," I told him, "you've gotta bet this horse, Native."

"Nope, I've already done my betting," he answered.

So I went up to the window and put $500 on Native to win. "This horse is gonna win by a mile," I thought. "He's raced against so many classier horses, there's nothing with him, I've seen him walking in the paddock ... he's gonna kill this race. And he's 10-to-1!"

Sure enough, he won by a football field and I picked up $5,000 on the race. "How'd you know about this horse?" Dad asked. He's one of the best handicappers I've ever met in my life, but if he makes a $5 bet it's gotta be at Christmas time and everything's gotta be just right.

The Pick-Six King

I know a guy named Larry Speck who has hit 317 Pick-Sixes in his life. As a bettor, he's the greatest horse man I've ever met. They had this horse that they kept back, made him lose two or three times, and they took him up to River Downs in Ohio and ran him in a race. They placed bets on this horse with just about every bookmaker in the United States. The horse won the race, but somehow he got disqualified. I think they might have taken him down because they figured out that Larry was trying to put something over on them.

Well, don't worry, it didn't bother Larry at all. He waited six months, took the horse to California where it went off at 8-to-1 against supposedly classier horses. But of course, he knew what he had. His horse won just as easy as pie and he hit all the California bookmakers. They do this stuff all the time — hold back a horse, looking for the right field — but the public doesn't know about it.

The Tournament in Tyler

Back in the early '80s, we decided to have a tournament at a home game in Tyler, Texas. There were about 60 or 70 players and about 30 wives and girlfriends, so we had right around 100 people in this house that Henry Bowman had just bought — we had moved him in that very day, although we had played poker in the house before because Henry had bought it from Lambert. I was selling the chips and we had about a $12,000 to $15,000 bankroll.

We had just sat down to play when all of a sudden they started coming at us from everywhere — the FBI, the City police, the State troopers — they were all coming in the front door. "Have you got the bankroll?" Henry asks me.

"Yeah," I answered, "I've got it under my baseball cap here on my head."

We tried to get out the back door, but they were coming in over the fence by the pool with guns pulled and told us to get back into the house. Somehow I slipped the money to Grover. That was significant because they searched everybody in the whole house, but for some strange reason they didn't search Grover, so all our money stayed intact.

This incident was reported on TV and in all the news media from Dallas to Shreveport: "Known Gamblers, Gangsters and Dope Peddlers Taken In Illegal Game." But of course, it was nothing but a bunch of card players. The police took money from about the last fifteen people they searched, and they got the $15,000 that Harlan Dean had on him. These folks had to get an attorney and file for the return of their money. After hiring lawyers to free up their money, they all got it back ... less the third that the lawyers took, of course. But after all this stuff came down — after all the TV coverage and everything else — when it finally went to court, a $300 fine for holding a poker game was all that ever came out of the whole thing.

Grover was a rounder in Texas and I can't figure out to this day why they missed searching him, but I'm glad they did because if our bankroll had been left under my cap they would've gotten it. We figured that somebody must have tipped the police about our game, and we figured that it probably was the son of a local banker. The boy had been playing a lot of poker with us, losing a bunch of money.

Buck Buchanan, one of the old rounders, was there that night. He had busted out of the tournament and was playing a side game, but about 11:30 he got tired and decided to go back home to Killene, Texas. As he went out the door, the police grabbed him and put him in a car. We all thought that he gone on home, we didn't know that anybody who left the house between 11:30 and 12:00 (when they busted us) had been grabbed by the cops and kept in a car so that they couldn't come back in.

Just as the police were getting ready to break down the front door, we got a phone call from Dick Melvin saying, "You're gonna get hit." All you try to do when you get the tip is just get rid of the "sheet," the one sheet of paper that lists the people who are in the game and for how much. If the cops don't have that sheet, how can they prove that you were making any money off the game? You see, poker is legal as long as you're not making anything for running the game. Of course, I wasn't making anything off it and Henry's dead so it doesn't really matter. A lot of things happened back in the old poker days, you know.

The Owl & the Pussycat

Maybe I've told you about the time when Bobby Baldwin was playing Mike Akins heads-up in no-limit hold'em. Mike had about $5,000 or $6,000 left on fifth street. He was just starting to bet it when Bobby says to him, "Mike, don't bet it. I've got queen-high, no pair, and I'm gonna call you if you bet." Mike shoved it in anyway. Bobby shoved it in. Bobby showed him queen-high. Bobby took the pot.

That happened back when Bobby was called The Owl. As good as it came down the pike, The Owl could put a man on a hand when he was playing in his prime. Today he's playing very tight, A-B-C only.

When I told Tom this story he said, "Sorta like me, huh?"

Freddy the Chemist

When Freddy the Chemist (we also called him Red-Shirt Freddy) was sober, he was the tightest player in the lowball game at Artichoke Joe's in San Bruno in the old days. But for a guy who really knows how to play the game, when he was drunk Freddy was the *loosest* player who ever played lowball.

One night we were playing no-limit lowball without the joker and he was drunk. (I was pretty young, in my early twenties, when this hand came down.) I took one card. He took one card. I paired deuces. He bet me right around $6,000, just about what I had in front of me. "Freddy's done something different this time," I thought, "and I know he bluffs a lot when he's drinkin'." So I called him.

You see, Freddy always took time to make his bets. He would hem and haw and count out his chips before he put in a bet. But when he bet this particular hand, he just shoved all his chips in real quick. Of course, he could've just paired his ace and had me beat, but he had bet enough that I couldn't raise him off the hand. A good play in lowball is to raise a guy when you know that he's bluffing with something like a king or queen and you've got a pair, because then he can't call. I couldn't get an edge by raising him, because there was nothing left to raise.

And I had to be right — he couldn't be betting a king or queen in this pot, he had to be betting a pair bigger than deuces. But in this situation, I had it set in my mind that he was bluffing and so I flat-called him. He had two eights and I won the pot with two deuces.

Nick from New Jersey

This guy called Nick from New Jersey kept passing by me in a tournament saying, "I played perfect all day long, I don't know how I lost." That's so much bull squat. He's the same guy that I was playing with at the Rio Carnivale of Poker when we were down to two and a half tables. He had been raising a lot of pots, so he comes in for a raise from the first seat. I'm in the big blind and look down as the A♥ Q♥.

"I've been waiting for this," I'm thinking, "because I know he doesn't have a hand" and I called him. "I know he's bluffing, and I know he's gonna fire at the pot to show me strength so that I'll get out of the pot." I also knew that I had to bet the pot if it came with an ace or queen and not let him take it away from me.

The flop came Q-6-2. I bet $4,000 at the pot and here he came with all his chips. Boy, I beat him into the pot! "This is the perfect scenario, I've got him stone cold!" I'm saying in my mind. He had the J♠ 9♠. His hand was dead to runner-runner. But don't worry — after all the money was in, he caught a 10-8 to make the straight. I had the whole play figured out, everything I did was correct, and I still lost the hand.

It's called making the right play at the wrong time. That is the luck factor in poker. For five solid days he had been telling me, "T. J., I'm playing perfect poker, I never make a mistake." And now I'm playing at the same table with him and I've already seen him make ten mistakes. This time he really made one — but he got there anyway!

Of course sometimes you make the wrong play at the right time, which usually means that you're taking the worst hand and sucking out with it. There isn't a single poker player who hasn't sucked out on somebody or been sucked out on. I never feel bad when I put a bad beat on a player because I figure that for me to lose they had to have put a bad beat on me. When you're playing against eight other players, if you put one bad beat on them you've won one pot. But if eight of them put a bad beat on you, you're an 8-to-1 dog right there!

The King and Mike

A while back I was playing in a $50,000 guaranteed limit hold'em tournament. When we were down to about 21 players with three tables in play, this hand came down: Mike Laing was in the big blind for $1,000 and had an additional $5,000 in chips in front of him. It was passed to the button, who had $2,500, and he raised the pot. Looking down at his hand Mike saw the K♠ 6♠, called the $1,000 raise, and put the button all-in for the extra $500. He did this at a time when he was three places out of the money, but Mike isn't the type of player who wants to win 18th place so that he can cash — he's always trying to win the tournament. So he made the play, putting the man all-in.

I guess the average chip count was about $12,000 at the time and he only had $6,000 including his blind bet. In my opinion, he made a major mistake in this situation. When you're short on chips, I don't think that you should ever defend the blind without a decent hand. Mike wasn't dead yet, he still had enough chips that he would be right in the ball game if he doubled up in a pot. But with the call and reraise he only had $3,500 left and would have to put up $500 in the small blind in the next hand.

If you had been watching the play, you would know that the man on the button wasn't just taking a shot at the pot. He had just gone through the blinds and hadn't played either of them, so obviously he was waiting for a hand that he could play. So I think that in these circumstances, Mike made the wrong play. He played a hand that he didn't necessarily have to play and he doubled up the man on the button when he lost the pot to him. About five minutes later Mike was out of the tournament.

The point is that you have to have a hand to defend the blind. Players throw off more money in tournaments defending their blinds than any other way possible. And they do it with hands that are *nothing* — the K♠ 6♠ is nothing. Suppose that Mike had been up against a lone ace: He would be a 2-to-1 dog even if both his cards were live. But what if he's up against something like a pair of sevens? He only has one overcard. Any way you look at it, his hand is supposed to be a dog in this pot. Why would you put in an extra $1,500 when the $1,000 that you already have in the pot isn't yours anymore anyway? Even if he couldn't play his little blind, he still would have $4,500 to play any one of the six or seven hands that he would be dealt before he had to post the big blind again. In that spot you're most likely going to pick up something better than a K-6 suited or unsuited.

And here Mike probably is the best and most successful big-field limit hold'em tournament player alive. It just goes to show that even the best of us sometimes make plays that are pretty hard to comprehend. But he seemed to think it was the right play. "The man could've had anything," he told me later.

"Yeah, but *you* didn't have anything," I answered. "Sure, you're a favorite over queen-high or anything in between it, but that's all you're favored over. Suppose the man has K-Q — what kind of chance do you have now? All you're looking for is a six!"

A lot of what I'm talking about here is just plain common sense. But people try to force action. That's why the good players win so often: They usually aren't trying to force action. They react to the action, but they aren't forcing it by going in with bad hands. The whole idea is to let the weak players play the bad hands while you only play the strong hands. If you get lucky in the big blind when you have the K♠ 6♠ in an unraised pot, that's great, it's a little extra bonus for you. But when you first see that hand, you don't expect to win the pot before the flop if there's any action. So why would you expect to win it after the flop against a raise, no matter where the raise comes from?

Jack's Invitational

For three or four years in a row at the World Series of Poker, we played a game that we called "Jack's Invitational," in which Jack Binion would play poker with us in a side game. Jack's Invitational was by invitation only — you could only play in it if you were on the list, otherwise you couldn't take a seat. Jack Straus, Nick Banion, Bill Smith, Dewey Tomko, Doyle Brunson and I usually played in it.

The game was no-limit hold'em with a $5,000 buy-in and $50-$100 blinds. About the third year that we played it, one of the invitees hadn't arrived by the time we first started the game but he was on his way. So Manning Briggs comes over and sits down in the empty seat at our table. Although he had plenty of money to play it and he was a good player, Manning hadn't been invited into the game.

"You'll have to get up, Manning," Jack Binion says to him real nice. Manning just sits there.

"Manning, you'll have to get up," Jack politely repeats. "You're not one of the invitees in this game and that seat's taken. He's on his way."

"This is an open-house casino," Manning finally answers. "I've got every right to sit in this game." He's saying this to the owner of the joint, right?!

Jack Binion jumped out of his seat and stalked around the table. Unless my eyes were deceiving me, I thought I saw steam coming out of his ears. "I said get out of that goddamned seat, Manning!" That was the only time that I ever saw Jack really get hot. Since it was Binion's joint, he probably could've called enough security guards to throw the man off the roof, but Manning finally moved along.

Manning is a very good friend of mine, but he's very hotheaded and set in his ways — Manning's way is the *only* way. This story just proves it: He was willing to argue with the owner of the place to keep his seat in Jack's Invitational. It was a terrific fun game and we usually played it three or four nights in a row because back then Jack had enough time to spare that he could play with us. Since then, he's been way too busy for it.

The Betting Lines at the World Series of Poker

In the earlier years at the World Series three betting lines were put out before the tournament began. Jackie Gaughan made up an odds sheet; Jack Binion and Doyle had a line; and Bob Stupak posted a line. Players were listed at all sorts of different odds to win the Series and you could bet on your favorites. After each day the odds would change according to who had chips.

Going into the third day one year, Johnny Moss had very few chips and they made his 100-to-1, so Mickey Appleman and quite a few other players made a big bet on him at those odds. Well, Johnny won every hand that he played that day and by the end of the third day, he was either the chip leader or second in chips. These guys were getting 100-to-1 on big bets — one of them had bet $10,000 on Johnny.

So when Johnny Moss made the final table at the beginning of the fourth day, Jackie Gaughan was running around all over town settling all these bets at a percentage. Moss didn't win the tournament, but this was one year when the bookmakers didn't do too well.

Terry Rogers, the big Irish bookmaker, also ran a book at the World Series for quite a few years. In 1985 when I came in second to Bill Smith, he had a lot of money on other players but he had made me the favorite. So when Bill and I both got to the final table, Terry was sitting in the stands yelling, "All the way with T. J.!" Obviously he needed me to win because of the odds he had laid on the other players. He had bigger odds on the other players so he wanted me to win it because I had the least amount of odds against.

Then the betting stopped. Jackie and Doyle and Dewey and Bob no longer put out a sheet, but Terry continued for one more year making up an odds sheet and booking bets. The police came in and arrested him, saying that he wasn't legal, and actually put him in jail. About two years later Terry got everything worked out that it was OK for him to book bets so long as his bets were being backed by his betting shops in Ireland, so he came back and booked the Series one last time. He hasn't done it since.

The way the bookies set it up was that when it got down to the final six at the last table for TV purposes, you could take two players against two other players, or three against three, or one against one as to who would win it. They never had bets on who would last longer, only on who would win.

But the odds were real terrible — they didn't give anything away. At the best, the leader in chips might be even money. If you bet on him, you laid $500 (plus $50 juice) to win $500. Say that a known player was in third chip position out of the final six — they might make him 2-to-1. Although another guy might have had a lot more chips, the known player was given real low odds.

I could never make myself bet it because the odds just weren't right. It was something like betting a horse race without looking at the sheet in advance.

Slow-Rollin' for $1 Million

I'm telling this story just to show you how some people act at the poker table. Some act with class, others don't. One year at the World Series of Poker we were in the second day of play in the Big One when a huge hand came up. It was four-way action between Doyle Brunson, two other players, and Brent Carter. Two threes were on the board but there also were three diamonds on it.

The way the hand came down there were two side pots, but Doyle and Brent were in for all of the pot. After the hand was completely dealt and all the betting was done with, the dealer was making sure that he had all the money right in each of the side pots. While this was going on, Doyle says, "Brent, I've got the nut flush. Is it any good?" Brent doesn't answer. Ten or fifteen seconds go by and Doyle repeats, "Brent, I guess you didn't hear me. I've got the nut flush. Is it any good? That's all I want to know." Again Brent doesn't answer. This went on for about a minute and a half and still no answer.

Finally all the pots are square the way they should be and Doyle shows down his hand, the nut flush. Brent sits there for about a minute and finally turns over pocket threes — he has quad threes. Doyle, a man that you never see getting out of line against another player when he's playing poker, called Brent every name under the sun. Not because he beat Doyle in the hand — because he slow-rolled him.

I call that the ultimate slow roll. Here you're playing for $1 million first-place money and you don't have the courtesy to tell a man that he's beat. There are two slimy things that all poker players hate — slow-rolling and asking to see the losing hand. The next story is about what happened one time when a player asked to see the losing cards at the end.

Think Before You Speak

I'm telling this story for all you players who love to see the losing hand. For starters I think that it's the worst etiquette in poker for you to ask to see the cards after a man has lost a hand to you. Why add insult to injury?

In the old days in Texas we didn't have a center dealer and the hands weren't killed, unlike today when the house dealer will kill a hand and then show it when asked. If you're any kind of poker player at all, you're supposed to know just about what your opponent has anyway, right? So to ask to see the losing hand is just poor manners.

This story happened during two sessions in the old days in Dallas. We played at Art Whitaker's on a Tuesday night and Charlie Bissell's the next day, Wednesday. Manning Briggs beat Larry Tooker in a pot and said, "I want to see the losing hand." So Larry showed it over. Larry's a real nice guy and Manning's a nice guy too, but he plays real hard when he's playing poker.

The very next day Larry, Manning and Hugh Briscoe are in a pot together. Hugh used to overlook a lot of his hands, and in this hand he was drawing for a flush. Larry got raised out of the pot, but remembering the night before, he says, "Now I want to see both hands when this pot's finished."

Manning shows down two pair at the end. "That's good," says Hugh.

"Wait a minute," says Larry, "I told you that I wanted to see both hands."

So Hugh turns his hand over. Sure enough, he had overlooked it — he hadn't made the flush, but he *had* made the middle-buster straight and wound up winning this huge hand from Manning. I'll guarantee you that Manning Briggs never again asked to see the losing hand. See how it came back to haunt him?

There's no need for that in poker. You know, when we used to play in the back rooms there was all this cheating and stuff going on. But today we've grown above all that stuff. And now we need to go above asking for the losing hand to be shown and slow rolling the winning hand.

I believe that poker should be a gentlemanly game. I know that a lot of women play poker, but when I say "gentlemanly" you realize that I mean it in the highest sense of the word. The most ungentlemanly things you can do are to slow-roll the winning hand against somebody or ask to see the losing hand.

Whether your opponent is strong or weak, it's a bad idea to ask to see his losing hand. The strong opponent just gets hot about it, and the weak player gets embarrassed. You might even drive the live one right out of the game — but the real point is that it's poor poker etiquette.

The Biggest Pot I've Ever Dealt

I really liked it better when we didn't have center dealers, the way it was when I was brought up in Texas. Back then when you had the button, you dealt. And you were never worried about being cheated either, because everyone was sharp enough to catch a cheater.

We were playing no-limit hold'em back in those good ol' days and although I wasn't in the hand, I was the dealer. The board came Q♦ 10♦ 7♦. Four players were in this pot. One player had a set of queens, the second one had a set of tens, the third man had a set of sevens, and the fourth player flopped the nut flush!

The worst player of the four had the tens and dropped out on the flop. All the rest of the money got in three ways on the flop. At the river the board showed Q♦ 10♦ 7♦ 5♥ 5♠. The three queens won the pot.

Now here was a scenario where you would love to have the nut flush because your opponents basically were dead to either a queen, a ten, a seven ... or a running pair. You see, if the board pairs one of the flop cards, anybody else in that pot would make quads — but you're such a favorite with the nut flush. If the tens had stayed in the pot, he would have run second in the hand, the sevens would have run third, and the nut flush would have been fourth. What a hand! ♠

GLOSSARY OF
POKER TERMS

Backdoor a flush/straight

Make a hand that you were not originally drawing to by catching favorable cards on later streets. "I had been betting top pair, but when a fourth spade hit at the river, I *backdoored* a flush."

Backup

A card that provides you with an extra out. "If you have a drawing hand, you like to have a *backup* to your draw, a secondary draw that might make your hand the winner."

Beat into the pot

When an opponent bets an inferior hand, you gladly push your chips into the pot. "When three clubs came on the flop, Slim moved in. I *beat him into the pot* with my flush — he had a 10-high flush, mine was higher."

Behind

Other players will have to act before you do. "So long as you're sitting *behind* the other players, you have the advantage of position."

Big Ace

An ace with a big kicker (A-K or A-Q). "When the flop came A-6-2, I played my *big ace* strong."

Big flop

The flop comes with cards that greatly enhance the strength of your hand. "I caught a *big flop* that gave me the nut flush."

Boss hand

A hand that is the best possible hand. "When you have the *boss hand*, you should bet it as aggressively as possible, especially if you think your opponents have drawing hands."

Broken Board

The board cards are random with no pair and no flush or straight possibilities. "A *broken board* such as 9-5-2 is a fabulous flop to pocket jacks."

Bully

Play aggressively. "When I have a big stack in a tournament, I like being able to *bully* the entire table."

Change gears

Adjust your style of play from fast to slow, from loose to tight, from raising to calling, and so on. "When the cards quit coming his way, Will didn't *change gears*; instead, he kept on playing fast and lost his whole bankroll."

Cold call

Call a raise without having put an initial bet into the pot. "Bonetti raised, Hellmuth reraised, and I *cold called*."

Come over the top

Raise or reraise. "I raised it $2,000 and Sexton *came over the top* of me with $7,000."

Commit fully

Put in as many chips as necessary to play your hand to the river, even if they are your case chips. "If I think the odds are in my favor, I will *fully commit*."

Decision Hand

A hand that requires you to make a value judgment. "The great hands and the trash hands play themselves. It is the *decision hands* that will determine your profit at the end of the session, the day, the year. It is all of the marginal, in-between hands that are played with great ability that separate winners from losers."

Flat call

You call a bet without raising. "When he bet in to me, I just *flat called* to keep the players behind me from folding."

Flop to it

The flop enhances the value of your hand. "If you don't *flop to it*, you can get away from the hand."

Get into the Deck

Get a free card. "If you just check your one-pair hand, you allow your opponents to *get into the deck*."

Get away from it

Fold, usually what appeared to be a premium hand until an unfavorable flop negated its potential. "If you don't flop to your hand, *get away from* it."

Get the right price

The pot odds are favorable enough for you to justify calling a bet or a raise with a drawing hand. "Since I was getting the *right price*, I called the bet with a wraparound."

Get full value

Bet, raise and reraise to manipulate the size of the pot so that you will win the maximum number of chips if you win the hand. "By raising on every round, I was able to get *full value* when my hand held up at the river."

Get there

You make your hand. "When you *get there*, you might be able to start maximizing your bets."

Give them

You attribute a hand to your opponent(s). "When the flop comes with a pair and your opponent raises, what are you going to *give him*? A straight draw?!"

Gone Goose

You're a beaten player. "When an ace hit on the flop, I figured that I was a *gone goose* with my king."

Isolate

You raise or reraise to limit the action to yourself and a single opponent. "I raised on the button to *isolate* against the big blind."

Jammed pot

The pot has been raised the maximum number of times and may also be multiway. "You should pass with a weak hand if the pot has been *jammed* before it gets to you."

Key card

The one card that will make your hand a winner. "I knew that I needed to catch a ten, the *key card* to my straight draw."

Lay it down

Fold. "Many times, you can put enough pressure on the pot to blow everybody away and sometimes even get the raiser to *lay down* his hand."

Limp

Enter the pot by just calling rather than raising. "You might decide to just *limp* in with a pair of tens and see the flop as cheap as possible."

Limper

A player who enters the pot for the minimum bet. "With two *limpers* in the pot, a pair of jacks should be your minimum raising hand."

(Two) Limper Rule

Once two or more people have voluntarily entered the pot for the minimum bet, the pot already has shaped up to be multiway. "Small pairs and connectors become somewhat more attractive in middle to late position when *two or more players have limped* into the pot in front of you."

Live cards

Cards that you need to improve your hand and which probably are still available to you. "When three players who I knew to be big-pair players entered the pot in front of me, I thought that my middle connectors might still be *live* so I decided to play the hand."

Live one

A loose, inexperienced or bad player. "Very seldom do you get a *live one*, a person who can't play at all, in the big games but it does happen sometimes."

Long call

Take a long time to decide whether to call a bet with a marginal hand. "When you're studying whether to call, making a *long call*, your opponents can get a read on you."

Make a move

Try to bluff. "When the board paired sixes, Max *made a move* at the pot. I thought he was bluffing but I had nothing to call him with."

Middle buster

An inside straight draw. "If the flop comes A-10-4 and you have the Q-J, you're not going to draw to the *middle buster* to try to catch the king."

Nit and Supernit

A very tight player and a supertight player. "The *nit* is a person who plays tight and takes no chances. The *supernit* will drive from one county to the other, win one pot, quit the game and drive home."

(the) Nut draw

You have a draw to the best possible hand. "When two clubs come on the board and you have the A♣ J♣, you have the *nut* flush *draw*."

(the) Nuts

The best hand possible at the moment. "Remember that you can flop the *nuts* and lose it on the turn; for example, when you flop the nut straight and the board pairs making a full house for your opponent."

Nutted up

When someone is playing very tight. "Jackson was so *nutted up* at the final table, I stole pot after pot from him."

Out (an)

A card that completes your hand. "Always try to have an extra *out*, a third low card to go with your ace, when you're drawing for the low end."

Overpair

You have a pair in your hand that is higher than the highest card showing on the board. "When the board came Q-J-6, I flopped an *overpair* with my pocket kings."

Pay off

You call an opponent's bet at the river even though you think that he might have the best hand. "When the board paired at the river, I decided to *pay him off* when he bet because I wasn't sure that he had made trips."

Peddling the nuts

Drawing to, playing and betting the nut hand. "Players may not always be peddling the nuts in a heads-up situation, but in any multiway pot somebody's usually drawing at the nuts if he doesn't already have it."

Piece of cheese

A hand that is a loser. "If you raise and get reraised, your trip threes are probably *a piece of cheese*, so be very careful when you flop bottom set."

Play back

Responding to an opponent's bet by either raising or reraising. "If a tight opponent *plays back* at you, you know he probably has the nuts."

Play from behind

Checking with the intent of check-raising when you have a big hand. "I knew that Kevin usually *played from behind* when he had a big hand so when he checked, so did I."

Play fast

Aggressively betting a drawing hand to get full value for it if you make it. "Many players *play fast* in the early rounds of rebuy tournaments to try to build their stacks."

Play slow

The opposite of playing fast; waiting to see what develops before pushing a hand. "When you make the nut straight on the flop and there's a chance that the flush draw is out or possibly a set, why not play your hand *slow* to start with?"

Play with

Staying in the hand by betting calling, raising or reraising. "You should realize that you're going to *get played with* most of the time because hold'em is a limit-structure game."

Put on the heat

Pressure your opponents with aggressive betting strategies to get the most value from your hand. "You might consider *putting on the heat* when your opponent is slightly conservative or when he has a short stack against your big stack."

Put them on (a hand)

You assign a value to your opponent's hand. "Using my instincts and the way he had played the hand, I *put Stanley on* the nut low."

Rag (or blank)

A board card that doesn't help you and appears not to have helped anyone else, either. "The flop came with A-2-3 and then a *rag*, the 9♠, hit on the turn."

Rag off

The river card doesn't help you. "Then it *ragged off* on the end and he was a gone goose for all his money."

Rainbow flop

The flop cards are three different suits. "I liked my straight draw when the flop came *rainbow* and nobody could have a flush draw against me."

Read the board

Understand the value of your hand in relation to the cards on the board. "If you *read the board* correctly, you often can tell where you're at in the hand by the action."

Rock

A very conservative player who always waits for premium cards before he plays a hand. "Smith was playing like a *rock* so when she bet into me, I knew she had me beat."

Run over

Playing aggressively in an attempt to control the other players. "If they're not trying to stop you from being a bully, then keep *running over them* until they do."

Runner-runner

Catch cards on the turn and river that make your hand a winner. "As it turns out, you had a suited K-J, caught *runner-runner* to make a flush, and broke me!"

Showdown

When no one bets at the river and the cards are turned over to determine the winner. "If everyone checks to you at the river and you couldn't win in a *showdown*, why bet if you know that you will get called?"

Scoop the pot

You win both the high and low ends of a pot in a split game. "The whole idea of high-low hold'em is to play hands that you can *scoop the pot* with."

Shut down

Discontinue aggressive action. "When the board paired the second highest card, I decided to *shut down*."

Slowplay

You intentionally do not bet a strong hand for maximum value because you are hoping to trap your opponents. "I knew the rock in the third seat was *slowplaying* aces so I didn't bet my kings when he checked on the flop."

Smooth call

Call a bet without raising. "If someone bets into you, you might *smooth call* with this type of hand because you have an extra out."

Stand a raise

Call a raise. "I recently *stood a raise* in a cash game with 9-8 on the button. The board came 7-6-2, no suits. A guy led off with a decent bet and I called him with my overcards and a straight draw."

Stiffed in

Play a blind hand in an unraised pot. "The only time that you might play 7-2 in hold'em is when you are *stiffed in* in the big blind."

Surrender

Give up on your hand. Fold. "When the fourth flush card hit at the river, I had to *surrender*."

Take off a card

Call a bet on the flop. "I decided to *take off a card* and see what the turn would bring."

Takeoff hand

A hand that has the potential of beating a better starting hand because it is live. "In four-way action, I figured that my middle connectors might turn into a *takeoff hand*."

Take them off (a hand)

Beat a superior starting hand. "Any of those types of hands in which you have two straight cards and a pair will *take the aces right off* a lot of times."

Underpair

You hold a pair that is lower than a pair showing on the board. "Why would you ever want to call with an *underpair*?"

Wake up with a hand

You are dealt a hand with winning potential. "Just because a player is a maniac doesn't mean that he can't *wake up with a hand*. Over the long haul, everybody gets the same number of good hands and bad hands."

Weak Ace

You have an ace in your hand but you do not have a high kicker to go with it. "I won't bet a *weak ace* unless I am certain that I have the only ace at the table."

Where you're at

You understand the value of your hand in relation to the other players' hands. "Your opponent may not know for sure *where you're at* in the hand when you have played it in a deceptive way."

World's fair

A big hand. "Suppose the flop comes 8-8-4, no suits. You know you're up against either nothing or *the world's fair*."

Cardsmith Publishing

The Championship Series

Championship No-Limit & Pot-Limit Hold'em

T. J. Cloutier and Tom McEvoy

Cloutier and McEvoy, two of the most famous poker tournament champions in the world, team up to bring you their best advice on big-bet poker. The champs show you how to win pot-limit cash games and no-limit and pot-limit tournaments. They teach you how much to bet, how to out-psych your opponents, and how to use position and chip power to win money at the world's most exciting poker games. Includes 30 pictorials of no-limit and pot-limit hands with Cloutier's expert commentary on how to play them in various situations. Written in a conversational style, the text is easy to read and understand. One of the most famous road gamblers of all time, Cloutier tops off the strategy sections with stories recounted from his colorful past. 212 pages, paperback, $39.95

Championship Omaha

T. J. Cloutier & Tom McEvoy

The definitive guide to winning at Omaha high-low, limit high Omaha and pot-limit Omaha. Cloutier & McEvoy have won four WSOP titles in the Omaha tournaments. The 1998 Player of the Year, Cloutier won the pot-limit Omaha championship at the World Series in 1998 and finished third in the $10,000 no-limit hold'em event. He is the only player ever to win WSOP titles in all three Omaha games. The authors discuss cash game and tournament strategies for each type of Omaha. Includes 21 practice hands for each game, plus a few more of T. J.'s popular road stories. Photos and hand illustrations with play-by-play analyses. 230 pages, paperback. $39.95.

Championship Stud
(7-Card Stud, Stud 8-or-Better, Razz)
Max Stern, Tom McEvoy, and Linda Johnson

Stern won the Stud/8 championship and Johnson won the razz title at the 1997 World Series of Poker. The champs outline strategic concepts for medium-limit stud cash games and stage-by-stage strategies for winning tournaments in each of the three stud games. Explores similarities and differences in views on how to achieve success in today's highly competitive cash games and tournaments, plus a roundtable discussion of tournament strategies with the latest concepts for winning in any type of poker game including hold'em, stud and Omaha split. Foreword by Mike Sexton. Sample hands and play-by-play analyses. 200 pages, paperback, photos. $29.95

Championship Hold'em
Tom McEvoy & T. J. Cloutier

Championship Hold'em gives you the latest strategies for winning in limit hold'em cash games and tournaments written in the easy-to-read conversational style that McEvoy & Cloutier have become famous for. The authors recognize that the play of limit hold'em has changed dramatically during the past few years and offer their best advice on how to adjust to the "new hold'em," emphasizing adjustment to the type of game you're playing with strategy suggestions for ramming-jamming, kill-pot, bad-beat jackpot, shorthanded, and other types of games. Takes you through the thinking process before the flop, on the flop, on the turn, and at the river with specific suggestions for what to do when various things happen. The chapters on tournament play explore general limit-hold'em tournament strategy, plus 20 illustrated hands with advice on how to play them in various circumstances. Also includes some new road stories from T. J., tips on playing hold'em variations such as high-low, and a glossary. 320 pages, photos, illustrated hands with play-by-play analyses. $39.95

The Tournament Poker Series

Tournament Poker
Tom McEvoy

Endorsed by many World Series of Poker champions, this book outlines strategies for winning all the games in the WSOP. First published in 1995, it has been become the "Bible" of tournament poker and has been translated into French and German. Extensive discussions of seven-card stud, limit hold'em, pot-limit and no-limit hold'em, Omaha, Omaha high-low, and 7-card stud/8-or-better. The 1983 World Champion, McEvoy outlines techniques for winning rebuy tournaments, satellites, half/half tourneys and winning concepts for each stage of tournament play. Includes an insightful discussion of the lifestyle of big-league tournament players and how they negotiate deals at the final table. Foreword by Phil Hellmuth. *"One of the most important poker books of all time."* — Gamblers Book Club. 344 pages, paperback, photos. $39.95

Poker Tournament Tips from the Pros
Shane Smith

This book shows you how to win the increasingly popular low-limit rebuy tournaments sponsored daily by casinos across the nation. Smith gives you the winning advice of poker theorists and tournament winners including Mike Caro, Tom McEvoy, Mason Malmuth and Bob Ciaffone, plus examples from play in actual tournaments. The author discusses the Top 20 Tips for winning tournaments and details strategies for each of the Four Stages of Tournaments. Includes 26 Tournament Traps to avoid and a Poker Potpourri of winning poker tips. The perfect companion book to McEvoy's *Tournament Poker*. 102 large pages, spiral bound. $19.95

101 Tournament Hands

D. R. Sherer

Big hands, little hands, trouble hands, trash hands — you're dealt all of them in tournaments. The key to success is what you do with them after you get them. When do you raise with Big Slick? When do you fold it? How do you play pocket jacks? Suited connectors? Baby pairs? Sherer takes you 101 steps closer to the winner's circle by dealing you practice hands in various tournament scenarios that are carefully designed to help you improve your tournament skills. He analyzes the play of a hand factoring in the stage of the tournament, your stack size, table position, and the makeup of your opponents. Whether you agree or argue with these strategies, you will find yourself thinking in more depth about what works and what doesn't in hold'em tournaments. Endorsed by Cloutier and McEvoy. 100 pgs, illustrated, spiral bound. $14.95

The Low-Limit Poker Series

7-Card Stud (The Complete Course in Winning)

Roy West

Veteran Card Player columnist Roy West discusses the latest strategies for winning at $1-$4 spread-limit up to $10-$20 fixed-limit seven-card stud. The author's style is both informal and instructional as he outlines 42 Important Lessons on how to win in casino and home games. "Think of me as your favorite uncle, a professional poker player, who is sitting across the table teaching you how to win at poker," West says. Includes numerous thumbnail tips on poker strategy and psychology, and an in-depth analysis of correct strategies for third street through seventh street. Plus a chapter by WSOP champion Tom McEvoy on how to win seven-card stud tournaments. 160 pages, paperback. $24.95

Omaha Hi-Lo Poker
Shane Smith

Geared to low-limit players who want to improve their game, Smith's 1991 book has become the standard on "How to Win at the Lower Limits." Smith outlines winning strategies for playing the flop, turn, and river in ring games and Omaha high-low tournaments. Includes an in-depth discussion of starting hands and an odds chart. The book also discusses lessons taken from live casino action. "It's a gem!" said Lou Krieger in his review for Card Player magazine. 84 large pages, spiral bound, sample hand pictorials. $17.95

The Pro Poker Playbook
John Vorhaus

Poker strategist and columnist John Vorhaus gives you more than "223 Ways to Win More Money Playing Poker," the subtitle of his 1994 book. Endorsed by Mike Caro, who wrote the foreword, as "filled with great insight and solid insider tips." The Playbook begins with The 65 Commandments of Poker, an in-depth expansion of the winning principles espoused by Caro. Part Two explores 126 tools you can use to increase your profits at poker, followed by 42 Powerful Plays, and 33 ways to stay out of financial jeopardy at the tables. Includes a strong chapter on how to win at low-limit Omaha high-low, and a collection of Vorhaus' short stories, "Tales from Cimarron," with unique insights into the psyche of gamblers. 176 pages, paperback. $19.95

Cowboys, Gamblers & Hustlers
The True Adventures of a Rodeo Champion & Poker Legend
Byron "Cowboy" Wolford

Byron Wolford, better known in worldwide poker circles as "Cowboy," won over thirty belt buckles for calf roping in the 1940s-50s in competition with rodeo legends Casey Tibbs, Dean Oliver and hundreds of others. When Wolford retired from the pro rodeo circuit in 1960, it seemed natural for him to become a professional road gambler — after all, he had been playing poker on bales of hay in the rodeo barns for years. And so began his odyssey across countless miles of dusty backroads to play poker in smoky backrooms with poker legends Amarillo Slim Preston, Titanic Thompson, Johnny Moss, Bobby Baldwin, Doyle Brunson, Jack Straus and a thousand other road gamblers who later migrated to the big action in Las Vegas at their friend Benny Binion's joint, the Horseshoe Club.

In this vivid and fast-paced memoir about his life on the road, Wolford takes you on the ride of your life as he fades the white line from Dallas to Shreveport to Houston in the 1960s in search of a score. He lets you inside his mind as he feels the fear and frustration of being hijacked and getting arrested for playing poker — and the satisfaction of cleverly outwitting card sharps and scam artists. Through his accurate retelling of actual conversations he had with the world's most famous gamblers and rodeo riders and the predicaments they got into, you can live the excitement of yesteryear as cowboys lose by a tenth of a second and gamblers lose by the luck of the draw.

One thing's for sure: You'll get a kick out of the humorous and sometimes poignant tales — and one helluva education on hustling for a living — from the cowboy gambler who won the calf roping title at the Calgary Stampede two years in a row and three decades later pulled off the most famous bluff in World Series of Poker history. 300 pages illustrated with 80 vintage photos. $19.95